WISDOM *for* TODAY *from the* EARLY CHURCH

A Foundational Study

WISDOM *for* TODAY *from the* EARLY CHURCH

A Foundational Study

David C. Ford

MMXIX

Wisdom for Today from the Early Church: A Foundational Study

First Edition: 2014
Second Edition: 2019

Published by:
St. Tikhon's Monastery Press
175 St. Tikhon's Road
Waymart, Pennsylvania 18472
Printed in the United States of America

ISBN: 978–0-9974718–5-4

Cover design by Hierodeacon Marc, 2019. Church of St. Mary, Ephesus (5th century). Church historians believe it to be here that the 3rd Ecumenical Council of 431 was held. It was likely built upon the site of a Jewish synagogue and assembly of early Christians.

Now, therefore, you are no longer strangers and foreigners, but fellow citizens with the saints and members of the household of God, having been built on the foundation of the apostles and prophets, Jesus Christ Himself being the chief cornerstone, in Whom the whole building, being fitted together, grows into a holy temple in the Lord, in Whom you also are being built together for a dwelling place of God in the Spirit.

Ephesians 2:19–22

DEDICATION

This book is dedicated to all the students I've ever had in the Church History I course at St. Tikhon's Seminary—they have taught me much; and to Fr. Theodore Petrides, who heartily encouraged me to write this book.

CONTENTS

FOREWORD

by His Eminence, Archbishop Michael (Dahulich), Archbishop of New York and the Diocese of New York and New Jersey (OCA)

IN HIS CLASSIC WORK, *The Orthodox Church,* the renowned Fr. John Meyendorff, of blessed memory, reviews each epoch of Christian history. Of the first three centuries of the early Church, he writes:

> The cautious historian of course must be wary about painting too bright a picture of the early Christians and portraying them as perfect in all respects. Yet, as long as the fledgling status of the new Church lasted, as long as being a member of the New Covenant entailed a certain risk or at least a conscious effort to profess the faith, it was natural that the faithful should be more aware than later generations of the true nature of the Christian community. *In this sense and in this only, the Church of the first three centuries can be said to be the golden age of Christianity—and also, to a certain extent, a criterion by which to judge the rest of Christian history* (*The Orthodox Church* [Crestwood, NY: SVS Press, 1981], p. 17; emphasis mine).

Today, we members of the Orthodox Church, certainly at least in North America, find ourselves in a situation not unlike the one in which the early Christians lived. We are a small minority in what is fast becoming a non-Christian society. There is no government support or funding for the Church, as in the Byzantine Empire or Tsarist Russia. The science and philosophy of the university are most often presented with an anti-religious slant. The Church is asked to be "politically correct" rather than theologically true. Values are very much like those of the pre-Christian, pagan society. And the influence of secularism in people's lives is more powerful today than ever before. In this regard, this "golden age" of the Church provides essential keys for us in dealing with issues and circumstances in which we find ourselves two millennia later.

It is in this regard that Dr. David Ford's book, *Wisdom for Today from the Early Church: A Foundational Study,* is such an invaluable resource. It brings to life the first four centuries of the Christian era, along with the wisdom that the early Church has to offer to us who are "the recipients of the fullness of the Christian Faith that all the faithful witnesses, shining as lights upon the earth, have preserved through their lives and their writings century by century down to our own time" (as he writes in the Introduction).

Dr. Ford begins our journey through time with a study of the first book of Church history, the Acts of the Apostles. In this study he highlights certain key elements of very early Christianity, as revealed in Acts, that would develop into what we have in the Church today, such as the liturgical worship of the apostolic age; the three-fold ministry of bishops, priests, and deacons; the precedence of the first council of the Church; and the first indications of infant baptism. He continues our trek, examining the lives of the Apostolic Fathers—saints such as Clement of Rome, Polycarp of Smyrna, and Ignatius of Antioch—and their teachings on the full divinity and full humanity of Christ, His Real Presence in the Eucharist, the End Times, the hierarchical structure of the Church, veneration of relics, the centrality of water baptism, and regulations for fasting. He also examines the relevance of these Fathers and their teachings for us today.

He offers insight for us from the Apologists, writers from the second and early third centuries, who explained and defended the Faith to the non-Christian society surrounding them—not just to the poor of Palestine but also to the Roman emperor himself! The Apologists include the well-known St. Justin Martyr and the less familiar Minucius Felix. St. Justin's message is that the Word of God has disseminated many "seminal words" throughout the universe, so that all truth, wherever it is found and to whatever degree it exists, is ultimately from God Himself. As St. Justin writes, "there seem to be seeds of truth among all men" (*First Apology,* 44); and, "on some points we teach the same things as the poets and philosophers ... , and on other points we are fuller and more divine in our teaching" (*First Apology,* 20). What a way for us to share Christianity in our own time!

Dr. Ford further examines for us the life and teachings of St. Irenaeus of Lyons, who met head-on the challenge posed to Christianity by Gnosticism, considered to be the greatest doctrinal threat to traditional Christian teaching in its first 250 years. The tendencies of this "secret knowledge" have continued to threaten to distort the personal piety of Christians ever since. Dr. David not only summarizes Irenaeus's brilliant response to Gnosticism from his famous late second-century work called *Against Heresies,* but he also surveys Gnosticism throughout history to our own day, highlighting its present challenges to the Faith of the Church, the "pillar and ground of the Truth" (1 Tim. 3:15).

He then reviews the rise of Montanism, a late second-century sect that over-emphasized prophecy and immediate direct inspiration from the Holy Spirit. A rigorist movement, it was characterized by a fervent conviction that the very Last Days had come. Dr. Ford discusses the modern-day successors of this movement, Pentecostalism and the Charismatic Movement, and their teachings on the gifts of the Holy Spirit—from healing and working miracles to speaking in tongues and their interpretation.

He goes on to examine the life and teachings of Tertullian, "the father of Latin theology," whose rigorist and legalistic mind-set led him to eventually break away from the Church established by Christ and join a sect. Dr. Ford's work underscores the dangers of such a sectarian mind-set, even in our own day, and offers insight on its typical characteristics: spiritual pride and self-righteousness; judgmental contempt of the established Church; excessive rigorism and legalism regarding penitence, fasting, the status of women, marriage, and children; negative attitudes toward the non-Orthodox; and an over-emphasis on and fascination with the End Times. These traits are typical of so many sects in our own age!

Next, Dr. David delineates the process involved in the canonization of the New Testament—highlighting how the hierarchical Church decided which books came to be regarded as Scripture. The impetus provided by the heretic Marcion and the Montanists; the influence of St. Irenaeus, St. Dionysius the Great, and Bp. Eusebius of Caesarea; and the world-wide acceptance of the list of St. Athanasius are especially noted. Dr. Ford especially stresses the relevance of this story for Protestants: "for it is the very Church [of the first four centuries] that decided which books would comprise the New Testament that we have today."

Another aspect of the journey through Church history is what Dr. Ford calls "the rise of papal presumption." He traces the place of the Church of Rome in the canons of the first four Ecumenical Councils, and in the writings of the Apostolic Fathers. He then chronicles the major controversies concerning various efforts by certain bishops of Rome to extend their authority in unprecedented ways: Bishop Victor over the date of Pascha; Stephen of Rome over the baptism of schismatics and heretics; the claims of Bishop Julius, Bishop Innocent, and Bishop Celestine;

the expansion of papal authority over the Western Churches; Pope Hormisdas's claims even over the Churches of the East; and the indignant response of Pope Gregory the Great to the "blasphemous" title of "Ecumenical Patriarch" assumed by John of Constantinople. Dr. David gratefully acknowledges the moderation of Rome on some of its exclusivist views since the Vatican II Council, and expresses hope that there might be progress made toward reconciliation through dialogue, if there is a firm resolve to return to the teachings and practices of the undivided Church before the Great Schism of 1054.

Dr. David examines the accounts of the holy martyrs, who lived and died for Christ in every generation—the Roman government's demands, persecutions by the emperors, and the resulting glory of Christian martyrdom. He offers us familiar stories, such as the account of the martyrdom of St. Polycarp, and lesser known ones, such as that of St. Perpetua. He shares these so that we might be encouraged to "always be strengthened and inspired, in the midst of whatever suffering we may be called to endure, by the example and the prayers of the vast army of Christ's holy martyrs, who are ever with us in prayer and spirit."

Finally, he guides our study of the rise of "the new martyrdom"—monasticism—and the wisdom of the Desert Fathers and Mothers. He examines the rise of the monastic movement and the prominent roles of Saints Anthony, Pachomios, Macarios, Basil, Martin of Tours, John Chrysostom, and John Cassian, as well as many Desert Fathers and Mothers. To help us, Dr. David quotes Metropolitan Anthony (Bloom), who wrote: "If we wish to understand the sayings of the Desert Fathers, let us approach them with veneration, silencing our judgments and our thoughts to meet them on their own ground and perhaps to partake ultimately … in their own silent communion with God."

This ten-chapter journey is by no means a dry read. Dr. Ford is well known for his passionate teaching of Church History. For 25 years at St. Tikhon's Seminary, he has instructed hundreds of students, who are now lay leaders, deacons, priests, bishops, and a metropolitan of the Church; he has served as the Chair of the Department of Church History and Patristics; and he has been promoted to the rank of full Professor. His commitment to the school and to his field of study flows from his great love for Christ and His Church—and her two millennia-old story.

If you were to speak with any of his students, you would find that they all agree on his incredible devotion to teaching, his unwavering faithfulness to the Church and her Tradition, his respect for her Scriptures, his obedience to her teachings, his veneration of her Saints. He literally relives the moments that he is teaching, with all their drama, joys, and sorrows. He makes the pages of Church History come alive in his classroom—and it is no different in this book.

For a quarter of a century, David Ford has taught not only seminarians, but also laypersons who have come to his lectures at St. Tikhon's and across the country. His presentations have always been more than mere recitation of the facts of history; they are in fact an entrance into the Patristic spirit and experience through entrance into the Saints' relationship with the Lord. He is a son of the Church, possessing brilliant scholarship yet child-like faith, an incredible gift for sharing what he has learned and doing it out of selfless love, and the ability to write clearly and concisely—the very same way he teaches in his classroom.

In *Wisdom for Today from the Early Church,* he challenges us to approach his subject matter in ways that stretch our faith and imagination. He beckons us to wonder: "Have you ever wondered what happened in the Early Church after the Book of Acts? That book ... gives various highlights in roughly the first 35 years of the history of the Church ... But what happened after that? ... Who were the leaders of the Church after [the Apostles]? What writings did they leave? And what do these writings reveal about the teachings, the worship, the spirituality, and the structure of the Church in the decades immediately following the era of the original Apostles?"

He also urges us to begin the reading of his work with prayer: "the Apostolic Fathers provide us many pages of tremendously edifying spiritual reading. I would recommend starting with the *Account of the Martyrdom of St. Polycarp.* Ask him to be with you as you accompany him through his arrest; his two-hour prayer in the midst of his captors for everyone he ever knew; his refusal to deny Christ as he stood in the stadium—'I have served Him eighty-six years and in no way has He dealt unjustly with me; so how can I blaspheme my King Who saved me?' ... Radiating throughout the account are his steadfast faith and quiet endurance through all of this, such that many of the onlookers were astounded. As the text says, 'and the whole crowd was amazed that there was so great a difference between unbelievers and the elect.'" Dr. Ford invites to experience the events that history has recorded through faith in Christ, and in fellowship with the Saints.

Saint Gregory the Theologian once wrote, "One cannot give another what one does not possess oneself." What Dr. Ford, a consummate teacher, offers his students in his classes, and his readers in this book, is the knowledge of God and communion with the Saints that he himself possesses—not merely from books but from actual experience. That is why he can share it with us so freely, so clearly, so naturally.

It is his hope and prayer "that this study of major themes in the history of the Early Church will inspire us to get to know better the Saints of this formative, foundational period.... May we all flourish more and more in our Christian growth, in fellowship with them." In our own era, when the Church is challenged by a new onslaught—secularism—the wisdom that he offers us from the early centuries of Church history is much needed and deeply appreciated. May his sharing of that experience guide our dealings with the non-Orthodox and help us to share with them "the pearl of great price," our Faith in our Lord God and Savior.

Dr. David concludes our journey with this hope: "May we also be inspired to continue our study of Church History through all the centuries down to our own time. As we do so, may we seek to get to know better the Saints of all the ages. And may we marvel to see Christ's Hand throughout the Story, as He has guided and protected His Church in the midst of a myriad of attacks by the Evil One. Surely we will become more and more convinced that Christ's promise has been and ever will be indeed true, that 'I will build My Church, and the gates of hell will not prevail against her' (Matt. 16:18)."

May it be so for us all, through the prayers of all the Saints of the Early Church.

PREFACE

THE BASIC SHAPE OF THIS BOOK has arisen from nearly 25 years of teaching Church History at St. Tikhon's Orthodox Theological Seminary in South Canaan, Pennsylvania. It has arisen specifically from the Church History 1 course, which begins with the grand theme of Christ's Preparation of the World for His Coming, and concludes with the Sixth Ecumenical Council (680–681). Every time I've had the opportunity to retell the glorious story of the history of Christ's Church with another new group of eager students, the importance of the story has become more evident to me—and especially the ten themes covered in this book, which have arisen naturally through the repeated telling of the history of the Church through the first five centuries.

Even more important than the basic historical facts involved with these ten themes are the lives and teachings of our brothers and sisters in Christ who lived the Faith, and often died for the Faith as martyrs, during the early centuries of the Christian era. They are alive in Christ, and they are constantly inviting us to get to know them personally, to ask them for their prayers, and to have active fellowship with them. As St. John of Kronstadt, an extremely beloved priest in Russia who died in 1908, writes in his diary, called *My Life in Christ,*

> We ought to have *the most lively spiritual union* with the dwellers in heaven—the apostles, prophets, martyrs, saintly bishops, confessors, with all the saints, as they are all members of the one body, the Church of Christ, to which we sinners also belong, and the living Head of which is the Lord Jesus Christ Himself. This is why we call upon them in prayer, converse with them, thank and praise them. It is *urgently necessary for every Christian* to be in union with them if he desires to make Christian progress; for the saints are our friends, our guides to salvation, who pray and intercede for us (*The Spiritual*

> *Counsels of Father John of Kronstadt*, ed. W. Jardine Grisbrooke [SVS Press, 1981 (Crestwood, NY: SVS Press, 1981)], p. 64; my emphasis).

So may this book be an avenue for all of us to closer, more fruitful, more intimate communion with the Saints of the early Church. For truly "God is wondrous in His Saints" (Ps. 67:36, Septuagint [LXX]).[1]

The subtitle of the book says it's a "foundational" study. This is so in two ways: first, in the sense that the history of the Church is so profoundly *cumulative*, with each generation of Christians, in cooperation with Christ and the Holy Spirit, building directly upon the witness and work of the preceding generations (see Eph. 2:19–22); and second, in the sense that what is conveyed in this book is very *basic*, describing and emphasizing things that are *foundational* to a proper understanding of the spiritual, theological, liturgical, and organizational life of our Orthodox Church to this day. Hence, the attempt has been made to write this book simply, in a reader-friendly way, to help make it as accessible as possible to every Orthodox Christian, as well as to any others who may be interested in learning more about the Early Church. (Part of this effort has been simplifying many of the translations of quotations given from primary sources, especially the Victorian English used in the *Ante-Nicene Fathers* and *Nicene and Post-Nicene Fathers* volumes.)

I wish to thank heartily all the alumni of St. Tikhon's Seminary who have taken the Church History I course with me, through whose interest and input my knowledge of the history of the Early Church has greatly increased, and my love for it has deepened. I also wish to thank Fr. Theodore Petrides, pastor of the Holy Cross Greek Orthodox Church in Stroudsburg, Pennsylvania, for strongly encouraging me to pursue this project through to its completion, especially by convincing me that there is a great need for such a book in helping our parishioners and inquirers to learn more about the origins and roots of our Holy Orthodox Faith. In addition, I want to thank Fr. Sergius (Bowyer), Abbot of St. Tikhon's Monastery and director of the St. Tikhon's Monastery Press, for publishing this book, and for encouraging and guiding me as the project unfolded. And I thank His Grace, Bishop Michael (Dahulich), Bishop of New York and New Jersey for the OCA, and Rector of St. Tikhon's Seminary, for being so graciously willing to write the foreword.

I would also like to offer special thanks to Metropolitan Herman and Fr. Daniel Donlick for giving me the opportunity to teach Church History at St. Tikhon's Seminary, when they made the decision to hire my wife Mary and me back in

[1] All references in this volume from the Book of Psalms is given according to the Septuagint (LXX) numbering, which differs slightly from the numbering found in the Authorized Version and most modern Bible translations.

the summer of 1989. What a great joy and privilege it has been all these years to share the history of our beloved Church with many whom our Lord has raised up through the years to serve His Church as dedicated laity, deacons, priests, monks, and even a bishop—Metropolitan Tikhon of the OCA!

Finally, as always, I give thanks to my beloved wife Mary, who helps me in everything I do in more ways than I can possibly know!

It is my hope and prayer that our All-Gracious Lord will use this book to help many of our parishioners to grow more deeply in their Orthodox Faith and their love for our Holy Church—and especially for our brothers and sisters, the Christians of the Early Church. And may this book also be of assistance to many who are looking into Holy Orthodoxy as they seek the fullness of the Christian Faith.

To God be all the glory!

Great Lent, 2014

INTRODUCTION

FR. GEORGES FLOROVSKY, the greatest Orthodox Church historian of the 20th century, once wrote that "Christianity is basically a vigorous appeal to history, a witness of faith to certain particular events of the past" which are "acknowledged by faith as truly eventful." The Nicene Creed, the most important brief summary of the Christian Faith, moves in a series of quick steps from the beginning of Time (Creation) all the way to the End of Time (at Christ's Second Coming). Along the way it highlights the key moments in the history of God's work to save mankind from sin, death, and the devil—especially His Incarnation in human flesh as Jesus Christ, His redemptive death on the Cross, and His glorious, triumphant Resurrection from the dead. Hence, Fr. Georges goes on to say, quoting F. M. Powicke, "it may be justly contended that 'the Christian religion is *a daily invitation to the study of history*'" (*Collected Works*, vol. 2, [Belmont, MA: Nordland Pub. Co 1972], pp. 31–32; my emphasis).

For not only is our attention drawn to the work of Christ as He lived on this Earth, but to all the ways He has guided and protected His Body, the Church, ever since He left the Earth on the Day of His Ascension (Mark 16:19; Luke 24:50–52; Acts 1:9–11). Only ten days later, on the Day of Pentecost, He sent the Holy Spirit upon His followers, who only numbered about 120 at that time, as they were gathered in an upper room. This powerful infilling of the Spirit is understood by many to be the formative moment for the Church, Her very Birthday, so to speak. For on that day, the first public Christian preaching takes place, and about 3,000 people respond with faith and are baptized (Acts 2). From that tremendously dramatic beginning, the Holy Spirit during the succeeding centuries empowers Christians to carry the Gospel, the Good News about eternal salvation in Christ, to the farthest corners of the world.

This book is an invitation to study the history of the Church in Her formative years—roughly the first five centuries. It is in this era that Christianity, through the guidance of the Holy Spirit, gradually takes the basic shape—in terms of spirituality, liturgical life, doctrine, and organizational structure—that it still has in the Holy Orthodox Church today.

As we reflect upon how the Gospel spreads and how the Church gradually takes shape in the cities and countryside of the Roman Empire and beyond during the first five centuries or so of the Christian era, certain key themes or stories stand out as being especially important. They are vital both for understanding the dynamics of Church life in these years, and for helping us to be stronger and wiser Orthodox Christians in our own day. For it is greatly strengthening to see how virtually every aspect of our life as Orthodox Christians is already present in the Church by the end of the 5th century.

In this book we will briefly consider the highlights of ten of these major themes or stories. As we do so, it will become evident that these stories can greatly enlighten, inspire, edify, and strengthen us as we strive to be faithful Orthodox Christians in the 21st century. And at the end of the book, a number of selected resources for further reading and study will be suggested.

As Christians, each one of us owes so much to our forefathers and foremothers in the Faith—all those who lived the Faith and passed it down whole and intact from generation to generation. Many of these, our spiritual ancestors, literally gave their lives in defending the Faith from doctrinal errors (heresies) arising from within the Church, and in the face of persecution from the outside. It is truly marvelous to see how the Holy Spirit, working in and through faithful Christians yielded to the will of God, has guided Christ's Church "into all Truth"—just as Christ promised (John 16:13).

Today, we as Orthodox Christians are the recipients of the fullness of the Christian Faith which all these faithful witnesses, shining as lights upon the earth, have preserved through their lives and writings century by century down to our own time. May we be ever more thankful for the treasure of this glorious inheritance, and may we ourselves be faithful in doing our part, in whatever ways we can, large or small, to pass the Faith whole and intact to the next generation.

And as we begin this study of key themes in the first five centuries of the Christian era, may we be open to receive all the wisdom that the Early Church has to offer us!

Chapter One

AN ORTHODOX UNDERSTANDING OF THE BOOK OF ACTS

INTRODUCTION

THE BOOK OF ACTS—or as it is known in the Orthodox Church, The Acts of the Apostles—was written by St. Luke, author of the third Gospel. It can be seen as the direct continuation of the Gospel of St. Luke—or in other words, the Gospel of St. Luke, Part II. After the Gospels, it is the first history book of the Church, recording many highlights of the history of the Christian movement from the Day of the Ascension of Christ in about 30 AD up until about 65 AD.

We see in the Acts of the Apostles a tremendous emphasis on the guidance of the Holy Spirit in leading the early Christians in their lives, and especially in their extensive missionary work, which is also dramatically described in this book. The Spirit is so much present in the account that the book could well be called The Acts of the Holy Spirit. This is a great reminder to all of us Christians that our lives, too, should be actively guided by the Holy Spirit day by day. As St. Paul writes to the Galatians, "If we live in the Spirit, let us also walk in the Spirit" (Gal. 5:25); and also, "For he who sows to his flesh will of the flesh reap corruption, but he who sows to the Spirit will of the Spirit reap everlasting life" (Gal. 6:8).

We're also reminded by this emphasis on the guidance of the Holy Spirit in the Book of Acts that the Orthodox Church has always retained an understanding of the importance of the Holy Spirit in the doctrine of the Church and in everyday life. One of the most commonly used prayers in the Church is this one addressed to the Holy Spirit:

O Heavenly King, the Comforter, the Spirit of Truth,
Who art everywhere present and fillest all things,
Treasury of blessings and Giver of Life:
Come and abide in us, and cleanse us from every impurity,
And save our souls, O Good One.

The Book of Acts has long been particularly popular among the more independent-minded Protestant Christians, some of whom have established entire, separate denominations based on an attempt to hearken back to Acts as a model or template for how to "have church," or how to get back to or restore "the pristine, primitive Church." Acts is especially popular among Pentecostal and Neo-Pentecostal (Charismatic) Christians because of its emphasis on the workings of the Holy Spirit. Of particular interest to them is the description of the Holy Spirit coming upon the Apostles on the Day of Pentecost, appearing as fiery tongues resting on each one of them, and prompting them to proclaim the Good News of Jesus Christ in all the languages of the known world—languages that they themselves did not know. These Christians also make much of several instances in the book which they consider to be examples of the bestowal of the Holy Spirit on particular believers through an experience known as the "Baptism of the Holy Spirit." In this chapter, we will interpret these passages from an Orthodox point of view, within the sacramental understanding of our Church.

Since the Book of Acts is so popular with so many Protestant Christians, it is all the more necessary for us as Orthodox Christians to embrace the book and appreciate its importance in indicating several crucial ways in which the Early Church would develop through the centuries into the Orthodox Church today. Hence, as we go through the book, we will emphasize the ways in which the first Christians continued to observe the liturgical life of the Jews, centered in Temple worship; the first indications of the developing structure of the Church, centered in the three-fold ministry of bishops, presbyters/priests, and deacons; the account of the first council of the Church, which becomes the prototype for all the local and general councils of the Orthodox Church ever since; and the first indications of infant baptism.

If we find ourselves rather ignorant of the contents of this book, perhaps we won't be too surprised to learn that St. John Chrysostom, the greatest Biblical commentator in the history of our Church, found the same problem among the Christians of his day—the late fourth and early fifth centuries—in the great urban centers of Antioch and Constantinople. As he says in the very beginning of his introduction to his line-by-line commentary on the Acts of the Apostles,

> To many persons this Book is so little known, both it and its author, that they are not even aware that there is such a book in existence. For this reason especially I have taken this narrative for my subject, that I may draw to it those who do not know it, and not let such a treasure as this remain hidden out of sight. For indeed it may profit us no less than even the Gospels—so replete it is with Christian wisdom and sound doctrine, especially in what is said concerning the Holy Spirit (*Nicene and Post-Nicene Fathers*, ed. Philip Schaff [Grand Rapids, Mich.: Wm. B. Eerdmans, 1980, reprint], first series, vol. XI, p. 1).

So let's proceed to our observations about certain selected passages in the book.

CHAPTER 1

Verses 9–11: The Ascension—one of the Twelve major Feastdays of the Orthodox Church, forty days after Pascha (Easter) and ten days before the Day of Pentecost. And in the words of the angels in verse 11—"*this same Jesus* ... will so come in like manner as you saw Him go into Heaven" (my emphasis)—we have one of the strongest Scriptural affirmations of the Second Coming of Christ, and the fact that He will still have His human body when He returns.

Verse 20: "Let another take his office (*episkopen*)"—quoting Psalm 108:8 (LXX). The Greek word means "bishopric"—which would be a more appropriate way to translate it, and which would point towards the development of the office of bishop in the early Church.

Verses 23–26: A selection process followed by a drawing of lots, leaving the ultimate decision to the Lord. This is the very way the new patriarch of Moscow and All-Russia was chosen at the Great Council of the Russian Church held in Moscow in 1917–1918. An election process narrowed the number of possible candidates down to three; those names were then put into a chalice, and after fervent prayer a monk drew Metropolitan Tikhon of Moscow's name—the future St. Tikhon of Moscow and Enlightener of America (for he served as Archbishop of the Orthodox Church in America from 1898 to 1907).

CHAPTER 2

Verses 1–41: The Day of Pentecost—another of the twelve great Feastdays of the Church. Originally it was one of the three major Jewish Feasts, along with the Passover and the Feast of Tabernacles (see Ex. 23:14–17; 34:18–23; and Deut. 16:1–17). It was celebrated at the beginning of the harvesting of the grain (Ex.

34:22), when the Hebrews offered the first fruits of the harvest to the Lord at the Tabernacle. It was always celebrated exactly fifty days after the Passover—hence the name *Pentecost,* derived from the word for "fiftieth." This is a great example of how the Lord filled a key part of the Jewish yearly liturgical cycle with tremendous new meaning in Christ—just as He did in being slain for the salvation of the world on the eve of the Day of Passover, becoming our new *Pascha* (the Greek word for Passover). Hence, the Orthodox Church to this day continues to celebrate these originally Jewish Feasts, but now filled with new meaning in Christ and the Holy Spirit—just as St. Paul and the other earliest Christians did (see, for example, Acts 20:16).

Many Christians consider the Day of Pentecost to be the birthday of the Church, since 3,000 new members were gained that day, greatly expanding the number of Christians from the 120 (Acts 1:15) there were when the day began. But in a certain sense, the Church has existed ever since the creation of the angels, who may be said to have been the first "parishioners" worshiping Christ the Lord. Hence the Book of Hebrews describes the Church in this way: "But you have come to Mount Zion and to the city of the living God, the heavenly Jerusalem, to *an innumerable company of angels* ..." (Heb. 12:22; my emphasis). Probably for this reason the sermon in the writings of the Apostolic Fathers known as 2 Clement says that "by doing the will of God our Father, we shall belong to the first Church, the spiritual one, which was *created before the sun and the moon*" (2 Clement 14:1; my emphasis; see also the *Shepherd of Hermas,* Vision II.4.1).

Verses 16–21: Here St. Peter publicly interprets what has just happened as being a fulfillment of a prophecy from the Hebrew Scriptures (what will become the *Old Testament* for the Christians). The other two references he makes in this speech to the Hebrew Scriptures—in verses 25–28 and 34–35—he says were directly prophetic of Christ, as he explains in verses 29–33 and verse 36. So we see illustrated in this, the very first Christian sermon, *the central Christian hermeneutical (that is, interpretive) key* to understanding the entire Old Testament—seeing it all as being, in one way or another, prophetic of Christ and of other aspects of the Christian Faith and life.

Verse 38: This same pattern or order for the reception of adult converts into the Church is followed to this day in the sacramental life of the Orthodox Church: repentance comes first, which is solidified in a formal way through a lifelong Confession just before one's baptism; then comes water Baptism; and this is immediately followed by the sacrament of Chrismation, in which the Holy Spirit is bestowed and received through the prayers and the anointing with holy oil (called "chrism"). In Chrismation, the newly baptized one is "*sealed* with the gift of the Holy Spirit"; as St. Paul says, "Now He Who establishes us with you in Christ and has anointed us (*chrisas*) is God, Who also has *sealed us* and given us the Spirit in our hearts as a guarantee" (2 Cor. 1:21–22; my emphasis).

Verse 42: Four tremendously important aspects of the Christian life are mentioned in this one verse: apostolic *doctrine*—the teachings of the Faith which the Apostles learned from Christ and through the Holy Spirit (see John 14:25–26); *fellowship*—spending time together both in Church and outside the services (see Heb. 10:24–25); *the breaking of bread—the Eucharist,* which Christ had commanded them to celebrate on a very regular basis (Luke 22:19); and *prayers,* which in the Greek is literally "*the* prayers," referring to the set liturgical prayers said in the services held in the Temple and in the synagogues, which the early Christians were still attending. All of these, of course, are central aspects of the life of Orthodox Christians to this day.

CHAPTER 3

Verses 1–3: This passage gives an indication of how the early Christians, most of whom were ethnically Jewish, continued their centuries-old practice of participating in formal prayer four times each day—at the first hour (6:00 AM), the third hour (9:00 AM), the sixth hour (noon), and the ninth hour (3:00 PM). The Orthodox Church to this day has services called The Hours, one for each of these four times. In monasteries, they are celebrated regularly; in parishes they are typically celebrated only on the most major Feastdays (the Royal Hours at Christmas, Theophany/Epiphany, and Great and Holy Friday).

Verses 18–26: St. Peter, in this second sermon as recorded in Acts, again quotes Old Testament prophecies which he asserts are fulfilled in Christ. Indeed, he declares, "Yes, and all the prophets, from Samuel and those who follow, as many as have spoken, have also foretold these days" (v. 24).

CHAPTER 4

Verses 10–11: St. Peter again quotes an Old Testament prophecy as being fulfilled by Christ. This time he's preaching to the rulers, elders, and scribes of the people (v. 5), as well as to the high priest (v. 6).

Verses 25–26: The early Christians even quote an Old Testament prophecy *in their prayer,* as they are convinced that the prophecy has just been fulfilled, at least in part, in the fierce interrogation of Peter and John at the hands of the Jewish leaders.

Verse 31: This is an additional filling, or a renewal of the filling, of the Spirit that the disciples had received on the Day of Pentecost, *for a specific task*—to preach the Gospel boldly in the face of persecution. This kind of thing should be a typical occurrence in the lives of all Christians who have received the Holy Spirit in Baptism and Chrismation.

CHAPTER 5

Verses 12, 20–21, 25, and 42: The link between the Temple of the Jews and the life, worship, and evangelism of the first Christians is seen again in these verses. Even the angel of the Lord commands the Apostles to proclaim the Christian message *in the Temple* (v. 20). This connection with the Temple very much helps to explain the origins of the highly liturgical worship which developed in the Church during the fourth century, after the era of the great persecutions, when the Church was free to develop without interference or oppression from the governmental authorities. This is when the Church could hearken back to the Temple worship with all of its elaborate trappings such as incense, the altar, and the decorated priestly vestments—all of which had been ordained/commanded by the Lord Himself to Moses (see Ex. 25–28). Now She could incorporate these things into Her own worship in grand cathedrals similar to the Temple in size and beauty.

CHAPTER 6

Verses 1–6: Here we see the selection and ordination of the first seven deacons, foremost of whom was St. Stephen, who hence becomes known as the Protodeacon of the Church. Thus the office of deacon is permanently established in the Church. We observe the very high credentials expected of the first deacons—"men of good reputation, full of the Holy Spirit and wisdom" (v. 3)—even though their first duty was only to "wait on tables," so to speak! We also observe that while the people as a whole selected the candidates, it was the Apostles who laid hands on them to formally set them aside for this ministry. To this day in the Orthodox Church deacons are only ordained *by a bishop*—since the office of bishop came to succeed the office of the apostles. And the Sacrament of Ordination to this day involves the laying on of hands by the bishop upon the head of the new deacon (or priest).

At first, the deacons were only involved with social services in and beyond the community. But in time, they came to have a liturgical role in the worship services of the Church. Also in time, it would become the practice in the Orthodox Church that all those who would be made priests would first serve as deacons.

Verses 8–15: Stephen the Protodeacon disputes with the non-believing Jews so persuasively that they have him arrested and brought before the Jewish council, before the elders and scribes and the high priest (7:1), where they give him a chance to explain what he is talking about.

CHAPTER 7

Verses 2–53: So Stephen proceeds to give the longest sermon recorded in Acts. Most of the sermon is a rehearsal of the highlights of *the history* of the Hebrew people, which reminds us how centrally important our Christian history is to the proper understanding of our Faith. We worship a God Who has been directly engaged in the history of His people ever since He created Adam and Eve.

Verses 54–60: However, St. Stephen ends his sermon with such a direct and piercing accusation of the Jewish leaders that they stone him to death—but not before he says he sees "the heavens opened and the Son of Man standing at the right hand of God" (v. 56). This was a singular honor bestowed by the Lord on His first martyr, for the Nicene Creed says that the Lord Jesus "ascended into Heaven and *sits* at the right hand of God the Father." So besides being St. Stephen the Protodeacon, he is also known with great reverence in our Church as St. Stephen the Protomartyr. His Feastday is December 27.

CHAPTER 8

Verses 14–17: The new Christians in Samaria had been baptized by the deacon St. Philip (v. 12; he was first mentioned in Acts 6:5). But when the Apostles Peter and John came to see the results of Philip's ministry, they saw that something was missing—the newly baptized had been wooed and drawn to Christ by the Holy Spirit, but they had not yet received the Holy Spirit internally. So the Apostles bestowed the Spirit upon them through laying their hands on them. This shows that from the beginning it was understood that the Spirit is given through a separate sacramental action with Apostolic/ Episcopal authority. In the Orthodox Church to this day, the Spirit is conveyed in the Sacrament of Chrismation, as we noted above, which is administered immediately after Baptism by the celebrant—either a bishop, or a priest who always ministers in the name of his bishop. And when a priest performs this sacrament, his bishop's authority is present through the oil—*the chrism*—that's used, which is only prepared and consecrated through the authorization, and under the supervision of, his bishop (or his archbishop, or metropolitan, or patriarch).

Verses 18–20: The crime of buying or selling an office of the Church is called *simony,* from the name *Simon.* This Simon later became known as Simon Magus (Simon the Great), who, after rejecting Christianity, returned to sorcery, and gathered a large following in Rome. According to St. Hippolytus, a writer in Rome in the early third century, Simon perished dramatically in Rome after being repeatedly opposed by St. Peter (*The Refutation of All Heresies,* Book VI, ch. 15; in *Ante-Nicene Fathers,* ed. Alexander Roberts and James Donalson [Grand Rapids, Mich.: Wm. B. Eerdmans, 1981], vol. V, p. 81).

Verses 26–35: This incident is a great demonstration in the Scriptures of *our need for assistance* in interpreting the Scriptures. Just as the Ethiopian eunuch needed Philip, who was well-versed in the Hebrew Scriptures, so we, too, need guides who are steeped in the historic Christian Tradition, which holds and preserves the proper interpretation of the Scriptures. As St. Peter says, "knowing this first, that no prophecy of Scripture is of *any private interpretation*" (2 Peter 1:20). In this statement by the Apostle Peter, we see that the classic Protestant claim of "*Sola Scriptura*" ("Scripture alone")—meaning that the Scriptures are meant to be interpreted by each person by himself or herself, without the need for guidance in and through Holy Tradition—is overturned by the Scriptures themselves. St. Peter also overturns the typical Protestant claim that the Scriptures are *easy to be understood by anyone* when he says in this same letter, "our beloved brother Paul, according to the wisdom given to him, has written to you, as also in all his epistles, speaking in them of these things, *in which are some things hard to understand,* which untaught and unstable people twist to their own destruction, *as they do also the rest of the Scriptures*" (2 Peter 2:15–16; my emphasis).

Verses 36–39: The conversion and baptism of the Ethiopian eunuch, treasurer for Candace the Queen of Ethiopia, marks the beginning of the Christian movement in black Africa. In time, the Church in Ethiopia becomes known as the Ethiopian Orthodox Church.

Verse 40: In one of the most dramatic of all the interventions of the Holy Spirit in the Acts of the Apostles, St. Philip the Deacon is lifted into the air and taken by the Spirit to Azotus, at least ten miles away, where he suddenly finds himself.

CHAPTER 9

Verses 3–6: The Lord Jesus, His holy Mother Mary the Theotokos (the Bearer of God), and many of His Saints have made appearances to many through the centuries. In our own time, Jesus appeared to a young Muslim in Indonesia as he was reading the Koran. This man became Fr. Daniel Byantoro, the first Indonesian

Orthodox convert, and later priest and apostle to his homeland. Through him, Holy Orthodoxy became established in Indonesia for the first time.

Verse 10: Ananias was the first bishop of the city of Damascus.

Verse 11: The Orthodox Church and Patriarchate of Antioch currently has its headquarters on the Street called Straight in Damascus; the Patriarchate was moved from Antioch to Damascus for strategic reasons in 1322. The present Patriarch of Antioch is John x (Yazigi).

Verse 31: This verse shows how far the Church had spread in the first several years after the Day of Pentecost.

CHAPTER 10

Verses 44–48: This is considered to be the Pentecost of the Gentiles, since Cornelius and his family and friends are the first non-Jewish Christian converts, as recorded in Acts. Here we see a reversal of the usual pattern of repentance, baptism, and then the filling with the Holy Spirit, as the Holy Spirit Himself comes down upon the listeners *before* they are baptized. This undoubtedly was *necessary* for the sake of the Jews accompanying St. Peter—and probably St. Peter himself—who had to witness something very dramatic in order to be fully convinced that the Gospel of Christ was meant for all the peoples of the world, and not just the Jews. Perhaps something similar happened with Ananias and St. Paul in the previous chapter (Acts 9:17–18), so that Ananias would be fully convinced that it was proper to baptize Saul, the fierce persecutor of the Christians. Certainly Saul must indeed have been totally transformed through his encounter with Christ on the road if he's now miraculously receiving his sight and being filled with the Holy Spirit before being baptized! In both these cases, the new converts were baptized immediately afterwards, showing how crucially important water baptism was for the early Church, as it still is today in the Orthodox Church.

According to Church Tradition, Cornelius eventually became a bishop, either of Caesarea or of Scepsis in Lysia. He is commemorated as a Saint in our Church on September 13.

CHAPTER 11

Verses 1–18: Again, it was the tremendously wondrous and dramatic way that St. Cornelius and his household were brought to belief in Christ and were then baptized into the Church, as recounted by St. Peter himself, that convinced the Jewish Christians in Jerusalem that the Gospel was meant for everybody—Jews and Gentiles alike.

Verses 20–24: As the young Church began to flourish in Antioch, the Apostles in Jerusalem saw fit to send one of their number to Antioch to provide some apostolic oversight—to see what was happening and to make sure everything was being done "decently and in order" (1 Cor. 14:40). The person they chose was a remarkable man named Barnabas, whose name very appropriately means "Son of Consolation." He is venerated in the Orthodox Church as St. Barnabas, one the Seventy Apostles. His Feastday is June 11.

Verses 25–26: Here we see the tremendously important role that St. Barnabas played in going to Tarsus to find St. Paul and bring him to Antioch, where he greatly assisted the Church there with his inspired preaching and teaching. It's very significant that Paul did not promote himself. Rather, it was an Apostle who went all the way to Tarsus to seek him out, and then bring him to Antioch to help with the ministry there.

Verse 30: The word translated as "elders" is *presbyterous* in the Greek. This is the first reference to "presbyters"—or as they later come to be also known, "priests"—in the New Testament.

CHAPTER 12

Verse 12: "John whose surname was Mark" is St. Mark the Evangelist, the writer of the Gospel of St. Mark. At first a companion of the Apostles Paul and Barnabas, who was his uncle or cousin (see Acts 12:25; 13:5; 15:36–39; Col. 4:10), John Mark later was such a close companion of St. Peter that Peter calls him "my son" at the end of his first epistle (1 Peter 5:13). This Mark eventually became the first bishop of the Church of Alexandria, Egypt; the Orthodox Patriarchate of Alexandria and All Africa is known as the throne of St. Mark. Martyred by pagans in 63 AD, his Feastday is April 25. He was succeeded by Bp. Annianos, who governed the Church of Alexandria from 63 to 82 AD. The current patriarch of Alexandria, through the direct line of apostolic succession, is Theodoros II.

Verse 15: Here is an indication that every human being has a guardian angel assigned to him or her by the Lord (see also Matt. 18:10). Some Orthodox prayerbooks include a prayer addressed to one's guardian angel.

Verse 17: This James is known as St. James, the Brother of the Lord—more precisely, the *foster-brother* of the Lord Jesus, since according to the Eastern tradition he was the son of St. Joseph the Betrothed by an earlier marriage. By this time this James is functioning as the first bishop of the Church in Jerusalem. We see his headship of the community there indicated in this verse. He is also the author of the Book of James in the New Testament. His Feastday is October 23. He was succeeded by Symeon, who led the Church of Jerusalem from 62 to 106 AD. The current patriarch of Jerusalem, Theophilos III, is the 141st head of this Church in the line of apostolic succession.

CHAPTER 13

Verse 1: The office of prophet existed in the Church for several generations (see Acts 11:27–28 and 21:10–11 concerning the prophet Agabus; Acts 15:32 concerning Judas [Barsabas] and Silas; and Acts 21:9 about St. Philip the Deacon's "four virgin daughters who prophesied. See also Luke 2:36–38; 1 Cor. 12:29 and 14:3; and Eph. 4:11 for further references to prophesying in the New Testament. For references to this office in the Old Testament, see Ex. 15:20–21 for Miriam; Judges 4:4 for Deborah; 4 Kingdoms 22:14 for Huldah; and Is. 8:3 for the Prophet Isaiah's wife).

However, over time there proved to be difficulties with regulating the activities of the traveling prophets, as we see in the mid-second century document known as the *Didache* (11:3–12). Also, the rigorist, schismatic movement of the later second century known as Montanism based its authority upon the prophecies of Montanus and two female prophetesses, whose prophecies were claiming further authority than the Gospels and the letters of St. Paul, as we will see. So the office of prophet gradually comes to be subsumed within that of the bishop. This process is indicated in this verse from the early 2nd century document known as the *Didache*: "Ordain for yourselves, then, bishops and deacons who are worthy of the Lord—men who are unassuming and not greedy, who are honest and have been proved. For *they also are performing for you the task of the prophets* and teachers" (*Didache* 15:1; my emphasis).

Verses 4–12: Christianity had first come to the island of Cyprus a few years earlier, as recorded in Acts 11:19). Here we can imagine how the new Church there must have been strengthened and encouraged by this visit of St. Paul, St. Barnabas, and St. Mark! The great Greek collection of Saints' Lives, called the *Synaxarion*, includes a large number of Cypriot Saints in the first centuries AD, which gives a strong indication of the steady growth of the Church on Cyprus. In the early centuries the Church there was subject administratively to the more prominent Church of Antioch. But in 431, at the Third Ecumenical Council held in Ephesus, the Church of Cyprus was officially given Her full independence, headed by an archbishop, as She still is to this day.

Two of the Church's most distinguished Saints of the early centuries were St. Spyridon of Trimethos and St. Epiphanios, Archbishop of Salamis. St. Spyridon was a godly shepherd who was made a bishop by popular acclaim after his wife died. At the First Ecumenical Council at Nicea in 325, he performed a notable miracle there demonstrating the truth of the Holy Trinity. St. Epiphanios was a great fighter of heresies who died in 403. St. Spyridon's Feastday is December 12, and St. Epiphanios's is May 12.

Verses 16–41: Just as St. Stephen had done in his sermon (Acts 7), so St. Paul immediately rehearses key parts of the history of Israel leading up to the birth of the Messiah, Jesus. And just as St. Peter had quoted prophecies from the Hebrew Scriptures as being fulfilled in Christ, St. Paul does so as well.

CHAPTER 14

Verse 1: As noted in the *Orthodox Study Bible* (p. 1493), in the *Acts of Thekla*, written in the 2nd century, there is a description of St. Paul that was told to "a man from Iconium" (in central Asia Minor): "a small man in size with meeting eyebrows, a rather large nose, bald, bow-legged, but strongly built, full of grace, who at times seemed to have the face of an angel." This is basically how he is depicted in the icons of the Orthodox Church.

Verse 23: The word "appointed" should be translated "ordained," since this is exactly what the Greek word (*cheirotonesantes*) means. So here we see again the Sacrament of Ordination in the Acts of the Apostles. Also, the word "elders" again is *presbyterous* (see above for the note for Acts 11:30).

CHAPTER 15

Verses 1–2: One of the great advantages of having a hierarchical Church is that disputes can be taken to a higher level for consideration and adjudication. Here, and in verses 4, 6, 22, and 23, we see elders/ presbyters/priests mentioned further.

Verses 6–29: This passage describes the first council of the Church—the Council of Jerusalem—which took place in 49 AD. This council set the precedent for all the subsequent councils, whether local, regional, or ecumenical (worldwide), in the history of the Church up to the present. In nearly every case, discussion, deliberation, and adjudication have been followed by nearly unanimous acceptance, through prayer and the help of the Holy Spirit. As the participants in the council declared, "being assembled with one accord" (v. 25); and, "For it seemed good to the Holy Spirit, and to us …" (v. 28). We also notice very clearly the leadership/ headship of St. James, the Brother of the Lord, at this council, since he gives the final word (vv. 13–21). This is a key indication of St. James's position as the first bishop of the Church of Jerusalem.

CHAPTER 16

Verses 1–3: This Timothy had been raised in the Christian Faith by his ethnically Jewish mother, Eunice, who believed in Christ, as did her mother, Lois (2 Tim. 1:5). Becoming a "true son in the faith" of St. Paul (1 Tim. 1:2), Timothy received two letters from Paul which would become part of the New Testament. Eventually St. Timothy succeeded the Apostle John as bishop of Ephesus. His Feastday is January 22.

It's natural to wonder why St. Paul circumcised St. Timothy, since the Council of Jerusalem, as recounted in the immediately preceding chapter, stipulated that circumcision would not be required of Gentile converts to Christianity. But Paul did so in this case by way of an exception (or *economia*), for pastoral and evangelistic reasons, so that the Jews would be more likely to accept Paul's special relationship with Timothy, and so that the Jews might more readily accept all of Timothy's future ministry. This is an example of how the Orthodox Church to this day interprets and implements the *canons* (i.e., the ecclesiastical laws/rules/regulations) according to the unique circumstances of each particular case.

Verse 10: The shift to the first person plural by the author of Acts, St. Luke the Evangelist, is very significant, as it shows that he was with St. Paul, St. Silas, and St. Timothy at this point. At several further points in the Book of Acts this same thing occurs, showing that St. Luke is writing from his first-hand experience as an eyewitness when he records some of the events in Acts. Humanly speaking, this would add to the veracity of the Acts of the Apostles. But as St. John Chrysostom says, referring to St. Luke's authorship of the work, "So that there can be no mistake in attributing this work to him; and when I say to him, I mean, to Christ" (NPNF, first series, vol. XI, p. 2). In this way he testifies to the Divine inspiration of the writing of this book.

Verse 15: This is the second instance as recorded in Acts of an entire household being baptized. The first such instance was the household of the first Gentile convert, St. Cornelius (Acts 10:2). Most likely, these entire households included small children and perhaps infants, and presumably all of them received baptism.

Verses 30–34: Another entire household receives baptism, so here is another indication of the practice of the baptism of young children in the Early Church.

CHAPTER 17

Verses 1–10: Despite this tumultuous ending to St. Paul's very brief time of ministry in Thessalonica, this most major city in northern Greece, Paul will have special affection for the new Christians there, as seen in his two letters written to them not long after his visit there. As he tells them in his first letter,

> But we were gentle among you, just as a nursing mother cherishes her own children. So, affectionately longing for you, we were well pleased to impart to you not only the gospel of God, but also our own lives, because you had become dear to us. For you remember, brethren, our labor and toil; for laboring night and day, that we might not be a burden to any of you, we preached to you the gospel of God.... you know how we exhorted, and comforted, and charged every one of you, as a father does his own children, that you would walk worthy of God, Who calls you into His own kingdom and glory (1 Thess. 2:7–12).

And further, "For what thanks can we render to God for you, for all the joy with which we rejoice for your sake before our God, night and day praying exceedingly that we may see your face and perfect what is lacking in your faith?" (1 Thess. 3:9–10).

Most likely, St. Paul's two letters to the Church in Thessalonica, written around the year 51 AD, are the earliest of all the writings that eventually would become collected and canonized as the New Testament.

The Church in Thessalonica has flourished to this day. She is especially blessed to have in Her midst the relics of Her two most illustrious Saints—Great Martyr St. Demetrios the Myrrhgushing, and St. Gregory Palamas. St. Demetrios died in the Diocletian Persecution of the early 4th century. His relics, housed in the leading church of the city, have exuded divine myrrh ever since. St. Gregory is one of the greatest Church Fathers of all time. He was the archbishop of the Church in Thessalonica from 1350 till his death in 1359. Today, the Church there is administratively subject to the Archbishop of Athens.

Verse 34: This Dionysius eventually became the first Bishop of the Church of Athens. Orthodox Tradition considers him to be the author of a number of very mystical works, including *The Divine Names* and *The Celestial Hierarchy*. However, since these works never appeared in the history of the Church until the early 6th century, it is often thought that they were written by a later, unknown author. St. Dionysius the Areopagite is commemorated in the Church on October 3. The "woman named Damaris" is also venerated as a Saint. Her Feastday is October 2.

CHAPTER 18

Verses 1–4 and 11: St. John Chrysostom marvels at what it must have been like for Priscilla and Aquila to have St. Paul, "the tongue of the whole world," staying in their home for more than a year and a half:

> Priscilla and Aquila, then, were worthy of Paul. And if worthy of Paul, they were also worthy of angels. And their house I could confidently call a Church, or even Heaven itself. For where Paul was, there was Christ . . . And where Christ was, there the angels constantly gathered.
>
> For if the couple had already rendered themselves worthy to be hosts to Paul, think what they became in their two years of living with him, as they carefully watched his bearing, his walk, his look, his way of dressing, his comings and goings, and everything else. . . .
>
> Imagine how great it was to see Paul doing things like eating dinner, and reproving, and consoling, and praying, and crying, day in and day out! We have only fourteen of his letters, and we take them all over the world. So we can imagine how those living with him must have become like angels—they who had with them the wellspring of these epistles, the tongue of the whole world, the light of the Churches, the foundation of the Faith, the pillar and ground of the Truth!
>
> If the demons were afraid of his very garments, which possessed such power [cf. Acts 19:12]. how much grace of the Spirit would one have gained through living with him! Would not simply seeing Paul's chair, his bed, or his sandals have been enough to move one to continual compunction? If the demons trembled at seeing his clothes, how much more would the faithful, and especially those living with him, have been stirred to contrition by seeing them? (David and Mary Ford, *Marriage as a Path to Holiness: Lives of Married Saints*, second ed. [St. Tikhon's Monastery Press, 2013], pp. 153–154).

Verse 8: Here is another entire household coming to faith in Christ and being baptized.

Verse 18: We see here St. Paul's great esteem for his hosts, Priscilla and Aquila, as he takes them with him for the next stage on his very long missionary journey.

We also see here St. Paul taking a vow, probably some sort of Nazarite vow that included one's hair being shorn (see Numbers 6:1–21). This is another indication of the continuity between Judaism and early Christianity, especially for the Jewish Christians.

Verse 21: Here is another indication of this continuity, as St. Paul finds it extremely important to be back in Jerusalem in time for a major Jewish Feast (probably either Passover or Pentecost), which of course for the Jewish Christians was replete with additional meaning in Christ.

Verses 24–28: The critical Greek text has Priscilla listed before her husband Aquila in v. 26, which would imply that the woman was the leading one in further instructing Apollos. This is all the more noteworthy in that Apollos was already a powerful and effective preacher of the Gospel: "an eloquent man and mighty in the Scriptures ... fervent in spirit, ... [who] spoke and taught accurately the things of the Lord" (vv. 24–25).

This remarkable husband and wife missionary team remained in Ephesus for some time, where their home was a house-church (see 1 Cor. 16:19). Later we find them back in Rome, again with a house-church meeting in their home (see Romans 16:3–5). They are Saints in our Church, being commemorated on February 13.

CHAPTER 19

Verses 1–7: Again we see the sacramental pattern being followed—water Baptism followed by the laying on of hands to receive the Holy Spirit, which occurs in the Orthodox sacrament of Chrismation. Thus we see the error of modern Charismatic Christians when they pray for people to "receive the Holy Spirit" whether or not these people have been baptized.

Verses 11–12: In the Orthodox understanding of Creation, all of the natural, material, physical order is *good*; indeed, as the Lord fashioned it, He repeatedly declared that it was good (Genesis 1). Even further, since the natural order is good and God-given, *it can convey spiritual realities*. This understanding is at the heart of the Orthodox sacramental world-view, centered in our understanding of the *natural sacramentality*—or natural holiness—of the world.

In these verses we have an instance of some items from the material realm conveying spiritual reality—indeed, miracle-working power! In a comparable way, the woman with the issue of blood was healed simply by touching the hem of Jesus' garment (Luke 8:43–47). Jesus Himself once used clay to heal a blind man (John 9:6–7). And, of course, in our sacraments, or *mysteries*, bread, wine, water, and olive oil all convey Divine grace and power.

As an example of this same general principle from the Old Testament, the bones of Elisha the Prophet brought a dead man back to life (4 Kingdoms 13:20–21, LXX; 2 Kings 13:20–21, KJV). All of this, along with the lived experience of the Church, undergirds our practice of keeping and venerating the relics of the Saints, through which untold numbers of people have been healed of all kinds of ailments through the centuries.

CHAPTER 20

Verse 6: Again we see the importance of the Jewish liturgical cycle for the early Christians.

Verse 7: This is an indication that Sunday, the first day of the week, known as *the Lord's Day* (Rev. 1:10), was established *from the beginning* of the Christian movement as their main day of worship, rather than the Jewish Sabbath (Saturday). Thus it is an error to believe that Christians did not start worshiping on Sunday until this day in every week was made a legal holiday by Emperor Constantine the Great, the first Christian emperor, in the early 4th century. Rather than instituting something new, he was simply acknowledging and honoring the age-old Christian practice. And this Sunday worship always included the celebration of the Eucharist, which is referred to here in the words "to break bread."

Verse 16: Once again, we see St. Paul's determination to reach Jerusalem in time for a major Jewish, but also Christian, Feast—the Feast of Pentecost.

Verses 17–38: St. Paul's great love for the Church in Ephesus, where he had spent three years (v. 31), and their love for him (vv. 37–38), is demonstrated very vividly in this scene, as he calls for the elders (*presbyterous*; in the Greek he also calls them "bishops" in v. 28 [*episkopous*]) of that Church and meets with them in Miletus, about 30 miles away further down the seacoast. Later St. Paul would write one of his most magnificent letters in the New Testament to the Ephesians.

Some time after this, the Apostle and Evangelist John the Theologian came to Ephesus, where he lived the rest of his very long life as the bishop of that city, which was the most prominent city in the Roman province in southwest Asia Minor known as Asia. In around 90 AD, when John received his revelation as recorded in the Book of Revelation, one of the seven churches which received a message in chapters 2 and 3 of that work was the Church of Ephesus. Unfortunately, by then the Christians there were being chastised because "you have left your first love" (Rev. 3:4), even though they were praised for their hard work, perseverance, and patience (Rev. 3:2–3). They were also praised for rejecting false apostles (Rev. 3:2), as well as rejecting the sect of the Nicolaitans, who were probably an early libertine Gnostic group (Rev. 3:6; we will look at Gnosticism in Chapter Four).

Christianity flourished greatly in Ephesus in the early centuries. Indicative of this is the fact that the Third Ecumenical Council was held there in 431. But all of Asia Minor, the ancient heartland of the Early Church, was overrun by Islamic Seljuk Turks in the late 11th and early 12th centuries, and the churches there never fully recovered. Nearly all the Greek Orthodox Christians remaining there by the early 20th century were forcibly deported to Greece in the infamous population exchange of 1923–1924.

CHAPTER 21

Verses 8–10: This is the last reference to St. Philip the Deacon in the New Testament. He eventually became Bishop of Tralles on the northwest coast of Asia Minor. St. Ignatius of Antioch, one of the great Apostolic Fathers, wrote a letter to the Church there in about 107. St. Philip died a natural death in great old age. Considered to be one of the Seventy Apostles, he is commemorated on October 11.

Verse 18: Here is another indication of St. James being the first bishop of the Church of Jerusalem. This is the final reference to this great early Christian leader. St. Hegisippus (c. 60–c. 130; commemorated on April 7), the first historian of the Christian movement, wrote of him,

> He used to enter the Sanctuary alone, and was often found on his knees beseeching forgiveness for the people, so that his knees grew hard as a camel's from his continually bending them in worship of God and beseeching forgiveness for the people. Because of his unsurpassable righteousness, he was called "the Righteous" (quoted by Eusebius, the Bishop of Caesarea in Palestine, the first major Church historian, who wrote his great *Ecclesiastical History* in the early years of the 4th century; EH 2.23).

Also, his name is associated with the oldest and longest form of the Divine Liturgy, the Liturgy of St. James, the heart of which may well date back to his time. Today it is celebrated very rarely, if ever, in the Orthodox Church. Some parishes and monasteries celebrate it on St. James's two days of commemoration—October 23, and on the Sunday following Christmas.

Verses 23–26: This is another instance of St. Paul taking a special vow according to Jewish custom, in order to help his fellow Jews understand that following Christ did not mean forsaking all the customs of Judaism.

CHAPTER 22

Verses 17–21: Another instance of Paul spending time in the Temple. This time Christ Himself even appears to him!

CHAPTER 24

Verses 14–15: St. Paul here very clearly expresses *the unity* between the Old Testament—"the Law and the Prophets" and the worship of "the God of my fathers"—and the Christian gospel and way of life, which he calls here "the Way." For he knows that "the God of my fathers" is the very same God Who raised Jesus from the dead (Acts 13:29–37; cf. 17:31). Ananias, who would become the first bishop of Damascus, expressed this same truth directly to Paul when he told him, "The God of our fathers has chosen you that you should know His will, and see the Just One, and hear the voice of His mouth [referring to Christ]" (Acts 22:14).

CHAPTER 26

Verses 1–23: Again we see an historical account given in a speech as recorded in Acts. This time it's St. Paul's own autobiographical account—or as we could say, he gives his own *testimony*. So again we see the great importance of history for the spread of the Gospel message. And again we see an appeal to the Hebrew Scriptures, that many things about Christ were long ago foretold in those writings by "the prophets and Moses" (vv. 22–23; see also Acts 28:23).

CHAPTER 28

Verses 30–31: The Acts of the Apostles ends on a very positive note, for even though St. Paul was under house arrest, he had great freedom to receive guests, and to teach them and preach to them. All the rest of Christian history up to and including the present can be seen as the continuation of the Book of Acts, with the Holy Spirit empowering faithful believers to spread the Gospel message to, and establish churches in, all the world.

EPILOGUE TO THE BOOK OF ACTS

St. Paul, as is well-known, was beheaded for his faith in Christ under the crazed Emperor Nero (ruled 54–68 AD) in about 67 AD, on June 29.

St. Peter also died in the fierce persecution of Christians initiated and overseen by Nero, either on the same day as St. Paul, or on June 29 a year later. The account of Peter's martyrdom says, when the persecution rose up against the Christians of Rome,

> with tears the faithful entreated the apostle to save his life, which was so necessary for the holy Church, which was tempest-tossed amid the waves of tribulations caused by the ungodly. Yielding to this tearful plea of his reason-endowed flock, St. Peter [very reluctantly] promised to hide himself outside the city.
>
> On the following night, after praying with his spiritual children, he bade farewell to all and departed, alone. But when he was beyond the city gates, he saw the Lord Jesus Christ coming towards him. Bowing low before Him, the holy Peter said: "Whither goest Thou, Lord?" "I go to Rome, to be crucified anew!" the Lord said in answer, and then vanished.
>
> Astonished, the apostle knew that Christ, Who suffers in His servants, as in His own members, also desired to suffer in his body. The Savior had prophesied the crucifixion which would fall to Peter's lot, when He said: "'Amen, Amen, I say unto thee, When thou wast young, thou girdest thyself, and walkest whither thou wouldest. But when thou shalt be old, thou shalt stretch forth thy hands, and another shall gird thee, and carry thee whither thou wouldest not.' This He said, signifying by what death he should glorify God" (John 12:18–19)....
>
> Peter, therefore, returned to the faithful and was arrested by the soldiers and taken to his death.

When Peter was sentenced to be crucified, he

> requested that he be crucified head-downwards, saying, "I am not worthy to be crucified as my Christ, upright. For thus He was crucified, so as to look to the earth, where He would descend into hades to deliver the souls therein. Crucify me head down, that I may look to heaven, whither I will go" (*The Lives of the Holy Apostles*, compiled by Holy Apostles Convent [Buena Vista, Colo.: Holy Apostles Convent, 1988], pp. 21–23).

It is completely understandable that the Church in Rome would increase in prestige and honor through the fact that both of the two greatest Apostles were martyred there. And indeed, by the middle of the next century the city had already become a popular site of pilgrimage, as Christians from all over the Empire traveled there to venerate the graves and the relics of the great Apostles Peter and Paul.

They are commemorated together every year on June 29; and the preceding fasting period, known as the Apostles' Fast, is dedicated to them.

The Lives of all the rest of the original eleven Disciples of the Lord, as well as the Lives of St. Paul, St. Matthias (Acts 1:23–26), St. Mark, St. Luke, and St. James the Brother of the Lord, are all recounted in *The Lives of the Holy Apostles*, compiled by the Holy Apostles Convent, as just noted above. This book can surely be considered the direct sequel to the Book of Acts.

Chapter Two

THE APOSTOLIC FATHERS ENCOURAGE AND TEACH THE FAITHFUL

WHO WERE THE APOSTOLIC FATHERS?

HAVE YOU EVER WONDERED what happened in the Early Church *after* the Book of Acts? That book, as we've seen, gives various highlights of roughly the first 35 years of the history of the Church—up until about 65 AD. But what happened after that?

As we noted at the end of the previous chapter, we can read in the *Lives of the Holy Apostles* about the travels and the martyrdoms of the original Twelve Apostles, with St. Matthias taking the place of the traitorous Judas. This takes us up to about the year 100, when St. John the Theologian, the last of the Twelve Apostles, died in Ephesus.

But who were the leaders of the Church after that? What writings did they leave? And what do these writings reveal about the teachings, the worship, the spirituality, and the structure of the Church in the decades immediately following the era of the original Apostles?

The writings known as *The Apostolic Fathers* give us many answers to these questions. Dating from as early as the late first century up to the middle of the second century, these writings were composed by leaders in the Early Church, who addressed them to fellow Christians for their instruction, encouragement, and edification. This is just like the letters/epistles of the New Testament, which were written to the faithful for their spiritual benefit in the middle of the first century by St. Paul, St. James, St. Peter, St. Jude, and St. John the Theologian.

So the Apostolic Fathers, as their name suggests, stand in direct continuation with the Apostles. They were taught either by the Twelve Apostles or by those who worked with them. These are some of the "faithful men" whom St. Paul wrote of to his spiritual son St. Timothy: "And the things that you have heard from me among many witnesses, commit these to faithful men who will be able to teach others also" (2 Tim. 2:2).

We can trust the teachings of the Apostolic Fathers because Jesus Himself promised to His disciples, "When He, the Spirit of Truth, has come, He will guide you into all Truth" (John 16:13). And the Holy Spirit did come with mighty power on the Day of Pentecost, and He has continued to abide within and guide the Church ever since.

Also, Jesus had commanded the Apostles, "Go therefore and make disciples of all the nations, baptizing them in the name of the Father and of the Son and of the Holy Spirit, teaching them to observe all things that I have commanded you." Surely those whom He had personally taught for three years, both by His words and the example of His pure life, would be able to accurately convey His teachings to others! We can have even more confidence about this in light of Christ's promise to His followers when He adds, "and lo, I am with you always, even to the end of the age" (Matt. 28:19–20). And we recall that He had promised them earlier, "I will build My Church, and the gates of hell shall not prevail against it" (Matt. 16:18).

As we've indicated, the Apostolic Fathers immediately follow the first Apostles and their disciples. In fact, 1 Clement, the earliest of the writings of the Apostolic Fathers, was written in about 96 AD, when St. John the Theologian, the last of the original Twelve Disciples of Christ, was still alive!

ST. CLEMENT OF ROME

1 Clement was most likely written by St. Clement of Rome, the third bishop of that city, even though his name is never mentioned in the book. Clement's close association with the Apostles Peter and Paul is described by St. Irenaeus of Lyons, the great Church Father of the latter part of the second century, in these words:

> The blessed apostles Peter and Paul, then, having founded and built up the Church in Rome, committed into the hands of Linus the office of the episcopate. Paul makes mention of this Linus in his Epistles to Timothy [2 Tim. 4:21]. After Linus came Anacletus. And

> after him, in the third place from the apostles, Clement was allotted the bishopric. This man, as he had seen the blessed apostles, and had been conversant with them, might be said to have the preaching of the apostles still echoing in his ears, and their traditions still before his eyes. Nor was he alone in this, for there were many still remaining alive who had received instructions from the apostles (*Against Heresies* III.3.3).

1 Clement is a letter written to the Church in Corinth. It opens with the words, "The Church sojourning in Rome to the Church sojourning in Corinth." This, of course, was the same Corinthian Church to which St. Paul had written his two epistles (which were later included in the New Testament) just about 45 years earlier. So that means there surely were believers in that Church who in 96 AD could remember St. Paul's letters being received and first read in their Church!

St. Clement's letter was being read as Scripture in the Church of Corinth around the year 170. Also, it occurs in the Codex Alexandrinus, a very important manuscript of New Testament writings dating from the early fifth century.

ST. POLYCARP OF SMYRNA

St. Polycarp, another of the Apostolic Fathers, as a young man undoubtedly knew St. John the Theologian and was taught by him. Several years after St. John's death, Polycarp became Bishop of Smyrna in western Asia Minor (now Izmir, in Turkey). As St. Irenaeus writes,

> Polycarp also was not only instructed by apostles, and conversed with many who had seen Christ, but was also, by apostles in Asia, appointed bishop of the Church in Smyrna.

St. Irenaeus was born around the year 120 and grew up in the Church in western Asia Minor. As a young man, he knew Bp. Polycarp and was taught by him. As Irenaeus says,

> I saw Polycarp in my early youth, for he tarried on earth a very long time. When he was a very old man, he gloriously and most nobly suffered martyrdom. He departed this life, having always taught the things which he had learned from the apostles, and which the Church has handed down, and which alone are true (*Against Heresies* III.3.4).

St. Polycarp wrote a letter to the Philippians—the same church that St. Paul wrote an epistle to in the previous century. This letter by St. Polycarp is filled with references to verses in the Acts of the Apostles and in the Epistles of St. Paul, St. Peter, and St. James. This shows how these writings were already being treated as Scripture in Smyrna in the first half of the second century.

We also are blessed to have the remarkable account of St. Polycarp's martyrdom, which occurred in about the year 157. This account was written by the Church in Smyrna to the Church in the neighboring town of Philomelium. In this report, the events leading up to Polycarp's martyrdom are recounted, and his awesome martyrdom itself is described. The Early Church's understanding of martyrdom, and the importance of the veneration of Saints and their relics, are also presented.

ST. IGNATIUS OF ANTIOCH

St. Ignatius, another of the Apostolic Fathers, lived even earlier than St. Clement and St. Polycarp did. He was born around the year 30 AD. According to tradition, he was the child whom Christ took up into His arms (Matt. 18:2). In about the year 69 AD, he became the second bishop of the very important city of Antioch (where the followers of Christ were first called Christians, as it says in Acts 11:26). This was only about ten years or so after the Apostle Peter lived in Antioch, helping to strengthen the Church there.

In about 107, as St. Ignatius was taken by armed guards across Asia Minor on his way to be martyred in Rome, the soldiers and their captive stopped for a while in Smyrna, where St. Polycarp was bishop. There Ignatius was allowed to meet with Polycarp. Imagine the glorious and wonderful, yet poignant, fellowship they must have had together!

While in Smyrna, Ignatius took the opportunity to write letters to the Churches in Ephesus, Magnesia, and Tralles (all in western Asia Minor). He also wrote a letter to the Christians in Rome, urging them not to try to prevent his martyrdom by appealing to the civil authorities there. For he was utterly convinced that God had revealed to him that he should end his life on this earth as a sacrifice to Christ through being offered to the teeth of wild animals in the arena.

From Troas, on the western coast of Asia Minor, Ignatius wrote a letter back to Polycarp, highly praising him. He also wrote a letter to the Church of Smyrna as a whole, as well as one to the Church in Philadelphia, also in western Asia Minor.

So these are the famous seven letters of St. Ignatius, which give such a dramatic glimpse into the life of the Church in western Asia Minor, the heartland region of Christianity, in the early years of the second century. (We may remember that in the Revelation of St. John, John was commanded to write messages, dictated by Christ Himself, to the Churches in Ephesus, Smyrna, and Philadelphia [Rev. 2:1–11 and 3:7–13]. These messages were received by these Churches only about ten years before they received the letters written by St. Ignatius.)

Bishop Eusebius of Caesarea, the first great historian of the Church, writing in the early fourth century, calls St. Ignatius "one who to this day is universally remembered" (*Ecclesiastical History* 3.36). And St. Polycarp strongly proclaims the great worth of Ignatius's letters when he writes to the Philippians,

> We are sending you at your request the letters of Ignatius which he sent to us, and any others which we possess. They are attached to this letter. You will be able to benefit greatly from them. For they deal with faith and endurance and all the edification which belongs to our Lord (Polycarp, Epistle to the Philippians 13.2).

HERMAS OF ROME

The *Shepherd of Hermas* is the longest of the writings of the Apostolic Fathers. It was probably written by a married layman in Rome named Hermas, around the year 150 AD. Certain parts of the Early Church esteemed it so highly that in some local churches it was considered to be at the same level of inspiration as the Gospels and Epistles which were already becoming recognized as the heart of the New Testament. As the *Oxford Dictionary of the Christian Church* says of this work,

> In the Greek Church of the 2nd and 3rd centuries, the work was widely regarded as Scripture, e.g., by St. Irenaeus, Clement of Alexandria, and also by Tertullian in his pre-Montanist days, though there was no unanimity on the subject. It was, however, greatly esteemed for its moral value and served as a textbook for catechumens, as is testified by St. Athanasius. In the Codex Sinaiticus [a very important early manuscript containing the New Testament] it comes after the NT, together with the Pseudo-Barnabas (third, revised edition [2005], p. 764).

The *Shepherd of Hermas* consists of a series of visions which Hermas was granted, along with various extensive teachings that were conveyed through these visions. The first vision occurred in an isolated place in the countryside near Rome. In this vision, Hermas beheld "a great white chair made of snow-white wool; and an elderly woman in a brightly shining garment came up with a book in her hand, and sat down alone and greeted me" (Vision 1.2.2). This woman, who represents the Church (as he was told by "a handsome young man" in a later vision), chastises him for neglecting to properly instruct and discipline his children:

> God is angry with you, in order that you might convert your children who have sinned against the Lord and against you, their parents. For, being overly fond of children, you have not admonished your family, and you have allowed it to become terribly corrupt. It is for this reason the Lord is angry with you. But He will heal all of your evil deeds which have originated in your family.
>
> Because of their sins and iniquities you have been corrupted by the concerns of this life. But the great compassion of the Lord has been merciful to you and to your family, and will make you strong and will establish you in His glory. Only do not be remiss, but have courage, and strengthen your family. For just as a blacksmith, beating his work with a hammer, becomes master of the iron as he wishes, so also the righteous word daily repeated becomes master of all evil. So do not cease instructing your children. For I know that if they repent with all their heart, they will be inscribed in the Book of Life with the saints (Vision I.3.1–2).

With great vividness and candor Hermas describes how he felt in the midst of a subsequent vision:

> So, brethren, I went to the field, and I noted the hour, and I went to the place where I had arranged for the elderly lady to come, and I saw an ivory couch placed there, and on the couch there was a linen cushion, and spread out over it was a fine linen cloth. When I saw these things standing there, and no one at that place, I was utterly astonished, and a sort of trembling seized me and my hair stood on end. And a kind of shuddering came over me, because I was alone. Then when I came to myself and remembered the glory of God, I took courage, and kneeling down I again confessed to the Lord my sins, as previously.
>
> And she came with six young men, whom I had seen before, and she stood beside me and listened attentively while I prayed and confessed my sins to the Lord. And she touched me and said, "Hermas, stop asking all of these things concerning your sins. Ask also concerning righteousness, so that you may take some part of it to your family" (Vision III.1.4–6).

The further teachings contained in this book are given through "the shepherd, the angel of repentance," who appears to Hermas while he sits on his own bed. As he recounts,

> After I had prayed in my house and had sat down on the bed, there came in a man glorious in appearance, in the manner of a shepherd, wearing a white goatskin and with a bag on his shoulders and a staff in his hand. And he greeted me, and I returned his greeting. And he sat down beside me at once and said to me, "I have been sent by the most reverend angel to dwell with you the rest of the days of your life" (Vision V.1–2, 7).

So this is how the book comes to be called the *Shepherd of Hermas.*

THE DIDACHE

The *Didache* (pronounced dee-dah-KAY), whose full name is *The Teaching of the Lord through the Twelve Apostles,* is an early handbook of Christian morals and practices. It was probably compiled by several different anonymous editors. Parts of this short work may date from as early as around 60 AD—about the time the Holy Gospels were being written!

The *Didache* is the earliest of a series of similar, lengthier works known as "Church Orders." It contributed to the *Didaskalia Apostolorum* (*Teachings of the Apostles*), compiled in northern Syria in the first half of the third century. And it forms the basis for most of the seventh section of *The Apostolic Constitutions,* dating from the second half of the fourth century (also most likely from Syria).

2 CLEMENT

Another work among the writings of the Apostolic Fathers is known as 2 Clement, though it is generally recognized not to be the work of St. Clement of Rome. Dating from the first half of the second century, it probably was written in the area of Corinth. We find it attached, along with 1 Clement, to the Codex Alexandrinus manuscript of the New Testament. A sermon rather than a letter, it gives strong encouragement to Christians to live in repentance, in expectation of the Last Judgment at Christ's Second Coming.

THE EPISTLE OF BARNABAS

Then there is the Epistle of Barnabas. The writer of this letter does not give his name, but it has been traditionally attributed to St. Barnabas, St. Paul's close associate

(Acts 11:22–26; 13:1–15:4; 15:35). Clement of Alexandria, around the year 200, was convinced of this, and his Church in Alexandria regarded the letter as part of the New Testament. Its last four chapters, vividly describing the Way of Light and the Way of Darkness, are very similar to the first six chapters of the *Didache*, which describe the Way of Life and the Way of Death.

SOME KEY DOCTRINES AND PRACTICES TAUGHT IN THE APOSTOLIC FATHERS: THE FULL DEITY OF CHRIST

The full deity of Jesus Christ is emphasized in the letters of St. Ignatius. In the salutation/ introduction of his letter to the Ephesians, he says, "by the will of the Father and Jesus Christ our God." He uses the same phrase, "Jesus Christ our God," in the beginning of his letter to the Romans; and in that letter in chapter 3 he uses the phrase "our God Jesus Christ." In chapter 1 of his letter to the Smyrnaeans he says, "I give glory to Jesus Christ, the God who made you so wise." And in his epistle to the Ephesians he says, "For our God, Jesus the Christ, was conceived by Mary in accordance with the plan of God—of the seed of David and of the Holy Spirit" (18:2).

We also see Christ's full deity affirmed in the opening words of 2 Clement: "Brethren, we ought to think of Jesus Christ just as we do of God, as the Judge of the living and the dead" (1:1).

THE FULL MANHOOD OF CHRIST

St. Ignatius also affirms the real manhood of Christ. It was especially important to emphasize this in the face of Gnostic heretics who denied that Christ had a real human body. Ignatius exhorts the Trallians, "Be deaf, then, when anyone speaks to you apart from Jesus Christ, who was of the family of David, who was of Mary, who was *truly* born, ate, and drank, was *truly* persecuted under Pontius Pilate, was *truly* crucified and died" (9:1; my emphasis). And he emphasizes the real flesh of Christ several times in a long passage to the Smyrnaeans: "Become convinced concerning our Lord that He is *truly* of the family of David as to the flesh ... *truly* nailed for us in the flesh ... and He *truly* suffered, just as He *truly* raised Himself—not, as some unbelievers say, that He *appeared* to suffer" (chs. 1–2; my emphasis).

In a passage that sounds like a creedal statement and/or an early hymn, St. Ignatius powerfully affirms both Christ's full deity and humanity:

> For there is one Physician:
> Both flesh and spirit,

> Begotten and unbegotten,
> In man, God,
> In death, true life,
> Both from Mary and from God,
> First able to suffer [in His flesh], then unable to suffer [in His divine nature],
> Jesus Christ our Lord (Ignatius, Epistle to the Ephesians 7:2).

And also St. Polycarp, in order to emphasize the full reality of Christ's flesh, quotes John 4:2–3: "For 'everyone who does not confess that Jesus Christ came in the flesh is antichrist,' and anyone who does not confess the testimony of the Cross 'is of the devil'" (Polycarp, Epistle to the Philippians 7:1).

THE REAL BODY AND BLOOD OF CHRIST IN THE EUCHARIST

The central understanding of the historic, traditional Church about the Holy Eucharist is that the bread and wine, in a way beyond all comprehension, truly become the body and blood of Christ—just as Christ Himself said (Matt. 26:26–28). So it is natural to see this affirmed in the second generation of the Church, as we see in these quotations from St. Ignatius:

> Let no one deceive himself; unless a man is within the sanctuary, he lacks the bread of God (Ign., Ephesians 5:2).

> I take no pleasure in the food of corruption or in the pleasures of this life. I desire the bread of God [cf. John 6:33], which is the flesh of Jesus Christ (who was of the seed of David), and for drink I desire His blood, which is imperishable love (Ign., Romans 7:3).

> They abstain from Eucharist and prayer because they do not acknowledge that the Eucharist is the flesh of our Savior Jesus Christ which suffered for our sins (Ign., Smyrnaeans 7:1).

THE GREAT TRIBULATION BEFORE THE SECOND COMING OF CHRIST

> The fourth vision which I saw, brethren, twenty days after the former vision which came to me, was a foreshadowing of the impending tribulation … this beast is a foreshadowing of the great tribulation which is to come (*Shepherd of Hermas*, Vision IV.1.1 and IV.2.5).

THE SECOND COMING OF CHRIST

Let us then be on the watch hour by hour for the kingdom of God, in love and in righteousness, since we do not know the day when the Lord will appear (2 Clement 12:1).

Truly His purpose will be quickly and suddenly accomplished, just as the Scripture confirms when it says, 'He will come quickly and not delay, and the Lord will come suddenly to His Temple, even the Holy One Whom you expect' [Mal. 3:1]. Let us consider, beloved, how the Master continually points out that future resurrection which is to be, of which He made our Lord Jesus Christ the first-fruits when He raised Him from the dead [cf. 1 Cor. 15:20] (1 Clement 23:5–24:1).

THE RESURRECTION OF THE DEAD AND THE LAST JUDGMENT

Further, let none of you say that this flesh is not judged nor does it rise again. Consider: in what state were you saved, in what state did you regain your sight, if it was not in this flesh? Hence it is necessary to guard the flesh as the temple of God. For as in the flesh you were called, in the flesh you will come. If Christ the Lord who saved us was first spirit but became flesh and in that state called us, so we also shall receive our reward in this flesh (2 Clement 9:1–5).

This flesh is able to receive so great a life and immortality because the Holy Spirit is closely joined to it, nor can anyone express or declare 'what things the Lord has prepared' [1 Cor. 2:9] for His elect (2 Clement 14:5).

So let not the pious man be grieved if at the present time he is miserable. A time of blessedness awaits him. When he has come to life again with the fathers above, he will rejoice in an eternity that knows no grief [cf. Romans 8:18; James 5:7].... we are being trained by the present life that we may be crowned by that which is to come (2 Clement 19:4 and 20:2).

And anyone who perverts the sayings of the Lord to suit his own lusts and says that there is neither a resurrection nor a judgment—that man is the firstborn of Satan! (Polycarp, Epistle to the Philippians 7:1).

But be ready, for you do not know when our Lord is coming [cf. Matt. 24:42, 44; Mark 13:35; Luke 12:40].... The Lord will come and all His saints with Him [cf. Zech. 14:5]. Then the world will see the Lord coming on the clouds of heaven with power and dominion [cf. Mark 13:26] to repay each man according to his work [cf. Ps. 62:12; Matt. 16:27] with justice before all men and angels. Amen (*Didache* 16:2 and 6).

THE CENTRALITY OF THE BISHOP SURROUNDED BY THE ELDERS (PRESBYTERS/PRIESTS) AND DEACONS IN THE THREE-FOLD HIERARCHICAL STRUCTURE OF THE CHURCH

All of you are to follow the bishop as Jesus Christ follows the Father, and the presbytery as the apostles. Respect the deacons as the command of God. Apart from the bishop no one is to do anything pertaining to the Church. A valid Eucharist is to be defined as one celebrated by the bishop or by a representative of his. Wherever the bishop appears, the whole congregation is to be present, just as wherever Jesus Christ is, there is the whole Church. It is not right either to baptize or to celebrate the *agape* [meal] apart from the bishop; but whatever he approves is also pleasing to God—so that everything you do may be secure and valid (Ignatius, Epistle to the Smyrnaeans 8:1–2).

Therefore it is fitting for you to run your race together with the bishop's purpose—as you do. For your presbytery—worthy of fame, worthy of God—is attuned to the bishop like strings to a lyre. Therefore by your unity and harmonious love Jesus Christ is sung (Ign., Epistle to the Ephesians 4:1).

Since, then, I was judged worthy of seeing you through Damas your God-worthy bishop and the worthy presbyters Bassus and Apollonius and my fellow slave the deacon Zotion—whom I may enjoy because he is subject to the bishop as to God's grace and to the presbytery as to the law of Jesus Christ (Ign., Epistle to the Magnesians 2).

Since, then, in the persons already mentioned I have beheld the whole congregation in faith and have loved it, I exhort you: be eager to do everything in God's harmony, with the bishop presiding in the place of God; and the presbytery in the place of the council of the apostles; and the deacons, most sweet to me, entrusted with the service (*diakonia*) of Jesus Christ (*Ibid.*, 6:1).

When I was with you I cried out, I spoke with a loud voice, God's own voice: "Pay attention to the bishop and the presbytery and deacons." Some suspected me of saying this because I had advance information about the division of some persons; but He for whom I am in bonds is my witness that I did not know about it from any human being. The Spirit made the proclamation, saying this: "Do nothing apart from the bishop; keep your flesh as the temple of God [cf. 1 Cor. 3:16, 17; 6:19; 2 Cor. 6:16]; love unity; flee from divisions; be imitators of Jesus Christ as He is of the Father" [John 5:19]. I did what I could as a man devoted to unity. For God does not dwell where there is disunity and wrath. The Lord forgives all who repent, if they repent and turn toward the unity of God and the council of the bishop (Ign., Epistle to the Philadelphians 7:1–8:1).

If you have the will to do so, it is not impossible for you to do this for God's Name—just as the neighboring churches have sent bishops, and other presbyters and deacons (*Ibid.*, 10:2).

Pay attention to the bishop so that God will pay attention to you. I am devoted to those who are subject to the bishop, presbyters, and deacons; and may it turn out for me that I have a portion with them in God. Labor together with one another, strive together, run together, suffer together, rest together, rise up together—as God's stewards and assistants and servants (Ign., Epistle to Polycarp 6:1).

VENERATION OF RELICS

The devil "set about preventing even his poor body being taken by us, though there were many who wanted to do this and *to have fellowship with his holy flesh*" (Martyrdom of Polycarp 17:1; my emphasis).

Accordingly, we later took up his bones, more precious than costly stones and finer than gold, and deposited them in a suitable place. And there, in so far as it is possible, the Lord will grant that we come together with joy and gladness and celebrate the birthday of his martyrdom, both in memory of those who have contended in former times, and for the exercise and training of those who will do so in the future (*Ibid.*, 18:2–3).

CENTRALITY OF WATER BAPTISM

Now concerning baptism. Baptize as follows, after you have rehearsed the aforesaid teaching: Baptize in the Name of the Father and of the Son and of the Holy Spirit, in running water [cf. Matt. 28:19]. But if you do not have running water, use whatever is available. And if you cannot do it in cold water, use warm. But if you have neither, pour water on the head three times—in the name of Father, Son, and Holy Spirit. And prior to baptism, both he who is baptizing and he who is being baptized should fast, along with any others who can. And be sure that the one who is to be baptized fasts for one or two days beforehand (*Didache* 7:1–4).

"Look! Do you not see right before you a great tower [representing the Church] being built of lustrous square stones *upon the water*?" (*Shepherd of Hermas*, Vision III.2.4; my emphasis).

The stones "needed to *come up through the water in order to be made alive*, for otherwise they could not enter the kingdom of God [cf. John 3:5], unless they set aside the deadness of their former life. So even those who had fallen asleep received the seal of the Son of God and entered into the kingdom of God. For before he bears the name of the Son of God, the man is dead, but whenever he receives the seal he sets aside the deadness and receives life. So *the water is the seal*. Therefore they go down into the water dead and come up alive. So the seal was proclaimed to them also and they used it to enter into the kingdom of God" (*Ibid.*, Similitude IX.16.2–4; my emphasis).

GUIDELINES CONCERNING THE TRAVELING PROPHETS

> Now concerning the apostles and prophets. Act in accordance with the precept of the gospel. Every apostle who comes to you should be received as the Lord. But he should not remain more than one day, and if there is some necessity, a second as well; but if he should remain for three, he is a false prophet. And when the apostle departs, he should receive nothing but bread until he finds his next lodging. But if he requests money, he is a false prophet....
>
> And not everyone who speaks forth in the spirit is a prophet, but only if he has the kind of behavior which the Lord approves. From his behavior, then, will the false prophet and the true prophet be known. And every prophet who, in the spirit, orders a table to be spread shall not eat therefrom; but if he does, he is a false prophet. And every prophet who teaches the truth, but does not do the things he teaches, is a false prophet (*Didache* 11:3–10).

REGULATIONS FOR FASTING

> But do not let your fasts fall on the same days as the hypocrites [i.e., the Jews], who fast on Monday and Thursday. Rather, you should fast on Wednesday and Friday (*Didache* 8:1).

* * *

RELEVANCE OF THE APOSTOLIC FATHERS FOR TODAY

We can trust the Apostolic Fathers for guidance today because they stand closest in time to the Apostles and Christ Himself. They represent the leadership of the Church in the first few generations directly after Christ and His Apostles, from whom they learned the timeless, eternally relevant precepts of the Faith. And as we mentioned in the beginning of this chapter, we trust the Apostolic Fathers because of Christ's promise to send the Holy Spirit, the Spirit of Truth, to guide His Church into all the Truth (John 16:13), and His promise to build His Church, His very Body, so that the gates of hell would never prevail against Her (Matt. 16:18).

As we've seen, the outlines of basic Christian doctrine and practice are quite clearly visible in the writings of the Apostolic Fathers—things such as the full deity of Christ, the three-fold ministerial offices of the Church (bishop, priest, and deacon), the centrality of the Eucharist and the belief that it is truly Christ's body and blood, the centrality of water Baptism, the veneration of the relics of the Saints, the glorification of martyrdom, the Second Coming of Christ, and the resurrection of the dead and the Last Judgment.

Many modern-day Christians, in varying degrees, do not believe and practice these things. But may we suggest to them that if the Apostolic Fathers were mistaken about these things, this would mean that Christ had broken His promises very soon after His departure from this earth! It also would indicate that His immediate disciples were grievously inept in passing the Faith down to their followers in the way Christ had given them the Faith. So, in the midst of the countless multitude of competing Protestant denominations in our day, why not trust the united witness of the leaders of the Church in the first few generations after Christ and His Apostles? If they did not receive and then faithfully pass down to the subsequent generations the fullness of the Christian Faith, then where else can that fullness be found?

Besides, the Apostolic Fathers provide us with many pages of tremendously edifying spiritual reading. I would recommend starting with the *Account of the Martyrdom of St. Polycarp*. Ask him to be with you as you accompany him through his arrest; his two-hour prayer in the midst of his captors for everyone he ever knew; his refusal to deny Christ as he stood in the stadium—"I have served Him eighty-six years and in no way has He dealt unjustly with me; so how can I blaspheme my King Who saved me?" (9:3); the preparation of the pyre; his request not to be bound to the stake; the fire encircling him, taking "the form of an arch like the sail of a ship filled by the wind … and he was in the center of it not like burning flesh but like baking bread or like gold and silver being refined in a furnace" (15:2); the "fragrant odor like the scent of incense or some other precious spice" (15:2); and finally, his being stabbed by the executioner, whereupon a white dove flew out of him, and enough blood poured out to extinguish the fire (16:1). Radiating throughout the account are his steadfast faith and quiet endurance through all of this, such that many of the onlookers were astounded. As the text says, "and the whole crowd was amazed that there was so great a difference between unbelievers and the elect" (16:1).

Besides the glorious account of St. Polycarp's martyrdom, we also have his stirring letter to the Philippians, filled with strong exhortations to living the Christian life in purity of mind and heart. It is also replete with a multitude of quotations and/or references from the Book of Acts and the Epistles of St. Paul (including Hebrews), St. Peter, St. James, and St. John. So it stands as testimony to the general acceptance of these writings as parts of the New Testament, which was still in the process of being pieced together. There are also numerous quotations and/or references to 1 Clement and the epistles of St. Ignatius, which provide another indication of the importance of these writings in the early Church.

Next in importance come the celebrated seven letters by St. Ignatius of Antioch, which are filled with inspiring advice for sound Christian living that would be highly relevant in any age. His repeated emphasis on the centrality of the bishop as the hierarchical head of the church in each city—and having full jurisdictional authority over his flock—is decisive early testimony of this pattern which becomes the norm for the entire Early Church wherever She spreads. Also, St. Ignatius quotes what seem to be early hymns which exalt, succinctly and poetically, the two natures of Christ, Who is both truly divine and truly human. And his emphasis on the centrality of the Eucharist in Christian worship, with the bread and wine truly becoming Christ's body and blood, is valuable very early testimony to this all-important key aspect of Christian worship in the Orthodox Church to this day. Knowing that he is writing to two of the very same Christian congregations (in Rome and in Ephesus) that St. Paul himself wrote to about fifty years earlier is also, I think, especially thrilling.

Then we have 1 Clement, in which the Church in Rome gently and painstakingly urges the Christians in Corinth not to revolt against their legitimately elected leaders. With great pastoral tact and wisdom, the letter urges its readers to consider the example of the great Saints of the Old Testament, such as Abraham, Moses, David, and Daniel, who accepted the Lord's will for their lives with great humility and patience, quelling their self-will and their desire for self-aggrandizement in order to work for the greater good. It liberally quotes from the Psalms and the Book of Job along these same lines. And near the end of this letter we find a remarkably beautiful liturgical prayer, filled with heartfelt cries of repentance, and supplication for the Lord's help in this situation.

2 Clement gives a glorious summons to heartfelt repentance in preparation for the Second Coming of Christ and the Last Judgment. It also raises a battle cry to rally all of us Christians to the spiritual warfare that we must engage in if we are to keep our faith intact in the midst of a hostile world, and if we are to live purely in mind and heart while our flesh so often tempts us to sink down into unholy passions instead. This work is also filled with quotations and/or references from

the Old Testament, as well as from the books that will come to be canonized as the New Testament.

I would suggest reading the *Didache* next. It is filled with practical guidelines for Baptism, fasting, prayer, celebrating the Eucharist, discerning true from false prophets, Christian hospitality, and supporting the clergy. In varying degrees all of these guidelines are still followed in the Orthodox Church today. The *Didache* begins with an exposition on the way of life and the way of death (1:1–6:2), which is more relevant than ever in the face of the steady decline of Western society away from traditional moral values. Especially appropriate in this regard are the exposition's moral injunctions, such as "Do not be sexually perverted"; "Do not be sexually promiscuous"; "Do not murder a child by abortion, nor kill it at birth" (2:2). And it concludes with a highly relevant, rousing exhortation to be ready for the Second Coming of Christ and the Last Judgment (16:1–8).

The *Shepherd of Hermas* also is filled with edifying exhortations to and guidance for holy living, according to Christ's life-giving commandments. The book, by far the longest of the writings of the Apostolic Fathers, is comprised of descriptions of five visions, then a series of twelve sermons or mandates, and finally a collection of ten similitudes or parables. Almost all of this wisdom and exhortation is presented through the lips of "the elderly lady" who represented the Church, and through the Shepherd, the Angel of Repentance, sent by the Lord to guide Hermas, and through him, the Church as a whole. Hermas, a married layman who had difficulty instructing and disciplining his children in the ways of the Lord, struggled to understand many things about the nature of Baptism, repentance, and the Church. The imagery and guidance that Hermas received through God's gracious provision of the Church and the Angel are all as edifying to us today as they were to him, even though he lived many centuries ago.

Then we have the *Epistle of Barnabas*, probably written in the late first or early second century in the vicinity of Alexandria, Egypt. Like the *Didache*, it also has a graphic description of the way of light contrasted sharply with the way of darkness; in this portion of the book we find the same three moral injunctions which we quoted from the *Didache*: "Do not be sexually promiscuous"; "Do not be sexually perverted"; and "Do not murder a child by abortion, nor, again, destroy that which is born" (19:4–5). Most of the letter presents an intriguing allegorical/ typological interpretation of the Old Testament in the light of Christ. Included in this is a strong attack against the ritual requirements of the Mosaic Law, with the claim that they were never meant to be followed literally. In this instance, the *Epistle of Barnabas* clearly stands beyond the bounds of Church Tradition.

May we all be greatly edified and inspired as we read the writings of the Apostolic Fathers, written so long ago and yet radiant with the ring of the timeless Truth of the Gospel. May we allow our All-Gracious Lord to comfort and strengthen us in our faith through these writings, as He does through the Holy Scriptures themselves.

THE EPISTLE TO DIOGNETUS

Finally, some editions of the writings of the Apostolic Fathers include the *Epistle to Diognetus*, written by an unknown author, and addressed to an inquirer—someone interested in learning more about the Christian Faith. After chiding the Greeks for their idolatry and the Jews for their superstitions, the author presents a beautiful summary of the Christian Gospel—the Good News of the Son of God redeeming all of mankind through His sacrificial death and triumphant resurrection. The author marvels at God's goodness in all of this:

> In Whom was it possible for us lawless and ungodly men to have been justified, save only in the Son of God? O the sweet exchange! O the inscrutable creation! O the unexpected benefits—that the iniquity of many should be concealed in One Righteous Man, and the righteousness of One should justify many who are iniquitous! (ch. 9).

Also, this letter is famous for this passage:

> Christians are not distinguished from the rest of mankind either in locality or in speech or in customs.... But while they dwell in cities of Greeks and barbarians as the lot of each is cast, and follow the native customs in dress and food and the other arrangements of life, yet the constitution of their own citizenship, which they set forth, is marvelous, and confessedly contradicts expectation.
>
> For they dwell in their own countries, but only as sojourners; they bear their share in all things as citizens, and they endure all hardships as strangers. Every foreign country is a fatherland to them, and every fatherland is foreign. They marry like all other men and they beget children; but they do not cast away their offspring. They have meals in common, but not their wives. They find themselves in the flesh, and yet they live not after the flesh. Their existence is on earth, but their citizenship is in heaven. They obey the established laws, and they surpass the laws in their own lives. They love all men, and they are persecuted by all. They are ignored, and yet they are

> condemned. They are put to death, and yet they are endued with life. They are in beggary, and yet they make many rich. They are in want of all things, and yet they abound in all things. They are dishonored, and yet they are glorified in their dishonor. They are evil spoken of, and yet they are vindicated They are reviled, and they bless; they are insulted, and they respect. Doing good, they are punished as evil-doers; being punished they rejoice, as if they were thereby quickened by life. . . .
>
> In a word, what the soul is in a body, this the Christians are in the world. The soul is spread throughout all the members of the body, and the Christians are spread throughout the diverse cities of the world. The soul has its abode in the body, and yet it is not of the body. So Christians have their abode in the world, and yet they are not of the world (chs. 5 and 6).

May we Christians today respond to the tribulations and persecution, however subtle or not so subtle, of our own time in the same godly ways as this unknown author was able to describe our brothers and sisters in Christ doing in his day!

Chapter Three

THE APOLOGISTS EXPLAIN AND DEFEND THE FAITH TO THE SURROUNDING SOCIETY

INTRODUCTION

UNLIKE THE WRITINGS of the Apostolic Fathers, which were all addressed to fellow Christians—or in the case of the *Epistle to Diognetus,* to a serious inquirer into the Faith—the Apologists addressed their writings to the non-Christian society surrounding them. Actually, in many cases they went "right to the top," and addressed their work to the Roman emperor himself!

The name "Apologist" comes from an older meaning of the word "apology," meaning a *defense.* Hence, a Christian apologetical writing is one in which the Christian Faith is explained and defended to those who presumably know nothing or very little about it, and who may well be ill-disposed towards it, due perhaps to distorted information and/or rumors about it. So the Apologists often make sure to clear up typical misunderstandings about the Faith and about those practicing it, such as the charges that Christians are cannibalistic, incestuous, and traitorous to the Empire.

The first of these charges against the Christians undoubtedly sprang from a radical misunderstanding of the Eucharist. The second arose from a radical misunderstanding of the *agape* meal, or "love feast," that often followed the Liturgy; and of the kiss of peace, the completely innocent mutual kissing on the cheek done by brothers and sisters in the Faith. And concerning the charge of being traitors to the Empire, this was because the Christians did not participate in the worship of the

Roman gods and goddesses, or in the worship of the Emperor, that was part of the state/civil religion. While acknowledging that the Christians could not in good conscience participate in such worship, the Apologists hastened to assert that the Christians were actually the most loyal and most law-abiding citizens. This was so because—if they were seriously trying to live the Faith—the Christians never broke the laws of the Empire (as long as the laws did not go against their Christian conscience), they went about doing good to their neighbors, and they prayed faithfully to the TRUE God for the Emperor and all the civil authorities (see 1 Tim. 2:1–2). Besides, they were taught to honor the civil authorities as "appointed by God" for the restraint of evil, and they were taught to willingly "be subject" to the civil authorities, whoever they might be (Romans 13:1–7—and we should remember that St. Paul wrote this while the infamous, crazed, Christian-hating Emperor Nero was on the throne!). Obedience to the civil authorities was seen as one very important way to be obedient to God Himself.

The earliest Christian apologies were written around 125 AD, with the later ones being written in the first part of the third century. So the timeframe of the Apologists overlaps with that of the Apostolic Fathers, and continues for over a half century afterwards.

ST. QUADRATUS

As far as we know, the two earliest Christian apologies were both written around the year 125 AD, and both were addressed to Emperor Hadrian, who ruled from 117 to 138 AD. They were composed by St. Quadratus and Aristides. This Quadratus may also have been bishop of Athens. He and his work are described by Bishop Eusebius of Caesarea in Palestine, the first great Church historian, in his *Ecclesiastical History* in these words:

> When Trajan had ruled for six months short of twenty years, Aelius Hadrian succeeded to the throne. To him Quadratus addressed and sent a pamphlet which he had composed in defense of our religion, because unscrupulous persons were trying to get our people into trouble. Many of the brethren still possess copies of this little work; indeed, I have one myself. In it can be found shining proofs of the author's intellectual grasp and apostolic correctness. He reveals his very early date by the wording of his composition (EH IV.3.1–2).

Then Eusebius gives a quotation from the work, which is the only surviving excerpt from it:

> Our Savior's works were always there to see, for they were true—the people who had been cured and those raised from the dead, who had not merely been seen at the moment when they were cured or raised, but were always there to see, not only when the Savior was among us, but for a long time after His departure; in fact, some of them survived right up to my own time (EH IV.3.3).

St. Quadratus is commemorated in the Church on May 26.

ARISTIDES

The second of the two earliest Apologists, Aristides, was a Christian philosopher living in Athens in the early second century. Eusebius says of him, "Aristides again, a loyal and devoted Christian, has, like Quadratus, left us a Defense of the Faith addressed to Hadrian. Many people still preserve copies of his work also" (EH IV.3.3). It has been said that in his apology,

> Aristides sought to defend the existence and eternity of God, and to show that Christians had a fuller understanding of His nature than either the barbarians, the Greeks, or the Jews, and that they alone live according to His precepts (*Oxford Dictionary of the Christian Church*, third revised edition, p. 102).

As did St. Justin Martyr, the next Apologist, Aristides kept wearing the distinctive philosopher's garb after becoming a Christian, as a very tangible way of declaring that Christianity is indeed the True Philosophy, fulfilling and completing all the partial insights of all the various human philosophies of the world.

ST. JUSTIN MARTYR

Justin was born around 100 AD and raised by pagan parents in the ancient Samaritan town of Shechem. A very thoughtful young man, and a spiritual seeker, Justin was a devotee of the writings of Plato. But one day, at about the age of 30, as he looked for an isolated spot near the seaside to do some contemplation, he encountered "a certain old man, by no means contemptible in appearance, exhibiting meek and venerable manners," as Justin himself writes in his *Dialogue with Trypho* (ch. 3). This wise man spoke with Justin about the nature of philosophy, and about philosophers and their various inadequacies. Then Justin asks him, "Should anyone, then, employ a teacher? Or how may anyone be helped, if not even in the philosophers is there truth?" In response, the old man immediately began talking about the Hebrew Prophets:

> There existed, long before this time, certain men more ancient than all those who are esteemed to be philosophers, men both righteous and beloved by God, who spoke by the Divine Spirit, and foretold events which would take place, and which are now taking place. They are called Prophets. These alone both saw and announced the truth to men, neither reverencing nor fearing any man, nor influenced by a desire for glory, but speaking those things alone which they saw and heard, being filled with the Holy Spirit. Their writings are still extant, and he who has read them is very much helped in his knowledge of the beginning and end of things, and of those matters which the philosopher ought to know …
>
> For they did not use argumentation in their treatises, seeing that they were witnesses to the truth beyond all argument, and worthy of belief. And those events which have happened, and those which are happening, compel you to assent to the utterances made by them—although, indeed, they were entitled to credibility on account of the miracles they performed, since they both glorified the Creator, the God and Father of all things, and proclaimed His Son, the Christ who was sent by Him (ch. 7).

Justin then recounts,

> When he had spoken these and many other things, which there is no time for mentioning at present, he went away, bidding me to attend to them; and I have not seen him since. But immediately a flame was kindled in my soul. A love of the Prophets, and of those men who are friends of Christ, possessed me. And while pondering and reflecting upon the man's words in my mind, I found this Philosophy alone to be safe and profitable. It is because of this that I am a philosopher. Moreover, I would wish that all people, making a resolution similar to my own, would not keep themselves away from the words of the Savior. For His words possess an awesome power in themselves, and are sufficient to inspire with awe even those who have turned aside from the path of rectitude; while the sweetest rest is afforded to those who make a diligent practice of them (ch. 8).

And then he urges his listener, a Jew named Trypho, "If, then, you have any concern for yourself, and if you are eagerly looking for salvation, and if you believe in God, you may—since you are not indifferent to the matter—become acquainted with the Christ of God. And, after being initiated [i.e., baptized], you may live a happy life" (ch. 8).

St. Justin wrote two apologies. The *First Apology* is addressed "To the Emperor Titus Aelius Adrianus Antoninus Pius Augustus Caesar, and to his son Verissimus the Philosopher, and to Lucius the Philosopher, the natural son of Caesar and the adopted son of Pius, a lover of learning, and to the sacred Senate, with the whole people of the Romans." And the *Second Apology* is addressed to the Roman Senate in the early years of the reign of Emperor Marcus Aurelius (r. 161–180), the successor of Emperor Antoninus Pius (r. 138–161).

One of the most important points that he makes in both of these apologies is that the Word of God (*O Logos tou theou*) has disseminated many "seminal words" (*spermatikoi logoi*) throughout the universe, so that all truth, wherever it is found and to whatever degree it exists, is ultimately from God Himself. As Justin says, "there seem to be seeds of truth among all men" (*First Apology*, ch. 44). In a very noteworthy passage, Justin writes:

> I strive with all my might to be found a Christian, not because the teachings of Plato are different from those of Christ, but because they are not in every respect similar, as neither are those of the others, such as Stoics, and poets, and historians. For each man spoke well in proportion to the share he had in the spermatic word, seeing what was related to it. But those who contradict themselves on the more important points appear not to have possessed the heavenly wisdom, and the knowledge which cannot be spoken against.
>
> *Whatever things were rightly said among all men are the property of us Christians.* For next to God, we worship and love the Word who is from the unbegotten and ineffable God, since also He became man for our sakes, so that, by becoming a partner of our sufferings, He might also bring us healing. For all the writers were able to see realities darkly *through the sowing of the implanted word that was in them.* For the seed and imitation of something which is imparted to each one according to each one's capacity is one thing, and quite another is the thing itself, of which there is the participation and imitation according to the grace which is from Him (*Second Apology*, ch. 13; my emphasis).

Hence Justin readily admits that Plato and Socrates, and the Stoics, for instance, were right about many things. They just didn't have the fullness of the Truth. As he writes, "on some points we teach the same things as the poets and philosophers whom you honor, and on other points we are fuller and more divine in our teaching" (*First Apology*, ch. 20). In fact, Justin was so amazed that Plato was so accurate on so many things that he was convinced that Plato must have read the writings of Moses and the other Hebrew Prophets while spending time in Egypt:

> And that you may learn that it was from our teachers—we mean the account given through the Prophets—that Plato borrowed his statement that God, having altered matter which was shapeless, made the world, hear the very words spoken through Moses, who, as was shown above, was the first Prophet, and of greater antiquity that the Greek writers ... And the physiological discussion concerning the Son of God in the *Timaeus* of Plato, where he says, "He placed him crosswise in the universe," he borrowed in like manner from Moses (*First Apology*, chs. 59 and 60).

Justin also so highly values the virtuous life—living "reasonably" (or, "according to reason")—as being ultimately inspired by the Word of God that he can say, "We have declared above that *Christ is the Word of whom every race of men were partakers*; and *those who live reasonably are Christians*, even though they have been thought to be atheists—such as, among the Greeks, Socrates and Heraclitus, and men like them; and among the barbarians, Abraham and Ananias, and Azarias, and Misael [the Three Holy Children in the Furnace], and Elias [Elijah], and many others" (*First Apology*, ch. 46; my emphasis).

The *First Apology* is extremely noteworthy also for its quite detailed description of the Eucharistic celebration held every Sunday (chs. 65–67). This is the earliest such description that is extant. It provides very strong early testimony that the main day of the week for worship for the early Christians always was Sunday, and that on every Sunday the Holy Eucharist was celebrated.

Justin also emphasized the power of human free will over against any kind of Gnostic or Stoic determinism or fatalism (*First Apology*, ch. 43; *Second Apology*, ch. 7); the reality of the resurrection from the dead, the Last Judgment, and eternal punishment for the wicked (*First Apology*, chs. 8, 18, 19, 21, 45, and 68; *Second Apology*, ch. 9); the glory of martyrdom for Christ's sake (*First Apology*, chs. 14 and 57; *Second Apology*, chs. 2, 11, and 12); the gods and goddesses worshiped by the Romans are fictions inspired by "wicked devils" (*First Apology*, chs. 21, 25, and 54); and that having no moral standards is "the greatest profanity and wickedness" (*First Apology*, ch. 28), and is "contrary to every sound idea, reason, and sense" (*Second Apology*, ch. 7). He also gives references to the Holy Trinity (*First Apology*, chs. 13, 61, and 65).

Two more apologetical works by St. Justin are called *The Discourse to the Greeks*, and *The Hortatory Address to the Greeks*. In the first of these, Justin severely criticizes the gods and goddesses, as described by the various ancient poets, for their rampant immorality. For example, he writes,

> And as for Jupiter, he was an adulterer on numerous occasions ... And I say nothing of the masculine character of Minerva, nor the feminine nature of Bacchus, nor the fornicating disposition of Venus. Read to Jupiter, you Greeks, the law against those murdering their own fathers, and the penalty of adultery, and the ignominy of pedophilia. Teach Minerva and Diana the works of women, and Bacchus the works of men. What seemliness is there in woman's girding herself with armor, or in a man's decorating himself with cymbals, and garlands, and female attire, accompanied by a herd of bacchanalian women? (ch. 2).

How relevant is this passage to our own time, with the sins of fornication, adultery, homosexual activity, pedophila, and transvestism seemingly more rampant than ever before, and certainly with more societal approval than ever before!

In the second of these treatises, Justin quotes much from Plato and Homer—the great ancient Greek epic poet, author of *The Iliad* and *The Odyssey*. Justin says that Homer, like Plato, "received similar enlightenment in Egypt," in order to show that the Greek philosophers and poets themselves actually believed in One True God, Maker of heaven and earth. He quotes the great ancient Greek dramatist Sophocles as saying exactly this: "There is one God, in truth there is but one, Who made the heavens and the broad earth beneath, the glancing waves of ocean and the winds ..." (*Hortatory Address to the Greeks*, ch. 18). And he quotes the famous ancient Greek Oracle of Sibyl as saying: "There is one only unbegotten God, omnipotent, invisible, most high, all-seeing, but Himself is seen by no flesh" (ch. 16). In this work Justin also includes a short history of the writing of the Septuagint (LXX), the celebrated Greek translation of the Hebrew Scriptures done in Alexandria in the third century BC (ch. 13).

In one other work, called *On the Sole Government of God*, which consists almost entirely of quotations from the ancient Greek dramatists Aeschylus, Sophocles, Euripides, Menander, and Philemon, as well as the philosopher and mathematician Pythagoras, Justin follows the same tack. As he says, "This I shall do, not by a mere display of words, but by altogether using demonstration drawn from the old poetry in Greek literature, and from writings very common among all. For from these, the famous men who have handed down idol-worship as law to the multitudes shall be taught and convicted of great ignorance by their own poets and literature" (ch. 1). For example, he quotes Menander as writing, "'If there exists a God who walks outside with an old woman, or who enters into houses by stealth through the folding-doors, he never can please me—nay, but only He Who 'stays at home,' a just and righteous God, to give salvation to His worshipers" (ch. 5).

St. Justin Martyr, the most important of all the Apologists, ended his life in martyrdom for Christ—hence his epithet of "Martyr." In fact, the account of his trial, along with several fellow Christians, before the authorities in Rome in about 165 AD, comes down to us. Part of this account reads:

> Rusticus the prefect said, "Let us, then, now come to the matter at hand. Having come together, offer sacrifice with one accord to the gods." Justin said, "No right-thinking person falls away from piety to impiety." Rusticus the prefect said, "Unless you obey, you shall be mercilessly punished." Justin said, "Through prayer we can be saved on account of our Lord Jesus Christ, even when we have been punished, because this shall become to us salvation and confidence at the more fearful and universal judgment-seat of our Lord and Savior." This also said the other martyrs, "Do what you will, for we are Christians, and we do not sacrifice to idols." . . .
>
> The holy martyrs, having glorified God, and having gone forth to the accustomed place, were beheaded, and perfected their testimony in the confession of the Savior. And some of the faithful, having secretly removed their bodies, laid them in a suitable place, the grace of our Lord Jesus Christ having wrought along with them, to whom be glory for ever and ever. Amen (*The Martyrdom of the Holy Martyrs Justin, Chariton, Charites, Paeon, Hierax, and Liberianus*, chs. 4 and 5).

The greatly beloved St. Justin Martyr is commemorated in our Church on June 1.

TATIAN

Tatian was born and raised in Syria in the early part of the second century. He says he was initiated into one of the various "mystery cults" (each one dedicated to the worship of a certain god or goddess), but then turned to Christianity after being introduced to the writings of the Hebrew Prophets. In his *Address to the Greeks*, he says of these writings that they are "too old to be compared with the opinions of the Greeks, and too divine to be compared with their errors." Then he says,

> I was led to put faith in these writings by the unpretending cast of the language, the unartificial character of the writers, the foreknowledge displayed of future events, the excellent quality of the precepts, and the declaration of the government of the universe as centered in one Being. And my soul being taught by God, I discern that the former class of [pagan] writings lead to condemnation, but that these [writings of the Hebrew Prophets] put an end to the [spiritual] slavery that is in the world, and rescue us from a multiplicity of rulers and ten thousand tyrants (ch. 29).

By 150 AD Tatian was in Rome, where he became a student of the great Christian teacher St. Justin Martyr. Sadly, in his polemical writings Tatian lacks the gentleness, broad-mindedness, and magnanimity of his teacher. His most important apologetical work, called *Address to the Greeks,* is vitriolic in its disparagement of the entire Greco-Roman literary and cultural inheritance. Where it seems that St. Justin was as charitable to Plato, for instance, as possible, Tatian witheringly "rakes Plato over the coals," so to speak. As he asks the Greeks rhetorically, "What noble thing have you produced by your pursuit of philosophy? Who of your most eminent men has been free from vain boasting?" (ch. 2). He goes on to say, lambasting various ancient Greek philosophers,

> I laugh, too, at the old wife's talk of Pherecydes, and the doctrine inherited by him from Pythagoras, and that of Plato, an imitation of his, though some think otherwise.... Wherefore be not led away by the solemn assemblies of philosophers who are no philosophers, who dogmatize one against the other, though each one vents but the crude fancies of the moment. They have, moreover, many collisions among themselves; each one hates the other; they indulge in conflicting opinions; and their arrogance makes them eager for the highest places (ch. 3).

He also ridicules to scorn the vicissitudes and immorality of the gods and goddesses whom the Greeks and Romans profess to worship. For example,

> There are legends of the metamorphosis of men; with you, the gods are also metamorphosed. Rhea becomes a tree; Zeus becomes a dragon, on account of Persephone; the sisters of Phaedon are

> changed into poplars, and Leto into a bird of little value ... A god, forsooth, becomes a swan, or takes the form of an eagle, and, making Ganymede his cupbearer, glories in a vile affection. How can I reverence gods who are eager for presents, and get angry if they do not receive them? Let them have their Fate! (ch. 9).

Like Justin, Tatian often attributes the various false beliefs about divine things to "wandering demons" (ch. 9). He says, for example, that the oracles of the Greeks are merely "the trickeries of the frenzied demons" (ch. 12). And also like Justin, Tatian is extremely intent on emphasizing the antiquity of the writings of Moses, which predate Homer and the Trojan War by at least 400 years (ch. 39). As he says, "But the matter of principal importance is to endeavor with all accuracy to make it clear that Moses is not only older than Homer, but also older than all the writers who were before Homer" (ch. 41). And like his teacher, Tatian is convinced that the Greek philosophers "learned from Moses"; but rather than accepting his writings, they "endeavored to adulterate whatever they learned from Moses" (ch. 40).

Tatian's determined reluctance to allow for anything good and praiseworthy among the ancient Greeks is a "tip-off" to his highly judgmental and critical spirit. Hence, it is not surprising that he eventually turns this critical spirit against the Christian Church Herself. And as a result of his judgment that She was neither pure enough in Her morals nor rigorous enough in Her fasting and other forms of asceticism, he returned to Syria after the death of Justin Martyr and started his own sect, separate from the Church. Called the Encratites, meaning "the self-controlled ones," this sect emphasized asceticism to the point of disallowing newly baptized Christians to ever get married. They were later described and excoriated by many early Church Fathers, such as St. Irenaeus of Lyons, St. Hippolytus of Rome, Clement of Alexandria, and St. Jerome of Rome and Bethlehem. We will further consider this "sectarian mind-set" as seen in Tatian when we discuss Montanism and Tertullian in Chapters Five and Six.

On a much more positive note, Tatian is also remembered for compiling the first *harmony* of the four Gospels—meaning a single, running account formed from blending the various portions of the Gospels of Saints Matthew, Mark, Luke, and John. This work is called the *Diatessaron,* literally meaning "through the four." It became the Gospel Book used by the Syrian Church up until the fifth century. Its compilation is a very strong attestation to the prevailing prominence of these four particular Gospel accounts, and these four alone, in the late second century—since many other writings concerning the life of Jesus, such as the Gnostic-oriented

Gospel of Thomas, were in circulation at that time, as we will discuss further in Chapter Seven.

ST. THEOPHILUS

Like most of the Apologists, Theophilus was a convert to Christianity from paganism, so he was especially eager to win his relatives and friends, and indeed the entire surrounding society, to the true Faith. In his one work that survives to the present time, called *Apology to Autolycus,* we find him urging his pagan friend, Autolycus, to believe the Hebrew Prophets when they predict the general resurrection at the end of time, along with the eternal rewards and punishments—just as he himself had come to believe them. As he writes to Autolycus,

> Therefore, do not be skeptical, but believe. For I myself used to disbelieve that this would take place, but now, having taken these things into consideration, I believe. At the same time, I met with the sacred Scriptures of the holy [Hebrew] Prophets, who also by the Spirit of God foretold the things that have already happened, just as they came to pass …
>
> Admitting, therefore, the proof afforded by events happening just as predicted, I do not disbelieve, but I believe, in obedience to God—to Whom, if you would, please submit, believing Him, lest if now you continue disbelieving, you be convinced hereafter, when you are tormented with eternal punishments. These punishments, when they had been foretold by the Prophets, the later-born [Greek] poets and philosophers stole from the holy Scriptures, to make their doctrines worthy of credit (*Apology to Autolycus* I.14).

Here we see again the Apologists' emphasis on the antiquity of the Hebrew Prophets, in order to convince the Greeks that "our doctrine is not modern nor a fable, but more ancient and true than all poets and authors, who have written in uncertainty" (III.16). Theophilus is so determined to convince the Greeks of the antiquity of Moses that he gives a strict chronology, based on the Book of Genesis, to prove that Moses lived hundreds of years before the Trojan War and the earliest Greek poets, Homer and Hesiod (III.17–29).

Moreover, like Tatian, Theophilus asserts that the ancient Greek poets and philosophers are not worthy of being believed because they all disagree among themselves. Moreover, he points out that there are inconsistencies even within each one's writings:

> For all these, having fallen in love with vain and empty reputation, neither themselves knew the truth, nor guided others to the truth. For the things which they said themselves convict them of speaking inconsistently, and most of them demolished their own doctrines. For not only did they refute one another, but some, too, even undermined their own teachings, so that their reputation has resulted in shame and folly (III.3).

In stark contrast, for Theophilus, "the Prophets and the Gospels" all say the same things, "because they all spoke while being inspired by the one Spirit of God" (III.12; cf. III.17). He also describes the Prophets as being

> men of God carrying in themselves a holy spirit and becoming Prophets, being inspired and made wise by God, who became God-taught, and holy, and righteous. Wherefore they were also deemed worthy of receiving this reward, that they should become instruments of God (II.9).

While Theophilus can be as hard on the poets and philosophers as Tatian was, he also can still recognize that sometimes they "spoke things in harmony with the Prophets":

> And without meaning to do so, they acknowledge that they do not know the truth. Rather, being inspired by demons and puffed up by them, whatever they spoke was at the instigation of the demons. For indeed the poets—for instance, Homer and Hesiod, being as they say inspired by the Muses—spoke from a deceptive fancy, and not with a pure, but with an erring spirit....
>
> But sometimes some of them wakened up in soul, and, that they might be for a witness both to themselves and to all men, spoke things in harmony with the Prophets regarding the monarchy [oneness] of God, and the Last Judgment, and the like (II.8).

Elsewhere in this work, Theophilus emphasizes Creation being created *ex nihilo* (out of nothing) by the uncreated God (I.4; II.4, 10, and 13); Creation being made for man (II.10); man's purpose "being even to be declared a god" [the doctrine of deification] (II.24 and 27); God as being Trinity (II.10 and 15—here is the first mention of the word *Trinity* [*Trias/Triados*] in all of Christian literature); the world being sustained by "the law of God and the Prophets flowing and welling up sweetness, and compassion, and righteousness, and the doctrine of the holy commandments of God" (II.14); the crucial importance of being pure in heart and soul in order to perceive God (I.2; cf. III.9–15); and man's power of free-will to decide whether to obey God and live eternally in glory, or that by "disobeying God, he should himself be the cause of death to himself. For God made man free, and with power over himself" (II.27).

We also find in Theophilus's work, which was probably written some time in the 160s or 170s, the first quotations given from the four Gospels (III.13–14). And he refers to St. Paul's Epistles as being "the divine word" just before he quotes 1 Timothy 2:2 and Romans 13:7–8 (III.14).

Finally, Theophilus is emphatic in contrasting the purity and holiness of the lives of the Christians with the immorality of pagan life. As we see in this stirring quotation,

> Consider, therefore, whether those who teach such things can possibly live unaffected, as they are commingled in unlawful intercourse, or, most impious of all, eat human flesh, especially when we are forbidden so much as to witness shows of gladiators, lest we become partakers and abettors of murders. But neither may we see the other spectacles [in the theaters], lest our eyes and ears be defiled, participating in the utterances sung there. For if one should speak of cannibalism, in these spectacles the children of Thyestes and Tereus are eaten; and as for adultery, both in the case of men and of gods, whom they celebrate in elegant language for honor and prizes, this is made the subject of their dramas. But far be it from Christians to conceive any such deeds. For with them temperance dwells, self-restraint is practiced, monogamy is observed, chastity is guarded, iniquity exterminated, sin extirpated, righteousness exercised, law administered, worship performed, and God is acknowledged. Truth governs, grace guards, and peace screens them; the holy Word guides, wisdom teaches, life directs, and God reigns (III.15).

St. Theophilus ended his life as the seventh bishop of Antioch. He passed on to meet his Lord in about 181 AD. He is commemorated on October 13.

ATHENAGORAS

As his name suggests, Athenagoras was from Athens. Living a little later than St. Justin, he also had been a pagan philosopher who adopted the True Philosophy of Christianity. Like several of the earlier Apologists, Athenagoras addressed his apology, called *A Plea for the Christians,* to the ruling Roman emperor, who in his time was Marcus Aurelius (ruled 161–180).

Athenagoras opens his apology with an appeal to the Emperor's sense of fairness, as he asks on behalf of the Christians simply the same freedom to worship the Divine as everyone else in the Empire has:

> And accordingly, with admiration for your mildness and gentleness, and your peaceful and benevolent disposition towards every man, individuals live in the possession of equal rights; and the cities, according to their rank, share in equal honor; and the whole Empire, under your intelligent sway, enjoys profound peace. But for us who are called Christians, you have not cared in the same manner. For though we commit no wrong—rather, as will appear in the sequel to this discourse, they are of all men most piously and righteously disposed towards the Deity and towards your government—you allow us to be harassed, plundered, and persecuted, as the multitude makes war upon us for our name alone (ch. 1).

Athenagoras then presents a long and involved explanation of why the Christians are not atheists, as they are often accused since they did not worship the gods and goddesses of the Roman state religion. He makes the interesting point that the ancient Greek poets and philosophers often also question the existence of these deities and yet are not accused of atheism. He gives several examples from their writings along this line, and then he shows how the philosophers actually believed in only one true God, and yet were not accused of atheism on this account. As he writes,

> If, therefore, Plato is not an atheist for conceiving of one uncreated God, the Framer of the universe, neither are we atheists who acknowledge and firmly hold that He is God who has framed all things by the Logos, and holds them in being by His Spirit (ch. 6).

We can note here the clear Trinitarian language (seen also even more clearly in chapter 24), with the Logos referring to the Word of God (another name for the Son of God; cf. John 1:1–3).

Like the Apologists before him, Athenagoras appeals to the testimony of the Hebrew Prophets:

> The voices of the Prophets confirm our arguments—for I think that you also, with your great zeal for knowledge, and your great

> attainments in learning [Emperor Marcus Aurelius was very intelligent and well-educated, and is actually considered to have been the last great Stoic philosopher], cannot be ignorant of the writings either of Moses or of Isaiah and Jeremiah, and the other Prophets, who, being lifted in ecstasy beyond the natural operations of their minds by the impulses of the Divine Spirit, uttered the things with which they were inspired, the Spirit making use of them as a flute-player breathes into a flute (ch. 9).

And as to why the Christians do not offer sacrifice to the Deity, he says beautifully,

> The Framer and Father of this universe does not need blood, nor the odor of burnt-offerings, nor the fragrance of flowers and incense, forasmuch as He is Himself perfect fragrance, needing nothing else. But the noblest sacrifice to Him is for us to know *Who* stretched out and vaulted the heavens, and fixed the earth in its place like a center, who gathered the water into seas and divided the light from the darkness, Who adorned the sky with stars and made the earth to bring forth seed of every kind, Who made the animals and fashioned man (ch. 13; my emphasis).

He then says that the Christians do not offer sacrifices to the various deities of the Greco-Roman world because, for one thing, the heathen in different places believe in different deities. But more importantly, this is because they are unlike "the multitude" who "cannot distinguish between matter and God, or see how great is the distance which lies between them" (ch. 15).

Then Athenagoras quotes Homer and Orpheus as asserting that the various gods and goddesses all originated from water (Oceanus). Moreover, he points out that Orpheus "was the first to invent their names, and recounted their births, and narrated the exploits of each" (ch. 18). In stark contrast, the true God is not only *not* originated from matter, but is Himself *the Creator* of matter: "Neither again is it reasonable that matter should be older than God; for the efficient cause must of necessity exist before the things that are made" (ch. 19). He also points out, to further his arguments against the existence of the gods and goddesses, that according to the ancient historian Herodotus, "the gods had been men"—something Herodotus learned from "the priests at Heliopolis, and Memphis, and Thebes" while traveling in Egypt (ch. 28).

Concerning the charges of cannibalism and incest, Athenagoras indignantly asserts that it's the gods and goddesses who do such things. He gives a number of examples from the writings of the ancient poets and dramatists illustrating this, which demonstrate that for the gods and goddesses, "vice makes war on virtue." In stark contrast, the Christians believe in a Last Judgment, and in a God Who "is witness to what we think and what we say both by night and by day, and that He, being Himself Light, sees all things in our hearts." Hence, "so that each one of us may be blameless and irreproachable before Him, we will not entertain even the thought of the slightest sin" (ch. 31).

Hence, Athenagoras sees great irony in the fact that those in the surrounding society

> who have set up a market for fornication, and established infamous resorts for the young for every kind of vile pleasure—who do not abstain even from males, males with males committing shocking abomination, outraging all the noblest and comeliest bodies in all sorts of ways, and thus dishonoring the fair workmanship of God (for beauty on earth is not self-made, but sent here by the hand and will of God)—these men, I say, revile us for the very things which they do themselves, and which they ascribe to their own gods, boasting of them as noble deeds, and worthy of the gods. These adulterers and pederasts defame the eunuchs and the once-married, while they themselves live like fishes; for these gulp down whatever falls in their way, and the stronger chases the weaker. And in fact, this is to feed on human flesh: to do violence in violation of the very laws which you and your ancestors, with due care for all that is fair and right, have enacted (ch. 34).

He also declares that the Christians "regard the very fetus in the womb as a created being, and therefore an object of God's care," while it is the non-Christian "women who use drugs to bring on abortion" and therefore "commit murder" (ch. 35). So here again we see the direct relevance of the Apologists for our own time, when thousands of babies are legally murdered in their mothers' wombs every day in the United States.

He concludes his remarkable work with reference to the resurrection of the dead and the Last Judgment, which in themselves offer strong incentive to avoid sin, whereas those who do not believe in these things have no such incentive. As he says very eloquently,

> It is reasonable to suppose that those who think that they shall have no account to give of their present life, whether ill-spent or

> well-spent, and who think that there is no resurrection, but rather calculate on the soul perishing forever with the body, being as it were quenched along with it, will refrain from no deed of daring. But as for those who are persuaded that nothing will escape the scrutiny of God, and that even the body which has ministered to the irrational impulses of the soul, and to its desires, will be punished along with it, it is not likely that they will commit even the smallest sin (ch. 36).

And he ends his apology with these beautiful words addressed to Emperor Marcus Aurelius and his son and heir Commodus:

> And now, you who are in everything, by nature and by education, entirely upright, and moderate, and benevolent, and worthy of your rule, now that I have disposed of the several accusations [against us Christians], and have proved that we are pious, and gentle, and temperate in spirit, bend your royal head in approval. For who are more deserving to obtain the things they ask than those who, like us, pray for your government, that you may, as is most equitable, receive the kingdom, son from father, and that your empire may receive increase and addition, all men becoming subject to your sway? And this is also for our advantage, that we may lead a peaceable and quiet life [cf. 1 Tim. 2:1–2], and that we may ourselves readily perform all that is commanded of us (ch. 37).

The great Apologist Athenagoras also wrote an entire treatise defending and explaining the Christian doctrine of the resurrection of the dead. This extremely interesting and well-written essay is the only other work by Athenagoras that comes down to us.

MINUCIUS FELIX

We know very little about the life of Minucius Felix, other than that he most likely lived in western North Africa and that he wrote an elegant, persuasive, thorough apology for Christianity in Latin in around the year 210. Called *Octavius,* it consists of a description of a meeting between Octavius, a married Christian with children, and Caecilius, Octavius's educated pagan friend. In the first part Caecilius gives his objections to Christianity, and in the second part Octavius gives his brilliant refutation of Caelicius's charges.

In his opening remarks, Caecilius sounds remarkably like a modern-day, atheistic, Darwinian materialist in claiming that

> man, and every animal which is born, inspired with life, and nourished, is as a voluntary concretion of the elements, into which again man and every animal is divided, resolved, and dissipated. So all things flow back again into their source, and are turned again into themselves, without any artificer, or judge, or creator (ch. 5).

In his beautiful, eloquent response, Octavius states that

> we differ from the wild beasts, that while they are on all fours and tending to the earth, and are born to think about nothing but their food, we, whose countenance is erect, whose look is turned towards heaven, as is our disposition and our reason, whereby we recognize, feel, and imitate God, have neither the right nor any reason to be ignorant of the celestial glory which reveals itself to our eyes and senses. For it is as bad as even the grossest sacrilege to seek on the ground for what you ought to find on high. Hence, those who deny that the structure and adornment of the whole world was perfected by Divine Reason, and assert that it was heaped together by certain fragments randomly adhering to each other, seem to me not to have either mind or senses, or, in fact, even sight itself. For what can possibly be so manifest, so clear, and so evident, when you lift your eyes up to heaven, and look into the things which are below and around, than that there is some Deity of most excellent intelligence, by whom all nature is inspired, moved, nourished, and governed?
>
> Behold the heaven itself, how broadly it is expanded, how rapidly it is whirled around, either as it is distinguished in the night by its stars, or as it is lightened in the day by the sun, and you will know at once how the marvelous and divine balance of the Supreme Governor is engaged therein.... The very beauty of our own figure especially proclaims God to be its artificer: our upright stature, our upward-looking countenance, our eyes placed at the top, as it were, for better vantage, and all the rest of our senses as if arranged in a citadel (ch. 17).

Caecilius also asserts that the Christians' God must be non-existent because they are not supernaturally rescued when they are tortured and killed for their faith. Octavius responds, in another very noteworthy passage,

> How beautiful is the spectacle to God when a Christian does battle with pain; when he stalwartly endures threats, and punishments, and tortures; when, mocking the sounds of death, he treads underfoot the horror of the executioner; when he raises up his liberty against kings and princes, and yields to God alone, to Whom he belongs; and when, triumphant and victorious, he tramples upon the very man who has pronounced sentence against him! For he has conquered, when he has obtained that for which he contended (ch. 37).

Like St. Justin and Athenagoras, Minucius is very favorable towards the inheritance of the ancient Greek philosophers and poets, and quotes them extensively whenever this helps to substantiate his points. For instance, concerning the existence of the one True God, Octavius says,

> I have set forth the opinions of almost all the philosophers whose more illustrious glory it is to have pointed out that there is one God, although with many names; so that anyone might think either that Christians are now philosophers, or that the philosophers were then already Christians (ch. 20).

And again like St. Justin, Minucius attributes the worship of the gods and goddesses to the deceit of demons. In another memorable passage, Octavius appeals to the power of Christian exorcism, driving out demons from possessed persons:

> A great many people, even some of your own, know all those things that the demons confess concerning themselves, as often as they are driven out from bodies by us by the torments of our words and by the fire of our prayers. Saturn himself, and Serapis, and Jupiter, and whatever demons you worship, overcome by pain, speak out and confess who they are; and assuredly they do not lie to their own discredit, especially when any of you are standing by. Since they themselves are the witnesses that they are demons, believe them when they confess the truth about themselves. For when they are abjured by the only and true God, unwillingly the wretched beings shudder in the bodies they occupy, and either leap forth at once, or vanish by degrees, as the faith of the sufferer assists or the grace of the healer inspires (ch. 27).

When Caecilius accuses the Christians of not offering sacrifices to God, Octavius answers:

> He who cultivates innocence supplicates God; he who cultivates justice makes offerings to God; he who abstains from fraudulent practices propitiates God; he who snatches men from dangers slaughters the most acceptable victim. These are our sacrifices, these are our rites of worship. Thus, among us, the one who is most just is the one who is most religious (ch. 32; cf. Romans 12:1–2; James 1:27; Micah 6:8).

And concerning the resurrection of the dead and the Last Judgment, Octavius observes cogently,

> And I am not ignorant that many, being aware of what judgment they deserve, believe and desire that they shall be nothing after death. For they would prefer to be completely extinguished at death, rather than to be restored for the purpose of punishment (ch. 34).

How appropriate is this observation for many in our own contemporary society who live recklessly and promiscuously, apparently with few moral standards, since they've convinced themselves that there is no life or judgment after death. And then there are those who seek relief from the difficulties and suffering of this life through committing suicide or requesting euthanasia, since they're so convinced that there's no life or punishment to face after death.

Finally, when Caecilius charges that the poverty of many Christians indicates a lack of divine favor, Octavius responds that poverty is more conducive to spiritual growth, and that contentment with little is true wealth:

> But that many of us are called poor, this is not our disgrace, but our glory. For as our mind is relaxed by luxury, so is it strengthened by frugality. And yet who can be considered poor if he does not want or crave the possessions of others—and if he is rich towards God? Rather, he is really poor who, although he has much, desires more (ch. 36).

OTHER APOLOGISTS

A number of other important Christian writers of the late second and early third centuries wrote apologetic works addressed to those in the surrounding society. However, they are more well-known for their other writings—homilies, treatises on various Christian doctrines, liturgical poetry, commentaries on the Holy Scriptures, and so on—which were addressed to fellow Christians. Such writers are

St. Melito of Sardis, St. Irenaeus of Lyons, Tertullian of Carthage, Clement of Alexandria, and Origen of Alexandria and Palestine.

Chapter Four

ST. IRENAEUS MEETS THE CHALLENGE OF THE GNOSTICS

THE LIFE OF ST. IRENAEUS

BORN AROUND THE YEAR 120 AD, St. Irenaeus was raised in southwestern Asia Minor, probably in the city of Smyrna, where the bishop was the remarkable St. Polycarp during the first half of the second century. In his youth, Irenaeus had the great blessing to have known Bp. Polycarp personally. As Irenaeus wrote much later to a friend,

> For, while I was yet a boy, I saw you in Lower Asia with Polycarp, distinguishing yourself in the royal court, and endeavoring to gain his favor. I have a more vivid recollection of what occurred at that time than of recent events … so that I can even describe the place where the blessed Polycarp used to sit and talk—his goings out, too, and his comings in—and the general character of his life, and his personal appearance, together with the discourses which he delivered to the people.
>
> I also recall how he would speak of his fellowship with the Apostle John, and with the rest of those who had seen the Lord; and how he would repeat their words from memory. Whatever things he had heard from them concerning the Lord, both with regard to His miracles and His teaching, Polycarp, having received these things directly from these eyewitnesses of the Word of Life, would recount them in complete harmony with the Scriptures.

> These things, through God's mercy which was upon me, I listened to attentively, and treasured them up not on paper, but in my heart. And I am continually, by God's grace, accurately turning these things over in my mind (from *On the Ogdoad*, an anti-Gnostic work now lost; quoted by Bp. Eusebius of Caesarea in his *Ecclesiastical History* 5.20).

In these years there was an active trade between western Asia Minor and southern Gaul (today's France), and a Greek-speaking colony had been established up the Rhone River at Lyons. Most likely it was Bp. Polycarp who sent his young, ardently devout disciple Irenaeus to the Church in this colony as a missionary. Eventually he became a priest in this community.

In about 176 Irenaeus was sent by his Church community to Rome to consult with the bishop there, Eleutherius, about the newly rising movement led by Montanus in central Asia Minor. Partly because he was originally from Asia Minor, Irenaeus was at first prone to give the benefit of the doubt to this fervent, apocalyptic movement (which we will discuss in the next chapter). But in time he rejected it.

As it happened, while he was in Rome on this diplomatic mission, a fierce persecution broke out in Lyons and neighboring Vienne, in which many Christians were martyred, including the bishop of the Church in Lyons, Bp. Pothinus. Their story was recorded in a dramatic document called *The Gallic Martyrs of Lyons and Vienne*, written by the Christians there and addressed to the Christians in western Asia Minor and Phrygia, their original homeland (we will look at this document in Chapter Nine).

Returning home to Lyons after the persecution ended, Irenaeus was selected to succeed the martyred St. Pothinus as the new bishop. He held this position until his death in about the year 202. His Feastday is August 23.

THE CHALLENGE OF GNOSTICISM

It was most likely during the decade of the 180s that Bp. Irenaeus wrote his greatest work, usually referred to as *Against Heresies*. This book was mostly directed against various expressions of the general heresy known as Gnosticism, whose roots go back as early as the middle of the first century. Gnosticism is generally considered to have been the greatest doctrinal threat to traditional Christian teaching in the first two and half centuries—and its typical tendencies have continued to threaten to distort the personal piety of Christians ever since.

The name "Gnosticism" comes from the Greek word *gnosis*, meaning "knowledge." But for the Gnostics, their "knowledge" did not mean the traditional teachings taught by the Apostles and their successors, the bishops of the Church. Rather, it meant *secret knowledge*—teachings that either the Apostles had been unaware of, or that they had transmitted secretly to only a few select followers.

While the dozen or more rival Christian Gnostic sects that had coalesced by the middle of the 2nd century differed in the details of their teachings, they were all *dualist* in their basic worldview. This means that they valued only spiritual things, and denigrated everything in the material realm, including the sacraments of the Church. For them, all of Creation was the work of an incompetent and/or evil fallen angel, called the *Demiurge*. The grandiose cosmological myths concocted by the various Gnostic leaders disagreed in their accounts as to how the Demiurge came about and how the universe came into existence. But all the Gnostics agreed that the true God, being entirely spiritual in nature, could not possibly have created the physical realm.

Concerning the Incarnation of Jesus Christ, the Gnostics' presupposition that all matter is intrinsically evil demanded that the Son of God did not really take human flesh. Rather, they taught that He only *appeared* to be a man. Hence, this heretical belief is known as *Docetism*, coming from the Greek word *dokein*, meaning "to appear." And concerning man's salvation, again, if matter is evil, for the Gnostics it is only the soul that can be saved and participate in eternal life—not the body. So they discarded the profoundly Christian doctrine of the resurrection of the body at the Last Day (1 Cor. 15:12–54), which the Apologists so ardently and persuasively defended, as we have seen.

In fact, the Gnostics believed that only some people can ever be saved, since only some have a spark of divinity trapped inside them. These people were considered to be "the elect." Once these people realized that they had this divine spark lodged within them, their Gnostic teachers told them that their salvation was assured. And the Gnostics' understanding of salvation meant that when one of the elect died, that person's soul would be *freed from the prison* of his or her body, as Plato taught.

For the Gnostics, the elect were the "spiritual ones" (in Greek, the *pneumatikoi*), whereas all the rest of the Christians were the "carnal" or "soulish ones" (the *psychikoi*). In such a two-tiered view of the Body of Christ, it is virtually impossible for those who consider themselves to be in the upper tier not to look down upon and despise at least to some extent the average, ordinary Christians in the lower tier. Such a judgmental attitude so often leads to spiritual pride, a dangerous delusion that cripples true spiritual growth. We will encounter such a two-tiered outlook again when we study the Montanists in Chapter Five.

With their disparagement of the body and the entire material realm, most of the Gnostic groups tried to live in strict asceticism, including rejecting marriage, or at least marital relations. Other Gnostic sects, however, believing that the salvation of their souls was guaranteed no matter what they did with their bodies, went to the opposite extreme and indulged in orgies of the flesh. St. Jude the "brother of the Lord" may have had such early libertine Gnostics in mind when he wrote in his New Testament epistle that "certain men have crept in unnoticed, … ungodly men, who turn the grace of our God into lewdness … Likewise also these dreamers defile the flesh, reject authority, and speak evil of dignitaries." He also says that they "walk according to their own ungodly lusts. These are sensual persons, who cause divisions, not having the Spirit" (Jude 4–8, 18–19).

Hints of various incipient Gnostic tendencies can be seen in several other epistles of the New Testament. For instance, St. Paul tells his spiritual son St. Timothy, "O Timothy! Guard what was committed to your trust, avoiding the profane and idle babblings and contradictions of *what is falsely called knowledge*, for by professing it some have strayed concerning the faith" (1 Tim. 6:20; my emphasis). Paul also warns the Colossians, "Beware lest anyone cheat you through philosophy and empty deceit, according to the tradition of men, according to the basic principles of the world, and not according to Christ. For in Him dwells all the fullness of the Godhead *bodily*; and you are complete in Him" (Col. 2:8–10; my emphasis; see also Col. 2:16–23).

St. John the Theologian, in his first New Testament epistle, condemns even more strongly and explicitly all tendencies towards a *docetic* Christ who only *appeared* to be really human:

> Beloved, do not believe every spirit, but test the spirits, whether they are of God; because many false prophets have gone out into the world. By this you know the Spirit of God: every spirit that confesses that Jesus Christ has come in the flesh is of God, and every spirit that does not confess that Jesus Christ has come in the flesh is not of God. And this is *the spirit of Antichrist*, which you have heard was coming, and is now already in the world (1 John 4:1–3; my emphasis).

We recall, from Chapter Two, that St. Ignatius of Antioch gave particular emphasis in his letters to the real Incarnation of Christ. Undoubtedly this was at least partly in order to refute Christian Gnostics who were teaching about a docetic Christ. As he wrote so trenchantly to the Trallian Christians,

> Be deaf, then, when anyone speaks to you apart from Jesus Christ, who was of the family of David, who was of Mary, who was *truly* born, ate and drank, was *truly* persecuted under Pontius Pilate, was *truly* crucified and died ... He was also *truly* raised from the dead, when his Father raised Him up, as in similar fashion his Father will raise up in Christ Jesus us who believe in Him—without Whom we have no true life [cf. Rom. 8:11]. But if, as some godless men—that is, unbelievers—say, His suffering was only *apparent* (they are the apparent ones), why am I in bonds? Why do I pray to fight wild beasts? Then I die in vain. Then I lie about the Lord [cf. 1 Cor. 15:12–19] (*To the Trallians*, chs. 9–10; my emphasis).

ST. IRENAEUS' AGAINST HERESIES

This brings us back to St. Irenaeus, who wrote the most thorough and powerful refutation of Christian Gnosticism in his magisterial work called *Against Heresies*, which we mentioned above. In this book, he first summarizes the faulty views of each of the various Gnostic groups. Then, as he gives a very detailed refutation of these opinions, he brings forth a magnificent presentation of all the major doctrines of the Faith as taught by the Apostles and the bishops of the Churches.

In addition, St. Irenaeus makes three very powerful arguments against the various heretical teachers themselves. First, he points out that these teachers all disagree among themselves in their opinions—so how could any of them be correct? As he says,

> We have judged it well to point out, first of all, in what respects the very fathers of this fable [i.e., the cosmological myth] differ among themselves, as if they were inspired by different spirits of error. For this very fact forms an *a priori* proof that the truth proclaimed by the Church is immoveable, and that the theories of these men are but a tissue of falsehoods (*Against Heresies*, Book 1, ch. 9.5).

He then immediately gives the Church's *Rule of Faith*, a brief summary of the true Christian doctrine. And he emphasizes that this Rule of Faith is held unanimously across the whole Christian world:

> As I have already observed, the Church, having received this preaching and this Faith, although She is scattered throughout the whole world, yet, *as if occupying but one house*, She carefully preserves it. She

> also believes these points of doctrine *just as if She had but one soul, and one and the same heart.* And She proclaims them, and teaches them, and hands them down, with perfect harmony, *as if She possessed only one mouth.* For, although the languages of the world are dissimilar, yet the content of the Tradition is one and the same. For the Churches which have been planted in Germany do not believe or hand down anything different, nor do those in Spain, nor those in Gaul, nor those in the East, nor those in Egypt, nor those in Libya, nor those which have been established in the central regions of the world [probably meaning the Holy Land]. But as the sun, that creation of God, is one and the same throughout the whole world, so also the preaching of the truth shines everywhere, and enlightens all men who are willing to come to knowledge of the truth [cf. John 1:9 and 1 Tim. 2:4] (AH I.10.2; my emphasis).

Secondly, St. Irenaeus points out that the various founders of the heresies cannot trace any continuity of their teaching back to the Apostles. As he observes, "For, prior to Valentinus, those who follow Valentinus had no existence; nor did those who follow Marcion exist before Marcion" (AH III.4.3). And also concerning Valentinus:

> It is most obvious that he confesses the things which have been said to be his own invention, and that he himself has invented names in his scheme of things which had never been previously suggested by anyone else. It is also clear that he himself is the one who has had sufficient audacity to coin these names; so that, unless *he* had appeared in the world, the truth would still have been destitute of a name (AH I.11.4).

We can almost literally hear St. Irenaeus asking, "How could the fullness of the Truth of the Gospel only have appeared with Valentinus in the early second century, or with Marcion in the middle of the second century?" For as we know, Christ assured His disciples, "all things that I have heard from My Father I have made known to you" (John 15:15). And He promised them, "When He, the Spirit of Truth, has come, He will guide you into all Truth" (John 16:13).

Irenaeus observes that the true Churches, in stark contrast with the heretics, have always maintained the Truth which Christ and the Apostles taught, as ensured by the fact that they can trace their line of leaders (bishops), generation by generation, all the way back to the Apostles of Christ Himself. This is known as *Apostolic Succession*. As he writes,

> It is within the power of all, therefore, in every Church, who may wish to see the truth, to contemplate clearly the Tradition of the Apostles manifested throughout the whole world. And we are in a position to list those who were instituted as bishops in the Churches by the Apostles, and to demonstrate the succession of these men down to our own times—those who neither taught nor knew of anything like what these heretics rave about. For if the Apostles had known hidden mysteries, which they were in the habit of imparting to 'the perfect' privately from the rest, *they would have delivered them* ***especially*** *to those to whom they were also committing the Churches themselves*. For they were desirous that these men should be very perfect and blameless in all things, whom also they were leaving behind as their successors, delivering up their own places of government to these men. These men, if they discharged their functions honestly, would be a great boon, but if they should fall away, it would be the direst calamity (AH III.3.1; my emphasis).

Thirdly, St. Irenaeus also strongly insisted that the Gospels of Saints Matthew, Mark, Luke, and John are the only authentic Gospels—over against the heretics who used only one of these Gospels, or who altered them, or who wrote their own "Gospels" filled with their own new teachings. He observes that the Ebionites, for example, use only St. Matthew's Gospel, and the Marcionites use only a "mutilated" version of St. Luke's Gospel (AH III.11.7). And concerning Valentinus's *Gospel of Truth*, he writes,

> But those who are from Valentinus, being, on the other hand, altogether reckless, as they put forth their own compositions, boast that they possess more Gospels than there really are. Indeed, they have arrived at such a pitch of audacity as to entitle their comparatively recent writing 'the *Gospel of Truth*,' though it agrees in nothing with the Gospels of the Apostles, so that they really have no gospel which is not full of blasphemy. For if what they have published is really 'the Gospel of *Truth*,' and yet it is totally unlike those which have been handed down to us from the Apostles, then anyone who pleases may learn, as is shown from the Scriptures themselves, that that which

> has been handed down from the Apostles can no longer be reckoned the Gospel of truth (AH III.11.9; my emphasis).

In the face of such developments, St. Irenaeus adamantly insists that there are only four authentic Gospels. He even appeals to the four "zones of the world" and the four winds (the four cardinal points of the compass), as well as the four faces of the cherubim (Ezek. 1:10 and 10:14), to help make his point:

> It is not possible that the Gospels can be either more or fewer in number than they are. For, since there are four zones of the world in which we live, and four principal winds, while the Church is scattered throughout all the world, and the 'pillar and ground' of the Church [cf. 1 Tim. 3:15] is the Gospel and the spirit of life, it is fitting that She should have four pillars, breathing out immortality on every side, and vivifying men afresh. From this fact, it is evident that the Word, the Artificer of all, He who sits upon the cherubim and contains all things, He who was manifested to men, has given us the Gospel under four aspects, bound together by one Spirit.
>
> This also David indicates, when entreating Him to appear: "Thou that sittest between the cherubim, shine forth" [Ps. 80:1, KJV]. For the cherubim, too, were four-faced [Ezek. 1:6], and their faces were images of the dispensation of the Son of God. For, as the Scripture says, "The first living creature was like a lion," symbolizing His effectual working, His leadership, and royal power. "The second living creature was like a calf," signifying His sacrificial and sacerdotal order. "The third had, as it were, the face of a man," which is an evident description of His coming as a human being. And "the fourth was like a flying eagle" [Rev. 4:7], which points out the gift of the Spirit hovering with His wings over the Church. The Gospels are in accord with these things, among which Christ Jesus is seated (AH III.11.8).

The decision to accept these four Gospels alone as authentic was the first major step in the Church's formation of the canon of the New Testament (deciding which writings would be included in the New Testament, and which ones would be rejected). This crucial process (which we will look at further in Chapter Seven), along with the Church's Rule of Faith and the Apostolic Succession, were all of vital importance in the Church's victory over Gnosticism and the other heretical movements of the 2nd century.

St. Irenaeus is considered to be the first great Church Father, partly because his magnificent *Against Heresies* was so effective in helping to bring the various early Gnostic heresies to an end. His only other work that comes down to us is an apologetical treatise called *Proof (or Demonstration) of the Apostolic Preaching*. This work basically consists of a beautiful summary of all of salvation history, beginning with the Lord's first dealings with His chosen people, the Hebrews.

GNOSTICISM THROUGH HISTORY AND TO THE PRESENT

While the various Gnostic sects that St. Irenaeus laboriously refuted had withered up by about the middle of the 3rd century, certain characteristics of the Gnostic mind-set have been a constant temptation for Christians through the centuries. There has always been the temptation, for instance, to lean towards a more "spiritualized," "pure," "simplified," and/or "primitive" form of Christianity which would minimize the importance of, or eliminate altogether, the Sacraments; the icons and other forms of religious art; crosses, including making the sign of the cross; veneration of the Saints, including their relics; incense and censers; kneeling and prostrations; specific, regular periods of fasting; pilgrimages to holy places; doctrinal creeds; the various festal days of the Church Year; and the discipline and order of the established, hierarchical Church.

Through the centuries after the demise of the Gnostic sects, up to the Protestant Reformation, in one way or another, and to one degree or another, all of these concrete, material expressions of the Christian Faith have been either minimized or rejected altogether by such groups as the Euchites/Messalians, Priscillianists, Paulicianists, Iconoclasts, Bogomils, Waldensians, and Cathari/Albigensians; and by the various denominations of Protestantism, culminating in the most Gnostic of all the Protestant groups—Christian Science. These groups, generally speaking, have favored a greater emphasis on: advanced knowledge of spiritual things, and certain techniques for spiritual growth, over simple faith, belief, and practice; spiritual things over the various aspects of the material realm; holding an elitist, two-tiered rather than a unified view of the Church; having more concern for one's own spiritual life than for the ongoing life of the Christian community as a whole; understanding the Christian life more in terms of exceptional spiritual experiences than of slow, hard, diligent, faithful pilgrimage towards the Kingdom of Heaven; believing in instantaneous, *imputed* righteousness rather than in gradual growth in *actual* holiness through asceticism and self-control in conquering one's passions; pridefully rejecting rather than humbly submitting to the discipline of the visible

Church; preaching over ritual in Church services; a congregational rather than an episcopal structure for the visible Church; a diminished sense of Church History and its importance in the continuing life of the Church; a corresponding diminished role for the canonized Saints in the ongoing life of the believing community; and holding a spiritualized, merely symbolic understanding of the Sacraments rather than the Church's traditional substantive, holistic view.

In our own time, these Gnostic tendencies have infiltrated much of Protestantism to a greater degree than ever before. This fact is insightfully described and eloquently lamented by Rev. Philip J. Lee, a Presbyterian minister from New Brunswick, Canada, in a seminal book called *Against the Protestant Gnostics* (Oxford University Press, 1987 and 1993). Even though this book was written over twenty years ago, it is more relevant now than ever, since gnosticizing tendencies, with a few exceptions, have spread even further within nearly all of the Protestant denominations, both liberal and conservative, during these years.

Very interestingly and tellingly, the basic way that Rev. Lee suggests for Protestantism to extricate itself from these pervasive, debilitating, gnosticizing tendencies is to adopt practices that are already part of Holy Orthodoxy—things like devoting more time in the services to ritual; celebrating the Eucharist every Sunday; emphasizing the crucial role of water Baptism in incorporating people of all ages—including infants—into the Church; not having church school (i.e., Sunday School) conflict with the children being in the church services; reciting/singing the creed (he recommends the Apostles' Creed); following the lectionary for weekly Scripture readings; reaffirming the central role of the visible Church and the submission of the laity to its discipline; reinstituting celebration of at least the major festal days of the Church Year; interpreting the Scriptures within the context of the visible Church, following the teachings of the Apostles, rather than on one's own and by oneself; and encouraging regular family prayer and Bible study.

Concerning preaching and teaching, Rev. Lee urges particular emphasis on a number of themes that have been characteristic of Orthodox preaching and teaching going all the way back to Apostolic times: the innate goodness of the created order; the central importance of seeing oneself not in isolation, but as a crucial part of the Body of Christ; the Church as the New Israel; the Christian life primarily as a life-long, ongoing pilgrimage, rather than as a series of exceptional spiritual experiences; willingness to endure suffering in this fallen world, and working for bettering the physical as well as the spiritual condition of its inhabitants, rather than seeking escape from suffering and the responsibilities of social service; self-denial rather than self-glorification/indulgence; the resurrection of the body as well as the immortality of the soul; rehearsing and explaining the mighty acts of God in salvation history, rather than teaching techniques for people to use to obtain salvation; exhorting the people to resist "the constant brainwashing through television and other mass media" (p. 261); overcoming class distinctions within the Church; a positive view of human sexuality; and affirming and preserving the divine gift of the distinctions between the two sexes/genders, and their non-interchangeability.

Beyond the various Protestant denominations, neo-Gnostic tendencies have spread far and wide into contemporary western society, especially concerning this last point. Never in the history of the world has there been such widespread confusion over gender as we have today in the western world—to such an extent that the popular social media website Facebook now offers more than fifty possible gender designations for its users to choose from when they "customize" their gender. Much of the present-day confusion over gender identity has been spawned by the mainstream media, which has been used by politicizing homosexuals to popularize the idea that because the actual differences between males and females are supposedly so insignificant, or because males and females share human nature equally, that therefore their roles are *interchangeable*. This can help lead to the idea that a man's wife can be another man rather than a woman, or that a woman's husband can be another woman rather than a man. And this then leads to the acceptance of children being raised by two fathers or two mothers, in spite of the fact that the very conception of every new human being requires the input of a male and a female, and in spite of the fact that there is an ever-increasing amount of scientific evidence indicating that the best environment for raising children involves the complementary input of both the father and the mother.

The traditional Christian understanding is that in the very beginning the Lord Himself created humanity in two genders, whereby men and women, while indeed sharing the same human nature, still have distinct physiological, emotional, and psychological differences, for very specific reasons. According to Genesis 2, the principal reason was so that whatever was lacking in Adam (we recall how the Lord said, "It is not good for Adam to be alone") was complemented and completed by and through his wife, Eve, who was created to be his "helper." She was very much like him, sharing identically his human nature (as Adam said, "She is bone of my bones"), but she was also wondrously and gloriously different from him, so that she could provide all that was missing in Adam by himself.

The other main reason for the two distinct genders, of course, is for the conceiving and raising of children. And a crucially important part of God's wisdom in having both a man and a woman be the progenitors and parents of children is so that ideally boys would have their fathers to model mature manhood for them, and so that girls would have their mothers to model mature womanhood for them, and so that both boys and girls would have both their parents to model a good marriage for them, to prepare them to have good marriages themselves. All of this provides a crucial foundation for a healthy society, as has been recognized by all societies (of any size at least) on the face of the earth until very recent times.

Same-sex erotic behavior, which is becoming increasingly accepted in our contemporary society, is also related to our society's "new Gnosticism," which rejects all traditional moral standards regarding sexual behavior, and instead trumpets the message, "If it feels good, if there's mutual consent, and if there's no obvious immediate harm to the individuals involved, then anything goes!" What's not usually mentioned in the media is that such an attitude often leads to self-centered, reckless, self-destructive behavior—not to mention the spread of serious infectious diseases. In stark contrast, it's the traditional morality, which assigns erotic sexual activity only within traditional marriage, that provides the safest, most life-affirming, and most profoundly meaningful way to live.

It's also helpful to observe that many of the gnostic tendencies permeating our surrounding society have been promulgated through the very popular New Age Movement. This nebulous but powerful movement has precedents in various neo-Gnostic movements of the past several centuries: in the 17th century, the founding of Rosicrucianism; in the 18th century, the founding of Freemasonry, Emmanuel Swedenborg's Swedenborgian/New Church, and Ann Lee's United Society of Believers in Christ's Second Appearing (the Shakers); in the 19th century, Ralph Waldo Emerson's Transcendentalism, Allan Kardec's Spiritism, Madame Blavatsky's Theosophical Society, and Charles and Myrtle Fillmore's Unity School of Christianity; and in the 20th century, Rudolf Steiner's Anthroposophy, Edgar Cayce's Association for Research and Enlightenment, George Gurdjieff and the Gurdjieff Foundation, and his disciple P. D. Ouspensky and his Fourth Way, L. Ron Hubbard's Scientology/Dianetics, George King's Aetherius Society, Jose Silva's Silva Mind Control/Silva Life System, Paul Twitchell's and Harold Klemp's Eckankar, and Werner Erhard's Erhard Seminars Training (EST). Most of these manifestations of modern-day Gnosticism still exist, and still continue to lure people away from a more traditional world-view.

May we all continue to be guided by St. Irenaeus and all the Church Fathers, along with the Scriptures and the divinely inspired words of our Church services, to keep us grounded in the healthy "earthiness" of the True Faith within the ongoing life of the visible, hierarchical True Church, the "pillar and ground of the Truth"

(1 Tim. 3:15). Let us resist, by God's help, all gnosticizing temptations to be drawn away from the well-defined, disciplined, sacramental way of life of this visible, hierarchical, True Church—this way of life that leads, through life-long pilgrimage, to true life both now and in the future Kingdom of Heaven.

Let us likewise reject all gnosticizing temptations to flee from the challenges of "fighting the good fight" in the midst of this very fallen world, which is in such great need of Christians "letting their light shine forth" through their exemplary lives of faith, prayer, and service to their fellow man. Let us truly behold the image of God—and indeed, let us behold Christ Himself—in all of our fellow human beings, and let us love and serve Him, our truly Incarnate Lord, through loving and serving them in an incarnational ministry of being truly present with them in Christ's love.

Chapter Five

THE CHURCH MEETS THE CHALLENGE OF THE MONTANISTS

THE RISE OF MONTANISM

THE POWERFUL PSEUDO-PROPHETIC MOVEMENT known as Montanism arose in Phrygia around the year 160 AD. Phrygia, a region in west-central Asia Minor (modern-day Turkey), was long known as a seedbed of religious rigorism and even extremism. The cult of Cybele, the Earth goddess, flourished there. Phrygia bordered on the province of Galatia, and we recall that St. Paul sternly admonished the early Galatian Christians, chastising them for their tendency to fall back into various legalistic, Judaistic practices, with the words "O foolish Galatians! Who has bewitched you?" (Gal. 3:1). It was generally a rural area, with no large towns, though Philadelphia was nearby to the southwest, and a prophetess named Ammia had lived there not so long before.

By the year 160 there had not been a major sustained persecution of the Christians since the time of the Emperor Domitian (r. 81–96 AD), and the number of Christians had grown significantly. It may well have been that some of these Christians were not as fervent in their faith, or as disciplined in their spiritual life, as the very early Christians had been. And there may be an indication in the *Didache* that the office of traveling prophet was beginning to decline. This early document sternly warned against traveling prophets who stayed more than two days, who asked for money, and whose lives did not measure up to the prophecies they were giving (11:3–12). Verse 11:6 flatly states, "if he requests money, he is a false prophet." And the intense expectation of the Second Coming of Christ that marked the early days of Christianity also was probably waning, generally speaking, by the middle of the second century.

These various factors help to explain why Montanism erupts in Phrygia at this time. It begins when a certain man named Montanus begins prophesying, along with two women, named Priscilla and Maximilla. Montanus was a fairly recent convert to Christianity. Some speculate that before accepting the Christian Faith he had been a priest of the mystery cult of Cybele, the Mother Earth goddess of the Phrygians. This certainly would help explain how he fell into the grip of a lying spirit, becoming one of the false prophets whom Christ warned about: "Beware of false prophets, who come to you in sheep's clothing, but inwardly they are ravenous wolves" (Matt. 7:15; see also Matt. 24:11 and 24).

Montanus, Priscilla, and Maximilla all claimed to be directly inspired by the Holy Spirit. Some of Montanus's opponents asserted that he claimed to be the Holy Spirit incarnate. We see this in the following quotation by Bp. Eusebius of Caesarea in his *Ecclesiastical History*:

> Filled with hatred of good and love of evil, the enemy of God's Church left no trick untried in his machinations against mankind, and did his best to make a fresh crop of heretical sects spring up to injure the Church. Some members of these crawled like poisonous reptiles over Asia [i.e., western Asia Minor] and Phrygia, boasting of Montanus 'the Paraclete' and his female adherents Priscilla and Maximilla, alleged to have been his prophetesses (EH v.14).

This, I think, is too extreme an accusation. Montanus was probably simply prophesying using language such as "I, the Holy Spirit, say unto you, ..." Still, by way of comparison, the New Testament prophet Agabus declared, "'Thus says the Holy Spirit...'" (Acts 21:11).

The Montanists were claiming that with them a new age of the Holy Spirit had dawned, bringing a renewed emphasis on prophecy and on immediate, direct inspiration from the Holy Spirit. In their attempt to promote and maintain very high moral and spiritual standards, they were propounding a new legalism, as seen in their very strict penitential disciple and their rigid adherence to fasting regulations. This all was no doubt partly in reaction to what they perceived as growing moral and spiritual laxity in the Church. For them, a sign of such moral laxity was the Church's growing allowance for the possibility of repentance for the most heinous of sins—murder, adultery, and apostasy—as seen, for example, in the *Shepherd of Hermas*, which allowed for a one-time repentance for adultery (Vision IV.1.3, and

Mandate IV.1.7–8 and 3.1–7). After Tertullian became a Montanist, he called this document "The Shepherd of Adulterers" (in his *On Modesty*, ch. 1).

As the numbers of Christians steadily grew, certainly there was an increasing possibility that some of them would be more lukewarm or complacent in their faith. Claiming to be "filled with the Spirit," the Montanists referred to themselves as the "*pneumatikoi*" (the "spiritual ones"), while all other Christians they called the "*psychikoi*" (the "soulish ones"). How similar this two-tiered, judgmental approach is to the Gnosticism of the first and second centuries (as we saw in Chapter Four), and to present day Pentecostalism and the Charismatic Movement!

As part of their all-encompassing moral and spiritual rigorism, the Montanists strictly forbade fleeing in times of persecution—even though Christ Himself had said, "then let those who are in Judea flee to the mountains ... and pray that your flight may not be in winter" (Matt. 24:16–20; Mark 13:14–18; Luke 21:21). They also absolutely prohibited second marriages. St. Paul, they said, had allowed second marriages (1 Cor. 7:9 and 39; 1 Tim. 5:14) because Christianity was so new in his time that Christians weren't mature enough to all live according to his ideal of celibacy, or even to accept that people should only ever be married once (see 1 Cor. 7:6–8). But now, according to the Montanists, since so many years had passed since St. Paul was writing, and since the Holy Spirit, they thought, was now coming upon the Church with new power, all Christians should be ready and able to live according to stricter, higher standards.

As is typical of such rigorist movements, Montanism was also characterized by an avid apocalypticism—an absolute conviction that the Last Days, just before the Second Coming of Christ, had come. Maximilla, one of their prophetesses, proclaimed that after her there would not be another prophet, but rather, the End of Time. Montanus declared that two small towns in his area, Pepuza and Tymion, were a "new Jerusalem"—possibly because "the Prophets seemed to be trying to ensure in those places a purity of life and fervour of belief such as would characterise the Jerusalem of promise" (Christine Trevett, *Montanism: Gender, Authority and the New Prophecy* [Cambridge: Cambridge Univ. Press, 1996], p. 99). It was probably a later Montanist prophetess, named Quintilla, who prophesied about the descent of the heavenly Jerusalem (cf. Rev. 21:2), claiming that this would occur at Pepuza (Trevett, pp. 96–105). When word spread about this prophecy, Montanists by the hundreds came and set up tents on a plain near Pepuza, in expectation of the imminent arrival from above of the New Jerusalem. Hence, the Montanists were sometimes called Pepuzites.

By the 170s it was a substantial movement. It had taken over, for example, the entire church in Thyatira, one of the seven Churches in western Asia Minor which received messages in the Book of Revelation (see Rev. 2:18–29). Very interestingly, Rev. 2:20 says, "Nevertheless I have a few things against you, because you allow that woman Jezebel, *who calls herself a prophetess*, to teach and seduce My servants" (my emphasis).

THE CHURCH RESPONDS TO THE CHALLENGE OF MONTANISM

Various hierarchs and other churchmen tried to suppress the movement by confronting the false prophets and prophetesses directly, and by writing treatises against it. According to Bp. Eusebius of Caesarea, the first great Church historian,

> To counter the so-called Phrygian heresy, the Power which fights for truth raised up an effective and invincible weapon at Hierapolis, in the person of [Bp.] Apolinarius, already referred to in these pages. With him were associated many learned men of the day, who have left us ample material for reconstructing the history. At the beginning of his polemic against these heretics, one of these writers first indicates that he had also argued with them orally to refute their pretensions:
>
> "A little while ago I visited Ancyra in Galatia and found the local church deafened with the noise of this new craze—not prophecy, as they call it, but pseudo-prophecy, as I shall shortly prove. So far as I was able, the Lord helping me, I spoke out for days on end in the church about these matters, and replied to every argument they put forward. The church was delighted and confirmed in the truth, while the enemy was repulsed for the time being and the opposition demoralized. So I was asked by the local presbyters, with the support of my fellow-presbyter Zoticus of Otrus, to leave them a summary of what I had said against the opponents of the word of truth. This I could not do [at the time], but I promised that if the Lord allowed me I would write it here and send it to them without delay."

Eusebius goes on to quote this anonymous writer at length, as he describes the origins of Montanism and brings one of the most serious charges against it: that their prophets and prophetesses prophesied in *an unnatural, frenzied way*, falling "into a kind of trance and unnatural ecstasy"—unlike "the practice of the Church . . . from the beginning":

> There is, it appears, a village near the Phrygian border of Mysia called Ardabau. There it is said that a recent convert named Montanus, while Gratus was proconsul of Syria, in his unbridled ambition to reach the top, laid himself open to the adversary, was filled with spiritual excitement, and suddenly fell into a kind of trance and unnatural ecstasy. He raved, and began to chatter and talk nonsense [perhaps speaking in tongues], prophesying in a way that conflicted with the practice of the Church handed down generation by generation from the beginning.
>
> Of those who listened at that time to his sham utterances, some were annoyed, regarding him as possessed, a demoniac in the grip of a spirit of error [1 John 4:6], a disturber of the masses. They rebuked him and tried to stop his chatter, remembering the distinction drawn by the Lord, and His warning to guard vigilantly against the coming of false prophets [Matt. 7:15]. Others were elated as if by the Holy Spirit or a prophetic gift, were filled with conceit, and forgot the Lord's distinction [between true and false prophets]. They welcomed a spirit that injured and deluded the mind and led the people astray; they were beguiled and deceived by it, so that it could not now be reduced to silence. By some art, or rather by methodical use of a malign artifice, the devil contrived the ruin of the disobedient, and was most undeservedly honored by them. Then he secretly stirred up and inflamed minds close to the true Faith, raising up in this way two others—women whom he filled with the sham spirit, so that they chattered crazily, inopportunely, and wildly, like Montanus himself.
>
> On those who were elated and exultant about him the spirit bestowed favors, swelling their heads with his extravagant promises. . . . They were taught by this arrogant spirit to denigrate the entire Catholic Church throughout the world, because the spirit of pseudo-prophecy received neither honor nor admission into it. For the Asian believers repeatedly and in many parts of Asia had met for this purpose, and after investigating the recent utterances, pronounced them profane and rejected the heresy. Then at last its devotees were

> turned out of the Church and excommunicated (*Ecclesiastical History* 5.16).

Eusebius quotes from another refutation of Montanism, written by Miltiades, which further emphasizes how differently the Montanists prophesied in comparison with the prophets of the Old Testament and the Apostolic eras:

> But the pseudo-prophet speaks in a state of unnatural ecstasy, after which all restraint is thrown to the winds. He begins with voluntary ignorance and ends in involuntary madness, as stated already. But they cannot point to a single one of the prophets under either the Old Covenant or the New who was moved by the Spirit in this way—not Agabus [Acts 11:27–28 and 21:10–11], or Judas or Silas [Acts 15:32], or Philip's daughters [Acts 21:8–9]; not Ammia at Philadelphia or Quadratus; nor any others they may choose to boast about though they are not of their number (EH 5.17).

Even allowing for a certain exaggeration in how the opponents of the Montanists described their method of prophesying, it seems quite clear that they were not abiding by St. Paul's very important dictum, "The spirit of the prophets is subject to the prophets" (1 Cor. 14:32).

Eusebius also quotes from another refutation of the heresy, written by "an orthodox writer named Apollonius" around the year 200, who makes charges involving morally questionable practices in which Montanus was involved:

> What sort of person this upstart teacher is, his own actions and teaching show. This is the man who taught the dissolution of marriages [apparently he encouraged Priscilla and Maximilla to leave their husbands], who laid down the law on fasting, who renamed Pepuza and Tymion, insignificant towns in Phrygia, as Jerusalem, in the hope of persuading people in every district to gather there; who appointed agents to collect money; who contrived to make the gifts roll in under the name of 'offerings'; and who has subsidized those who preach his message, in order that gluttony may provide an incentive for teaching it (EH 5.18).

Montanism was condemned by the Church in Asia Minor at several local councils, and Bp. Zephyrinus of Rome condemned it sometime after the year 200. The most crucial reason for its condemnation was the fact that the Montanists were treating the "revelations" given through their prophets and prophetesses as higher in authority than the words of St. Paul—as seen most clearly in their absolute prohibition of second marriages. This led inescapably to further critical questions: How could this kind of thing ever be properly regulated? Who would determine which "prophecies" were legitimate, and which ones were not? What might the "spirit of the New Prophecy" say next in opposition to the writings of the New Testament?

The Montanists also held a narrow, rigorist, judgmental understanding of the Church as a kind of holy club, made up of those who claimed to be sanctified—with the virtually inevitable spiritual pride and delusion that goes with such a claim. This is the quintessential characteristic of *the sectarian mind-set,* which we will consider in the next chapter. This mind-set rejects the understanding that has prevailed in the Orthodox Church that the Church is meant to be *a hospital for sinners,* embracing all who come to Her for any reason, and recognizing that all Her members are sinful to one degree or another and need healing from the wounds of sin. Even St. Paul himself, as we remember, called himself "the chief of sinners" (1 Tim. 1:15).

Fr. Schmemann, while acknowledging that Montanism did have some praiseworthy characteristics, indirectly addresses both of these crucial issues mentioned just above when he concludes that in Montanism

> the Church was facing the enormous question of whether, ... without altering its final ideal, it was right to accept the masses and start their slow re-education. Should the Church remain outside the world and outside history [as a self-enclosed enclave with a fortress mentality against the surrounding society], or should it accept history as a field of heavy and prolonged labor? It was difficult to fight against Montanism, which was fired with so much sanctity, faith, and self-sacrifice; by condemning it, however, the Church condemned forever all attempts to dethrone the historical, visible Church and to incorporate it into a third Testament (*Historical Road of Eastern Orthodoxy* [Crestwood, N. Y.: SVS Press, 1977], p. 50).

AN ORTHODOX RESPONSE TO THE EMPHASIS OF PENTECOSTALISM AND THE CHARISMATIC MOVEMENT ON THE NINE GIFTS OF THE SPIRIT (1 COR. 12:8–10)

The nine gifts of the Spirit—all of them associated with manifestations of the wonder-working power of the Holy Spirit, and all of them overly emphasized by the very widespread Pentecostal and Charismatic Movements to this day—are listed by St. Paul in his first epistle to the Corinthians:

But the manifestation of the Spirit is given to each one for the profit of all: for to the one is given *the word of wisdom* through the Spirit, to another *the word of knowledge* through the same Spirit, to another *faith* by the same Spirit, to another *gifts of healings* by the same Spirit, to another *the working of miracles,* to another *prophecy,* to another *the discerning of spirits,* to another *different kinds of tongues,* to another *the interpretation of tongues* (1 Cor. 12:7–10; my emphasis).

In general, our response/interpretation would begin, I think, with remembering St. Paul's words:

> Are all apostles? Are all prophets? Are all teachers? Do all work miracles? Do all possess gifts of healing? Do all speak with tongues? Do all interpret? But *earnestly desire the higher gifts.* And I will show you *a still more excellent way.* If I speak with the tongues of men and of angels, but have not love, I am a noisy gong or a clanging cymbal.... So faith, hope, and love abide, these three; but *the greatest of these is love* (1 Cor. 12:29–13:13; my emphasis).

St. Paul is reminding us that the most important thing is to grow in virtue. We might even say that a true repentance, and living without sin, are the greatest miracles. And performing miracles in the sense of signs and wonders may actually be dangerous spiritually, for it can lead to spiritual pride and delusion. St. John Chrysostom (late 4th century; Antioch and Constantinople) makes these points in his Homily XXXIII on St. Matthew:

> Let the acquisition of virtue, then, be our goal, for abundant are her riches ...
>
> But if you would work miracles also, be rid of transgressions, and you will have very much accomplished this. Yes, for sin is a great demon, beloved; and if you exterminate this, you have wrought a greater thing than they who drive out ten thousand demons. Listen to St. Paul, how he speaks, and prefers virtue to miracles: "But covet earnestly the best gifts; and yet I show unto you a more excellent way" [1 Cor. 12:31]. And when he went on to describe this better way, he spoke not of raising the dead, nor of cleansing the lepers, nor of any other such thing; but instead of all these, he spoke of love.
>
> Hearken also unto Christ, Who said, "Rejoice not that the demons obey you, but that your names are written in Heaven" [Luke

> 10:20]. And again before this, "Many will say to Me in that day, 'Have we not prophesied in Thy name, and cast out devils, and done many mighty works?' and then I will say to them, 'I know you not'" [Matt. 7:22–23]. And when He was about to be crucified, He called His disciples, and said to them, "By this shall all men know that you are My disciples," not "if you cast out devils," but "if you have love one to another" [John 13:35]. And again, "Hereby shall all men know that Thou hast sent Me"—not, "if these men raise the dead," but "if they be one" [John 17:22–23].
>
> For as to miracles, they often, while they profited someone else, have injured him who had the power, by lifting him up to pride and vainglory, or perhaps in some other way (NPNF vol. 1, vol. X, pp. 218–219).

Because the danger of spiritual pride and delusion is so real, we see in the Lives of our Saints the very clear general pattern that they are granted "supernatural" gifts of healing, clairvoyance, discerning of spirits, and exorcizing demons only after many years of rigorous ascetic effort to overcome and control the passions, and to become deeply grounded in humility. Fr. Seraphim Rose says that

> according to St. Ignatius Brianchaninov [late 19th century; Russia], the gifts of the Holy Spirit "exist only in Orthodox Christians who have attained Christian perfection, purified and prepared beforehand by repentance." They "are given to Saints of God solely at God's good will and God's good action, and not by the will of men and not by one's own power. They are given unexpectedly, extremely rarely, in cases of extreme need, and not just at random" (quoting St. Isaac the Syrian [7th century]) (*Orthodoxy and the Religion of the Future* [Platina, Calif.: St. Herman of Alaska Brotherhood, 1990], p. 201).[2]

St. John Chrysostom also says, in the homily quoted above, that

> if we all lived as we ought to live, we would be admired by the children of the heathen more than they would admire workers of miracles. For miraculous signs often carry with them either a notion of mere fancy, or another such evil suspicion, even though our miracles

[2] How different is this understanding from that of at least certain sectors of the Charismatic Movement, as exemplified by the title of a lecture I once attended, given at a Full Gospel Businessmen's Fellowship International regional convention: "How You Can Have a Wonder-Working Ministry."

> are genuine. But a pure life cannot admit of any such reproach; yes, all men's mouths are stopped by the acquisition of virtue (Homily XXXIII on St. Matthew, NPNF vol. I, X, p. 218).

His words here can remind us that miraculous signs and wonders, including all "supernatural" manifestations such as the nine gifts listed in 1 Cor. 12:8–10, can be counterfeited by the devil, and to some extent can even be exhibited sheerly through the mental, psychic, and/or spiritual powers of man, quite apart from any reference to Jesus Christ or to the Holy Spirit. Shamans (medicine men), for instance, from virtually every primitive culture, have been able to work healings, foresee the future, and speak in tongues.

Bearing all this in mind, there is still a place in the ongoing life of the Orthodox Church for the nine gifts of the Spirit of 1 Cor. 12:8–10. They are manifested in the following ways:

the word of wisdom—sound spiritual teaching, preaching, and pastoral counseling.

the word of knowledge—basically the same as the word of wisdom, though perhaps with a more specific, narrow focus. Both of these gifts are most readily seen in the incisive words of clairvoyant elders, who see/perceive/understand by the Holy Spirit exactly what a certain person needs to hear at a certain moment in his or her life. Also, any particularly helpful insight given to the one confessing by the father-confessor during the Sacrament of Confession would be an example of one or both of these gifts.

the gift of faith—an extraordinarily fervent appeal to Christ for His help, most typically in an emergency situation. For example, the Martyrs no doubt have been granted an "extra measure of faith" to help them endure their tortures.

gifts of healing—prayers to the Saints have often brought physical and/or psychological healing to believers. Many of the Saints, having had healing gifts during their earthly lifetimes, often continue such wonder-working after their passing from this life. Healing often occurs through contact with their relics (which sometimes miraculously stream forth fragrant myrrh), or their icons—especially myrrh-streaming icons of the Theotokos. Altogether there are at least 418 different wonder-working icons of the Theotokos which have produced so many miracles of healing that they each are commemorated on a particular day in the Church Year. Also, the Sacrament of Holy Unction is specifically provided by the Church to provide physical and/or emotional healing. And the Holy Eucharist is received every time by the communicants "for the healing of soul and body."

working of miracles—the Lives of the Saints often abound with miracles of many different kinds. And there are many attestations of the Theotokos working miracles on behalf of the faithful—including in times of civil emergencies.

prophecy—clairvoyant holy elders have this gift today. In general, we understand that the role of the traveling prophets of the first two centuries of the Church was gradually assumed by the bishops (cf. *Didache* 15:1—"Appoint for yourselves, then bishops and deacons who are worthy of the Lord—men who are unassuming and not greedy, who are honest and have been proved. For they also are performing for you the task of the prophets and teachers"). Certain Saints, such as St. Cosmas the Aitolian (18th century; Greece) and St. John of Kronstadt (19th and 20th centuries; Russia), have made accurate prophecies concerning future historical events.

discerning of spirits—in the Sacrament of Confession and in pastoral counseling. This gift is also often seen in the work of clairvoyant elders. And the Church has a rite of exorcism that is used for the expelling of evil spirits from those who are afflicted by them.

different kinds of tongues—facility in known languages for missionary work. In exceptional circumstances, this gift can involve speaking and/or understanding a language not previously known. Fr. Paisios (1924–1994), on Mt. Athos, for instance, once had a conversation with someone in French, yet he did not know that language!

The "private prayer language" practiced by Pentecostal and Charismatic Christians, which they assume is mentioned by St. Paul in 1 Cor. 14:2–18 when he writes of speaking and singing in an "unknown language" (cf. 1 Cor. 13:1, Romans 8:26, and Jude 20), is no longer mentioned by the end of the second century (perhaps due to the problems with Montanism). No Saint or Father of the Church has ever espoused speaking in a private prayer language. The Jesus Prayer, however, has been found by many former Pentecostal and Charismatic Christians to take the place of the private prayer language in a deeply fulfilling way—and with a much more secure feeling, knowing what you are praying!

interpretation of tongues—in missionary work, perhaps specifically for translation work; and occasionally the ability to understand or speak a language one has never studied.

May this part of our study be helpful to all of us today to resist getting too absorbed with, or even fixated upon, spiritual gifts. There is always safety in the guidance of our Holy Church in this, as in all other matters relating to the Christian life. And it's comforting to remember that this guidance is based in and upon the unbroken wisdom of nearly two thousand years of spiritual experience, from the Apostolic era to our own time, in the Holy Orthodox Church.

At the same time, let us be appreciative of the many positive qualities of our Pentecostal and Charismatic friends, who most likely have a deep love for the Lord and the Holy Scriptures, and who endeavor to live in and for Christ in every aspect of their lives. For they are keenly aware that Christ is "alive and well," and always ready to provide His tangible strength, joy, peace, and clear guidance in even the small details of life. And this is all a very good beginning to the Christian life.

But in being so aware of the Lord's power and sensing it at work in their own lives and in the lives of many others, they sometimes can get too focused on the miracle-working power of physical healing and the exhilaration of certain powerful spiritual experiences, at the expense of the much more laborious ongoing work of deep inner healing, grounded in humility, and of personal purification from sin and the wounds of sin. And without the proper guidance and discernment, such powerful experiences can lead to spiritual pride and even delusion.

Like a fireplace safely containing the fire, it's the Holy Tradition of our Church that properly channels the fire of spiritual enthusiasm in ways that are most beneficial as we continue on the path of the Christian life. For our Tradition contains the accumulated spiritual wisdom and experience of countless Orthodox Christians for nearly twenty centuries, and it's this wisdom and experience by which our own spiritual experiences are to be measured and guided, to protect us from spiritual pride and delusion, and to ensure that our spiritual life flourishes in the safety of being in synchronization and harmony with the consistent experience of all the Saints of the Church through the centuries.

Chapter Six

TERTULLIAN AND THE DANGERS OF THE SECTARIAN MIND-SET

TERTULLIAN'S LIFE

QUINTUS SEPTIMIUS FLORENS TERTULLIANUS was born around the year 150 AD in the city of Carthage, the leading metropolitan center in all of western North Africa—which ever since the middle of the second century BC had been under the authority of the Romans. Tertullian was most likely a descendant of the Latin colonizers of the region, but he may have picked up something of the fiercely independent spirit of the surrounding native Berber population.

He was raised in a pagan family of moderate means, as his father was a centurion of the proconsular cohort. He received a fine education in Carthage, and then went to Rome for further studies in literature, rhetoric, and law. He also became well-versed in history, archaeology, medicine, and philosophy. After finishing his studies, he entered the practice of law. The great Church historian Eusebius writes that he was "an expert in Roman law, and famous on other grounds—in fact he was one of the most brilliant men in Rome" (EH 2.2.4).

While in his mid or late 30s, Tertullian was drawn to the Faith of the Christians living in Rome. As Rudolph Arbesmann writes in his introduction to a volume of Tertullian's works,

> His family was pagan, and he himself confesses that he followed pagan customs and drank deep from the cup of worldly pleasures until, as a mature man, he became a Christian at Rome. In his writings he does not give a clear explanation of the reasons for his conversion. It

> seems, however, that he was moved to embrace the Christian Faith by observing the perseverance of the Christians in the persecutions and the heroic courage of the martyrs. No early Christian writer has so emphasized the fact that the Church owed her triumph to [such] sufferings: "Crucify, torture, condemn, grind us to dust ... whenever we are mowed down by you, our number increases; *the blood of the martyrs is the seed of the Church*" (*Tertullian, Apologetical Works, and Minucius Felix, Octavius*, in the *Fathers of the Church* series, vol. 40 [Washington, D.C.: The Catholic University of America Press, 1950], p. viii; quoting *Apology* 50.12–13; my emphasis).

Soon after returning to his native Carthage, Tertullian began writing apologetical and anti-heretical works in which he defended and argued for the truths of Christianity with all the brilliant, relentless logic and cutting wit that he had previously used to win cases in the law courts. He ended up writing a great number of helpful works on many different themes. The most important of these are *The Apology, A Treatise on the Soul, The Prescription against Heretics, On the Resurrection of the Flesh*, and a magisterial refutation of the views of the leading Gnostic heretic Marcion in a very long work called *Against Marcion*. And since he was the first major Christian writer to write in Latin, he is considered to be "the Father of Latin theology."

However, Tertullian, the former lawyer, generally wrote his works with a trenchant, harsh, argumentative, militant, rigorist, judgmental spirit that eventually contributed to his leaving the Church which had given him new birth and nurture in the Faith, and to his joining in about 205 the rigorist sectarian group that we have already encountered—the Montanists. It's true that the Montanism that had spread to Carthage was not as extreme in some ways as the Montanism in Asia Minor where it originated; for instance, it did not have the extreme apocalypticism that characterized the Pepuzites. Montanism actually never spread much beyond these two regions of Asia Minor and western North Africa.

Very ironically and poignantly, before he became a Montanist, Tertullian had a very clear understanding of the universality of the Church and the consistency through time of Her doctrine, with the Church in every place tracing Her heritage back to Christ and the Apostles. For example, in his work called *Prescription against Heretics*, he wrote that the Apostles,

> after first bearing witness to the faith in Jesus Christ throughout Judea, and founding churches (there), next went forth into the world

> and preached *the same doctrine of the same Faith* to the nations. They then in like manner founded churches in every city, from which all the other churches, one after another, derived the Tradition of the Faith, and the seeds of doctrine, and are every day deriving them, that they may become churches. Indeed, it is on this account only that they will be able to deem themselves *apostolic,* as being the offspring of apostolic churches.
>
> Every sort of thing must necessarily revert to its original for its classification. Therefore the churches, although they are so many and so great, comprise but the one primitive Church, (founded) by the Apostles, from which they all (spring). In this way *all are primitive, and all are apostolic,* while they are all proved to be one, in (unbroken) unity, by their peaceful communion, and title of brotherhood, and bond of hospitality—privileges which no other rule directs than the one Tradition of the same mystery.... (ch. xx; *Ante-Nicene Fathers,* vol. III, p. 252; my emphasis).

In addition, Tertullian at first was very clear that the test of sound doctrine was always to measure any belief and/or practice against the unchanging doctrine of Christ and the Apostles as found in all the Churches:

> Whereas all doctrine which agrees with the apostolic churches—those molds and original sources of the Faith—must be reckoned for truth, as undoubtedly containing that which the (said) churches received from the Apostles, the Apostles from Christ, and Christ from God; and whereas all doctrine must be prejudged as false which savors of contrariety to the truth of the churches and Apostles of Christ and God; it remains, then, that we demonstrate whether this doctrine of ours, of which we have now given the rule, has its origin in the Tradition of the Apostles, and whether all other doctrines do not *ipso facto* proceed from falsehood. *We hold communion with the apostolic churches because our doctrine is in no respect different from theirs.* This is our witness of truth (ibid., my emphasis).

So this makes it all the more tragic that in his later years Tertullian, who always had a rigorist, purist kind of mentality with a sternly critical view of the surrounding society, was attracted by Montanism. What he found most appealing in Montanism was probably its emphasis on moral and spiritual purity, along with its strict asceticism, heightened eschatological expectations, and ongoing prophecy and other dramatic demonstrations of the gifts of the Spirit (cf. 1 Cor. 12:8–10). Like the Montanists, he was scandalized by the hierarchical Church's acceptance of the possibility of repentance for even the worst sins. For instance, he called the *Shepherd of Hermas* "the Shepherd of Adulterers" (cf. *On Modesty*, ch. 1; ANF IV, pp. 74–75) because it allowed for a one-time repentance for adultery. He was also disturbed by what he judged to be growing laxity in the spiritual life of many of the laity and clergy in the established Church.

Still, it is hard to understand how someone as knowledgable as Tertullian could have left the hierarchical Church—the very apostolic Church whose doctrine and way of life were the same as that of Christ and the Apostles, according to his earlier writing—to join a heretical sect that was condemned by that Church. For it had been officially condemned by local councils in Asia Minor in the 180s and 190s, and by the Church in Rome in the early years of the third century. But his decision was apparently well thought out. For example, hear how stringently he affirmed the Montanists' complete rejection of second marriage:

> Christ abolished the commandment of Moses [concerning the possibility for divorce; Matt. 19:3–8] ... why then should not the Paraclete [the Holy Spirit] have cancelled the indulgence granted by Paul ...? 'Hardness of heart' held sway until the coming of Christ; let weakness of the flesh bring its reign to an end with the coming of the Paraclete. The New Law abolished divorce ... *the New Prophecy abolished second marriage* (*On Monogamy*, ch. 14; Henry Bettenson, ed., *The Early Christian Fathers* [N. Y.: Oxford University Press, 1969], p. 132; ANF IV, pp. 70–71; my emphasis).

This quotation also reveals how Tertullian accepted the Montanists' view of history—that there has somehow been *a new Pentecost* with the Holy Spirit coming upon the Montanist prophets and prophetesses, and thereby inaugurating a new Age of the Spirit.

Furthermore, with startling judgmentalism, Tertullian made it very clear that he had fully accepted the Montanists' two-tiered view of Christians, dividing them into the *pneumatikoi* (the *spiritual ones*) and the *psychikoi* (the *soulish*, or *worldly, ones*). He adamantly concluded that the established, hierarchical Church was in the worldly category:

> Now what of that church of yours, worldly man? This power (of binding and loosing sin, in granting absolution) will adhere to spiritual powers, to an apostle or prophet *as far as they show the personal*

> *qualities of Peter.* For the Church is properly and primarily the Spirit, in whom is the Trinity of the divinity, the Father, Son, and Holy Spirit. The Spirit makes the assembly of the Church ... Therefore the Church will indeed remit sins; but *it will be the Church of the Spirit, by the agency of a spiritual man, not the Church as a number of bishops.* For the right of judgment belongs to the Lord, not the servant; to God Himself, not to the priest (*On Modesty,* ch. 21; Bettenson, p. 133; ANF IV, pp. 99–100; my emphasis).

And with chilling hardheartedness, he declared:

> But, you say, the Church has the power to remit sins? I have the more reason for acknowledging and asserting this, in that I find the Paraclete saying, through the New Prophets, "The Church has power to remit a sin; *but I will not do it, lest they commit other sins*" (*On Modesty,* ch. 21; Bettenson, p. 133; ANF IV, p. 99; my emphasis).

So we see how thoroughly Tertullian had gotten convinced that through the various prophecies of the Montanist prophets and prophetesses, the Holy Spirit was doing a new thing in the earth, which the established Church was by and large ignoring, to the great detriment of the spiritual growth of its members, in his opinion. Indeed, as we have said, he got convinced that the established Church had lost the clear guidance of the Spirit and the fervent piety of the Apostolic age. He came to the opinion that most of the members of the established Church were not living according to the strict standards of prayer, fasting, personal asceticism, and moral probity that characterized the life of the first Christians. He then concluded that this Church was beyond hope of rejuvenation and transformation from within. Hence, he broke away, and joined the Montanists.

In the words of Roy J. Deferrari,

> To be sure, Montanism did not bring about a radical change in Tertullian's moral teaching, because his asceticism was marked with a certain rigor and inflexibility from the beginning. Since his contact with Montanism, however, this rigor increased in strength until the ideal of austere virtue which he wanted to impose on the faithful as a whole became more Stoic than Christian.
>
> We may well wonder how a man of so rare intelligence as Tertullian—a man, in addition, who had defended so vigorously the concept of Tradition and stressed so much the apostolic succession

> of the Catholic hierarchy—could turn his back upon the Church and be led astray by an Oriental sect whose frenzied excesses could hardly attract him. Once he saw himself rebuffed in his demands for a severer and more rigid asceticism, he discovered in the Montanist tenets some ideas that appealed to him. In the feverish expectation of the imminent end of the world and in preparation for it, Montanus and his associates, the prophetesses Maximilla and Prisca (or Priscilla), had demanded the most severe asceticism. Second marriages were forbidden, and virginity strongly recommended; longer and stricter fasts were made obligatory, and only dry foods (*xerophagy*) permitted; flight from persecution was disapproved, and the joyful acceptance of martyrdom advocated; and reconciliation was denied to all those who had committed capital sins [i.e., the worst sins—adultery, murder, and apostasy]. Here, Tertullian found a moral code that satisfied his own desires for a more perfect and purer life. He could give his adherence all the more easily as it was divine authority, the 'Paraclete,' who, as Montanus claimed, spoke through him and the prophetesses.
>
> The memory of a brilliant man who had served the Church so well and then became her bitter enemy is always sorrowful. The ideal which Tertullian sought outside the Church proved to be a mirage. He died a disillusioned and embittered man (from the Foreword, in *Tertullian: Disciplinary, Moral and Ascetic Works*, FC, vol. 40, pp. 9–10).

THE SECTARIAN MIND-SET

Tertullian's willingness to break away from the established Church and join a sect is an example of the hallmark characteristic of what can be called the *sectarian mind-set*. Here is a list of other typical characteristics of this mind-set which, like the various gnosticizing tendencies which we studied in Chapter Four, has been a constant temptation for the members of the established Church through the centuries: a lack of love for the established Church, and a lack of trust that She is always being guided by the Spirit of Truth and being protected and built up by Christ Himself; the continuing existence of the sectarian group is justified/bolstered mainly by ongoing criticism and disparagement of the canonical Church; pridefulness and self-righteousness; judgmentalism of and even contempt for those in the established Church; excessive rigorism and a legalistic spirit concerning penitence, fasting, asceticism, the adornment of women, second marriages, fleeing in times of persecution, reception of converts, length of the worship services, head coverings for women in the services, and certain moral issues; a generally harsh attitude towards the non-Orthodox, spurning relations with them; a generally negative attitude towards the world and human accomplishments; a tendency to overly identify with one particular political and/or economic and/or social philosophy or movement; an over-emphasis on the End Times, with an insistence that Christ will return within one generation; the danger of the group becoming further extreme and even bizarre in practices and/or doctrine; and a tendency of the sectarian movement to break up into further segments (so typical of Protestant denominationalism), as the spirit of judgmentalism and criticism gets directed towards one's own group.

Tertullian and the Montanist movement which he joined exemplified many, if not all, of these typical traits of the sectarian mind-set. Since the lure of the sectarian mind-set is so strong in our day—especially, it seems, for new converts to Orthodoxy—I think it's prudent to take the time to show at some length how harsh and self-righteous this world-view really is, as seen in the extremely rigorous writings of Tertullian as a Montanist. And the lesson becomes all the more vivid for us when we see the tenderness and compassion that marked his pre-Montanist writings on certain selected themes, and compare those passages with what he wrote as a Montanist on these same topics. For example:

CONCERNING PRIDEFULNESS AND SELF-RIGHTEOUSNESS, AND JUDGMENTALISM OF AND EVEN CONTEMPT FOR THOSE IN THE ESTABLISHED CHURCH

Tertullian wrote as a Montanist:

> This too, therefore, shall be a count in my indictment against the Psychics [meaning the ordinary, soulish Christians—the *psychikoi*], and against the fellowship of sentiment which I myself formerly maintained with them .... But *repudiation of fellowship* is never an indication of sin. *As if it were not easier to err with the majority, when it is in the company of the few that truth is loved....* I blush not at an error which I have ceased to hold, because I am delighted at having ceased to hold it, and because *I recognize myself to be better and more modest.* No one blushes at his own improvement (*On Modesty*, ch. 1; ANF IV, p. 75; my emphasis).

> We indeed, on our part, subsequently withdrew from *the carnally-minded* upon our acknowledgment and maintenance of the Paraclete (*Against Praxeas*, ch. 1; ANF III, pp. 597–598; my emphasis).

> What harshness, therefore, is there on our part, if we renounce communion with those who refuse to do the will of God? (*On Monogamy*, ch. 15; ANF IV, p. 71).

Correspondingly, in all of his Montanist writings, it is scarcely possible to detect any note of personal humility concerning his own weakness and sinfulness. Yet in his pre-Montanist days, he did express his own sinfulness quite humbly and openly. For instance:

> That repentance, O sinner, like myself (... for pre-eminence in sins I acknowledge to be mine) ... (*On Repentance*, ch. 4; ANF III, p. 659).

> ...sinner as I am of every dye, and born for nothing save repentance (*On Repentance*, ch. 12; ANF III, p. 666).

> But so far as I, with my poor powers, understand, ... Only, I pray that when you are asking, you be mindful likewise of Tertullian the sinner (*On Baptism*, ch. 20; ANF III, p. 679).

> I fully confess unto the Lord God that it has been rash enough, if not even impudent, for me to have dared to compose a treatise on Patience, for practicing which I am entirely unfit, being a man of no goodness...
>
> So I, most miserable, ever sick with the heat of impatience, must of necessity sigh after, and invoke, and persistently plead for, that health of patience *which I possess not* (*On Patience*, ch. 1; ANF III, p. 707; my emphasis).

So it certainly appears that having adopted the two-tiered view of the Church held by the Montanists, Tertullian in his own life exemplifies the virtually inevitable danger of spiritual pride that goes along with this false, judgmental, sectarian understanding of the Church. How far has he departed from the understanding of the entire Tradition that "Humility is the root, mother, nurse, foundation, and bond of all virtue," in the words of St. John Chrysostom!

CONCERNING EXCESSIVE RIGORISM AND A LEGALISTIC SPIRIT REGARDING PENITENCE

A major issue which confronted the Early Church was whether or not after one's Baptism the possibility of repentance for the worst sins—generally considered to be adultery, murder, and apostasy—would be granted to Christians through the sacramental offices of the Church. At first, Tertullian agreed with the growing sentiment that such repentance would indeed be possible—but only once, and only if it were lengthy, heartfelt, and guided by the pastoral offices of the canonical Church. In referring to the repeated attacks of the devil, he says in his treatise *On Repentance*,

> These poisons of his, therefore, God, foreseeing them, although the gate of forgiveness has been shut and fastened up with the bar of baptism, has permitted it still to stand somewhat open. In the vestibule He has stationed *the second repentance* for opening to those who knock; but now *once and for all*, because now for the second time, but never more ... For is not even this *once* enough? You have what you now do not deserve, for you had lost what you had received. If the Lord's indulgence grants you the means of *restoring* what you had lost, be thankful for the benefit renewed, not to say amplified. For restoring is a greater thing than *giving*, inasmuch as *having lost* is more miserable than never having *received* at all.
>
> However, if anyone does incur the debt of a second repentance, his spirit is not because of this to be cut down and undermined by despair. Let it by all means be irksome to *sin* again, but let not to *repent* again be irksome. Let it be irksome to imperil oneself again, but not to be again set free. Let no one be ashamed. Repeated sickness must have repeated medicine. You will show your gratitude to the Lord by not refusing what the Lord offers you. You have offended, but you can still be reconciled. You have One whom you may satisfy, and He is willing (*On Repentance*, ch. 7; ANF III, p. 663; his emphasis).

And further,

> If you doubt, unravel the meaning of "what the Spirit saith to the churches." He imputes to the Ephesians "forsaken love"; He reproaches the Thyatirenes with "fornication," and "eating of things sacrificed to idols"; He accuses the Sardians of "works not full"; He censures the Pergamenes for teaching perverse things; He upbraids

> the Laodiceans for trusting to their riches. And yet He gives them all general admonitions to repentance—with warnings, it is true [Rev. 2:1–3:22]. But He would not utter warnings to someone *unrepentant* if He did not forgive the repentant one.... The heavens, and the angels who are there, are glad at a man's repentance. Ho! you sinner, be of good cheer! you see where it is that there is joy at your return....
>
> That most gentle father, likewise, I will not pass over in silence, who calls his prodigal son home, and willingly receives him repentant after his indigence, slays his best fatted calf, and graces his joy with a banquet. Why not? He had found the son whom he had lost; he had felt him to be all the dearer of whom he had made a gain. Who is that father to be understood by us to be? God, surely: for no one is so truly a Father; no one is so rich in paternal love. He, then, will receive you, His own son, back, even if you have squandered what you had received from Him, even if you return naked—just because you have returned. And *He will rejoice more over your return* than over the sobriety of the other (*Ibid.*, my emphasis).

However, once he became a Montanist, the possibility of repentance for fornication and adultery is denied by Tertullian. Here is his reaction to the news that the Bishop of Rome—Bp. Zephyrinus at the time—had announced in his Church that the possibility of repentance for the sin of adultery would be granted by the Church:

> I hear that there has even been an edict set forth, and a peremptory one, too. The *Pontifex Maximus*—that is, the bishop of bishops—issues an edict: "I remit, to such as have discharged (the requirements of) repentance, the sins both of adultery and of fornication." O edict, on which cannot be inscribed, "Good deed!"
>
> And where shall this liberality be posted? On the very spot, I suppose, on the very gates of the sensual appetites, beneath the very titles of the sensual appetites. There is the place for promulgating such repentance, where the delinquency itself shall haunt. There is the place to read the pardon ...
>
> But it is in the Church that this (edict) is read, and in the Church that it is pronounced; and She is a virgin! Far, far from Christ's betrothed be such a proclamation! She, the true, the modest, the saintly, shall be free from stain even of Her ears. She has none to

> whom to make such a promise. And if She had, *She does not make it,* since even the earthly temple of God can sooner have been called by the Lord a "den of robbers" than of adulterers and fornicators....
>
> We command excommunication for adulterers also and for fornicators, *dooming them to pour forth tears barren of peace, and to regain from the Church no more return than the publication of their disgrace* (*On Modesty,* ch. 1; ANF IV, p. 75; my emphasis).

In this same work *On Modesty,* Tertullian asserts that the parables of the lost sheep, the lost drachma, and the Prodigal Son all *do not refer* to Christians returning to Christ and being found by Him after grievously sinning after Baptism (chs. 7–9; pp. 80–83). He also bluntly states in this work that "the power of loosing and of binding committed to Peter *had nothing to do* with the capital sins of believers" (ch. 21; p. 99; my emphasis).

CONCERNING EXCESSIVE RIGORISM AND A LEGALISTIC SPIRIT REGARDING FASTING

Tertullian the Montanist boasts about the "manful" way rigorist fasting is commanded among the Montanists, over against the laxity of those in the established Church, whom he asks rhetorically and sarcastically,

> Men of soul and flesh alone as you are, naturally you reject spiritual things.... Why, then, do not you constantly preach, "Let us eat and drink, for tomorrow we shall die?" just as *we do not hesitate manfully to command,* "Let us fast, brethren and sisters, lest tomorrow perchance we die" (*On Fasting,* ch. 17; ANF IV, p. 114; my emphasis).

CONCERNING EXCESSIVE RIGORISM AND A LEGALISTIC SPIRIT REGARDING THE VEILING OF WOMEN

Tertullian states, speaking as a Montanist,

> Still, until very recently among us, either custom was, with comparative indifference, admitted to communion. The matter had been left to the choice of each virgin whether to veil herself or expose herself, as she might have chosen, just as (she had equal liberty) as to marrying, ...
>
> But when the power of discerning [i.e., the Montanist prophecies] began to advance, so that the license granted to either fashion

> was becoming the means whereby the indication of the better way emerged, immediately the great adversary of good things—and much more of good institutions—set to his own work. In opposition to the 'virgins of God,' the 'virgins of men' go about with their front quite bare, being excited to a rash audacity ...
>
> If modesty, if bashfulness, if contempt of glory, if being eager to please God alone, are good things, let women who are scandalized by such good things learn to acknowledge their own evil....
>
> Every public exposure of an honorable virgin's flesh is, to her, the same as being raped (*On the Veiling of Virgins,* ch. 3; ANF IV, pp. 28–29).

And he declares that married women should continue to wear the veil, and "not outgrow the discipline of the veil, not even for an hour" (*Ibid.,* ch. 17; p. 37).

CONCERNING EXCESSIVE RIGORISM AND A LEGALISTIC SPIRIT CONCERNING THE ADORNMENT/ATTIRE OF WOMEN

In *On the Apparel of Women,* written in his Montanist period, Tertullian objects to Christian women wearing any dyed clothing, since God did not

> order sheep to be born with purple and sky-blue fleeces! If He was *able,* then plainly He was *unwilling* to do so; and what God did not will of course should not be fashioned. Those things, then, are not the best by nature which are not from God, the *Author* of nature. Thus they are understood to be from *the devil,* from the *corrupter* of nature. For there is no other whose they can be, if they are not God's, because what are not God's must necessarily be His rival's' (*On the Apparel of Women,* Bk. 1, ch. 7; ANF IV, p. 17; his emphasis).

In this same work, he says of jewels that since they are not used in the construction of houses, "The only edifice which they know how to build is this silly pride of women" (*Ibid.,* 1.6; p. 16).

CONCERNING EXCESSIVE RIGORISM AND A LEGALISTIC SPIRIT CONCERNING FLEEING IN TIMES OF PERSECUTION

Even though Jesus Himself said, concerning the time of great tribulation in the End Times, "then let those who are in Judea flee to the mountains ... And pray that your flight may not be in winter" (Matt. 24:16–20), for Tertullian the Montanist, true Christians will never flee in a time of persecution:

> But it is said that the Lord, providing for the weakness of some of His people, in His kindness, suggested the haven of flight to them. For He [they think] was not able without offering flight—a protection so base, and unworthy, and servile—to preserve in persecution those whom He knew to be weak! *Whereas in fact He does not cherish, but always rejects the weak,* teaching first, not that we are to flee from our persecutors, but rather that we are not to fear them. "Fear not them who are able to kill the body, but are unable to do anything against the soul; but fear Him who can destroy both body and soul in hell" [Matt. 10:28].
>
> And then what does He allot to the fearful? "He who will value his life more than Me, is not worthy of Me; and he who takes not up his cross and follows Me, cannot be My disciple" [cf. Matt. 10:38–39]. Last of all, in the Revelation, He does not propose flight to the "fearful," but a miserable portion among the rest of the outcast, in the lake of brimstone and fire, which is the second death [cf. Rev. 21:8] (*On Flight in Time of Persecution,* ch. 7; ANF IV, p. 120; FC 40, pp. 290–291; my emphasis).

Tertullian goes on to say in this treatise,

> Paul bids us to support the weak, but most certainly it is not when they flee. For how can the absent be supported by you? By bearing with them? Well, he says that people must be supported, if anywhere they have committed a fault through the weakness of their faith, just as (he enjoins) that we should comfort the faint-hearted, but not to encourage them to run away....
>
> He who bids us to shine as sons of light does not bid us to hide away out of sight as sons of darkness. He commands us to stand steadfast, certainly not to act the opposite part by fleeing; and to be girded [for battle], and not to play the fugitive or oppose the Gospel. He points out weapons, too, which persons who intend to run away would not require. And among these he notes the shield, too, that you may be able to quench the darts of the devil [Eph. 6:13–16], when doubtless you resist him, and sustain his assaults in their utmost force. Accordingly John also teaches that we must lay down

> our lives for the brethren [1 John 3:16]; much more, then, we must do it for the Lord. This cannot be fulfilled by those who flee....
>
> For indeed, it [the Montanist prophetic utterance] incites almost all to go and offer themselves in martyrdom, not to flee from it (*Ibid.*, ch. 9; ANF IV, p. 121; FC 40, pp. 292–294).

CONCERNING EXCESSIVE RIGORISM AND A LEGALISTIC SPIRIT REGARDING SECOND MARRIAGES

As a Montanist, Tertullian readily accepted their absolute prohibition of second marriages, thereby overturning the specific teaching of St. Paul who allowed for second marriage, especially for young widows with children (see 1 Cor. 7:8–9 and 39; 1 Tim. 5:14; cf. Rom. 7:3). As he states,

> Christ abolished the commandment of Moses ... why then should not the Paraclete have cancelled the indulgence granted by Paul? ... 'Hardness of heart' [cf. Matt. 19:8] reigned until Christ's time; let 'infirmity of the flesh' [cf. Gal. 4:13] be content to have reigned until the time of the Paraclete. The New Law abrogated divorce ...; the New Prophecy abrogates second marriage (*On Monogamy*, ch. 14; ANF IV, pp. 70–71).

Tertullian also writes, "accordingly, with the utmost strictness, we excommunicate digamists [i.e., those who have entered a second marriage], as bringing infamy upon the Paraclete by the irregularity of their discipline" (*On Modesty*, ch. 1; ANF IV, p. 75). In *On Exhortation to Chastity*, he calls second marriage "a species of fornication" (ch. 9; ANF IV, p. 55) and "a species of inferior evil" (ch. 3; ANF IV, p. 52); and in *On Monogamy* he calls it "adultery" (ch. 9; ANF IV, p. 66). And in response to the charge that this mandate is too harsh, he accuses those in the established Church of a lack of willpower and a lack of faith in the power of the Holy Spirit—Who is now being poured out in extra strength—to help them abide by this new prohibition (*Ibid.*, ch. 14; ANF IV, p. 71).

According to William P. Le Saint,

> In the *Exhortation to Chastity* his earlier counsel has already become an uncompromising demand, while in the work *On Monogamy* he speaks of all second marriage as adultery, and attacks, with savage violence, the 'sensualists' and 'enemies of the Paraclete' who justify it by appeals to Holy Scripture and especially to the authority of St.

> Paul. Thus, what should be a matter of personal preference or personal ideals is made a matter of conscience; ascetical is confused with moral theology, discipline with doctrine; and a way of life which in some circumstance is of value to some individuals becomes a strict and essential obligation imposed upon all Christians. It is well to remind ourselves that such warped and exaggerated views were not the views of the Catholics. These views were heretical errors and were condemned by the Church as heretical, along with similar excesses in the direction of an unnatural rigidity propounded by Marcionites, Manicheans, Priscillianists, and other avowed enemies of sex and marriage (Introduction to *Tertullian: Treatises on Marriage and Remarriage, Ancient Christian Writers,* vol. 13 [Mahwah, NJ: Paulist Press, 1978] p. 4).

CONCERNING A GENERALLY NEGATIVE ATTITUDE TOWARDS THE NON-ORTHODOX (AND TOWARDS THOSE IN THE ESTABLISHED CHURCH)

The Montanist Tertullian accuses the women in the non-Montanist Church of

> exhibiting in their gait *the same appearance as the women of the nations,* in whom *the sense of true modesty is absent,* because *in those who know not God, the Guardian and Master of truth, there is nothing true.* For if any modesty can be believed (to exist) among the Gentiles, it is plain that *it must be imperfect and undisciplined* to such a degree that, although it be actively tenacious in the mind up to a certain point, yet it allows itself to relax into licentious extravagances of attire *in accordance with Gentile perversity* (*On the Apparel of Women,* Bk. II, ch. 1; ANF IV, p. 18; my emphasis).

CONCERNING A GENERALLY NEGATIVE ATTITUDE TOWARDS THE WORLD IN GENERAL

As a Montanist, Tertullian writes to Christians in prison about to be martyred:

> Do not let this separation from the world alarm you; for if we reflect that the world is more really the prison, we shall see that you will have gone out of a prison rather than into one. The world has the greater darkness, blinding men's hearts. The world imposes the more grievous fetters, binding men's very souls. The world breathes out

> the worst impurities—human lusts. *The world contains the larger number of criminals, even the whole human race*" (*To the Martyrs*, ch. 2; FC 40, pp. 19–20; my emphasis).

Even before becoming a Montanist, Tertullian, as we saw in Chapter Three, was very critical of the non-Christian society around him, and its Greco-Roman philosophic and literary heritage. This attitude is clearly demonstrated in his famous rhetorical outburst, "What has Athens to do with Jerusalem? What concord is there between the Academy and the Church?" (*Prescription against Heresies*, ch. 7; ANF III, p. 246). As we also saw in Chapter Three, this is very different from the holistic, discerning approach of other Apologists such as St. Justin Martyr, Athenagoras, and Minucius Felix (and Clement of Alexandria, and later, for example, of the Cappadocian Fathers, St. Photios the Great, St. Innocent of Alaska, and St. Nikolai [Velimirovich] of Serbia).

In this same passage in *Prescription against Heresies,* Tertullian says that all "heresies are instigated by philosophy," and then he castigates Aristotle in particular:

> Unhappy Aristotle! He invented dialectics for these philosophers—the art of building up and pulling down—an art so evasive in its propositions, so far-fetched in its conjectures, so harsh in its arguments, so productive of contentions, embarrassing even to itself, retracting everything and really treating of nothing! From where spring those "fables and endless genealogies" [1 Tim. 1:4] and "unprofitable questions" [Titus 3:9], and "words which spread like a cancer"? [2 Tim. 2:17].... the Apostle Paul expressly names philosophy [as their source] [cf. Col. 2:8] (*Ibid*).

Concerning the popular entertainments of his day, Tertullian's rigorist negative attitude is described by Roy J. Deferrari:

> In view of Tertullian's uncompromising attitude toward everything that, in his opinion, was related to idolatry, it is hardly surprising that his treatise, *On the Spectacles,* contains an out-and-out indictment of the performances given in the circus, theater, stadium, and amphitheater, such entertainments being absolutely incompatible with the faith and moral discipline of Christianity (in the Foreword, FC 40, p. 8).

Deferrari also says that "in the treatise, *The Chaplet,* Tertullian declares unlawful not only military service, but also the acceptance of any public office" (Foreword, FC 40, p. 9).

CONCERNING A NEGATIVE VIEW OF MARRIAGE AND MARITAL RELATIONS

Tetullian strongly expresses the Montanists' sharply negative views concerning marriage and human sexuality in his work called *On Monogamy,* in which he absolutely forbids second marriage for any reason, as we saw above:

> But (as for the question) whether monogamy [meaning only ever having one marriage] be "burdensome," let the still shameless "infirmity of the flesh" look to that. Let us meantime come to an agreement as to whether it be "novel." This (even) broader assertion we make: that even if the Paraclete had in this our day definitely prescribed virginity or continence to be total and absolute, so as not to permit the heat of the flesh to "foam itself down" even in single marriage, even then He would seem to be introducing nothing of "novelty"—seeing that the Lord Himself opens "the kingdoms of the heavens" to "eunuchs," as being Himself, after all, a virgin. And seeing this, the apostle also—himself too for this reason remaining abstinent—gives the preference to continence [1 Cor. 7:8–9]. ("Yes"), you say, "but he still preserves the law of marriage." Preserving it, plainly, and we will see under what limitations; nevertheless, he already ***destroys it,*** in so far as he gives the preference to continence. "Good," he says, "(it is) for a man not to have contact with a woman" [1 Cor. 7:2]. It follows *that it is evil to have contact with her;* for nothing is contrary to good except evil. And accordingly (he says), "It remains, that both they who have wives so be as if they have not" [v. 29], that it may be the more binding on those who do not have wives to abstain from having them" (*On Monogamy,* ch. 3; ANF IV, p. 60; my emphasis).

With similar invective Tertullian links marriage with fornication, as he claims that marital relations are inevitably tinged with concupiscence, in this passage from *Exhortation to Chastity*:

> What is the thing which takes place in all men and women to produce marriage and fornication? Commixture of the flesh, of course—the *concupiscence which the Lord made equal to fornication.* "Then,"

> someone says, "are you now destroying first, that is, single marriage, too?" *Not without reason, for it too consists of that which is the essence of fornication* (ch. 12; ANF IV, p. 55; my emphasis).

Even when writing to his own wife, Tertullian can exclaim, "How far better it is neither to marry nor to burn!" (*To His Wife*, Bk. 1, ch. 3; ANF IV, p. 40; ACW 13, p. 13). And in the same work, concerning the future life, he writes, "There will at that day be no resumption of voluptuous disgrace between us. No such frivolities, no such impurities, does God promise to His (servants)" (*To His Wife*, I.1; ANF IV, p. 39; ACW 13, p. 10).

Once again, we see that in his thinking on this topic as well, Tertullian was infected by his association with the Montanists, since before being influenced by them he had a distinctly more positive view of marriage and marital relations. For example, he clearly asserts in *Against Marcion* that marital relations *do not by nature involve concupiscence*:

> concupiscence, however, *is not ascribed to marriage even among the Gentiles,* but to extravagant, unnatural, and enormous sins. The law of nature is opposed to luxury as well as to grossness and uncleanness; *it does not forbid connubial intercourse, but only concupiscence*; and it takes care of our vessel by the honorable estate of matrimony (V.15; ANF III, p. 462; my emphasis).

CONCERNING A NEGATIVE VIEW OF WOMEN

Tertullian the Montanist also succumbed to a negative view of women in general, linking each woman directly to Eve's transgression in the Garden of Eden. He states that *every woman* should "go about in humble garb, and be drab in appearance, walking about like Eve, mourning and repentant, in order that by every bit of penitential clothing she might the more fully expiate that which she derives from Eve—the ignominy, I mean, of the first sin, and the odium (attaching to her as the cause) of human perdition." He goes on to address each woman personally:

> And do you not know that you are (each) an Eve? The sentence of God on this sex of yours lives in this age: the guilt must of necessity live too. *You* are the devil's gateway; *you* are the unsealer of that (forbidden) tree; *you* are the first deserter of the divine law; *you* are she who persuaded him whom the devil was not valiant enough to attack. *You* destroyed so easily God's image, man. On account of *your* deserved punishment—that is, death—even the Son of God had to

> die. And do you think about adorning yourself over and beyond your tunics of skins? (*On the Apparel of Women*, Bk. I, ch. 1; ANF IV, p. 14; his emphasis).

The natural beauty of womanhood he sees preeminently as being dangerous for men to behold:

> Even the real beauty of natural grace must be obliterated by concealment and negligence, as equally dangerous to the glances of the beholder's eyes" (*Ibid.*, II.2; ANF IV, p. 19).

And he goes on to say in this work,

> because the use and fruit of beauty is voluptuousness, ... [You may ask,] "May we not enjoy the praise of beauty alone, and glory in a bodily good?" Let whoever finds pleasure in "glorying in the flesh" see to that.... such exaltation [in the flesh] is incongruous for those who profess humility" (*Ibid.*, II.3; p. 20).

CONCERNING A NEGATIVE VIEW OF CHILDREN

With rigid consistency, Tertullian as a Montanist continues to rant against the natural rhythms of daily life, even though he himself was married!—in railing against the bearing and raising of children. For example, he exclaims, "No wise man would ever willingly have desired sons!" (*Exhortation to Chastity*, ch. 12; ANF IV, p. 57). In this same work he says sarcastically, "Marry we, therefore, daily. And marrying, let us be overtaken by the last day, like Sodom and Gomorrah—that day when the 'woe' pronounced over 'those who are with child and giving suck' [Matt. 24:19] shall be fulfilled—that is, over the married and the incontinent; for from marriage result wombs, and breasts, and infants" (*Ibid.*, ch. 9; p. 55). And in *On Monogamy*, he says with great sarcasm, "Let them accumulate by their repeated marriages fruits exactly seasonable for the last times—breasts heaving, and wombs qualmish, and infants whimpering" (ch. 16; ANF IV, p. 72).

Very tellingly, in writing years earlier against the Gnostic Marcion, Tertullian expressed great sensitivity and compassion regarding child-bearing and child-raising, as he addressed Marcion directly:

> Describe the womb as it enlarges from day to day, heavy, troublesome, restless even in sleep, changeful in its feelings of dislike and desire. Inveigh now likewise against the shame itself of a woman in travail which, however, ought rather to be honored in consideration

of that peril, or *to be held sacred in respect of (the mystery of) nature.* Of course, you are horrified also at the infant, which is brought into life with the embarrassments which accompany it from the womb. You likewise, of course, loathe it even after it is washed, when it is dressed out in its swaddling-clothes, graced with repeated anointing, smiled on with the nurse's fawning glances.

This revered course of nature, you, O Marcion, (are pleased to) spit upon; and yet, in what way were you born? You detest a human being at his birth; then after what fashion do you love anybody? Yourself, of course, you had no love for, when you departed from the Church and the faith of Christ.... Well, then, in loving mankind He loved his nativity also, and his flesh as well....

Our birth He reforms from death by a second birth from heaven; our flesh He restores from every harassing malady. When leprous, He cleanses it of the stain; when blind, He rekindles its light; when palsied, He renews its strength; when possessed with devils, He exorcises it; when dead, He reanimates it. So then, shall *we* blush to possess it? ... believing in a God Who has been born, and that of a virgin, and of a fleshly nature too, Who wallowed in all the before-mentioned humiliations of nature? (*On the Flesh of Christ*, ch. 4; ANF III, 524; my emphasis).

CONCERNING AN OVEREMPHASIS ON THE END TIMES

Undoubtedly, Tertullian's negative perspective on marriage, marital relations, child-bearing, and raising children was colored by the avid apocalypticism which characterized the Montanist movement—and which has been so typical of nearly every sectarian movement to this day. For if Christ's Second Coming is indeed expected to occur any day, why would one be thinking about having children?

Here is an example of his thinking concerning the imminent return of Christ and the resultant consequences for marriage, as he says sarcastically:

Let us marry daily, and in the midst of our marrying let us be overtaken, like Sodom and Gomorrah, by that day of fear! For *there* it was not only, of course, that they were dealing in marriage and merchandise; but also, when He says, "They were marrying and buying" [cf. Luke 17:26–30], He denounces *the very leading vices of the flesh and of the world*, which call men away the most from divine

> disciplines—the first through the pleasure of rioting, and the other though the greed of acquiring. And yet that "blindness" *then* was felt long before "the ends of the world." What, then, will the case be if God *now* keep us from the vices which *of old* were detestable before Him? "The time," says (the apostle), "is compressed. It remains that they who have wives act as if they do not have them" [1 Cor. 7:29] (*To His Wife*, Bk. I, ch. 5; ANF IV, p. 42; my emphasis).

As he says in *On Monogamy*,

> But now, when "the extremity of the times" has *cancelled* the command "to grow and multiply," the Apostle Paul superimposes another command: "It remains that they who have wives to be as if they do not have them," because "the time is compressed" (ch. 7; ANF IV, p. 64; my emphasis).

Furthermore, he refers to "Antichrist now close at hand, and gaping for the blood, not the money, of Christians" (*On Flight in Time of Persecution*, ch. 12; ANF IV, p. 124). And also, with very little humility, he asserts, in reference to his own Montanist group,

> We are they "upon whom the ends of the ages have met, having ended their course." We have been predestined by God, before the world was, (*to arise*) *in the extreme end of the times.* And so we are trained by God for the purpose of chastising ... the world. We are the circumcision—spiritual and carnal—of all things; for both in the spirit and in the flesh we circumcise worldly principles (*On the Apparel of Women*, Bk. II, ch. 9; ANF IV, p. 23; my emphasis).

CONCERNING THE TENDENCY TO DIVIDE INTO MORE, SMALLER GROUPS

There is some evidence that near the end of his life, Tertullian became disillusioned with the main body of Montanists, and broke away from them to form his own group, which became known as the Tertullianists. Again, such a pattern is quintessentially typical of the sectarian mind-set. But how ironic, tragic, poignant—and telling—it is that the "Founder of Latin theology" actually dies outside the Church, as a Montanist—or perhaps even as a Tertullianist—a member of a sectarian, schismatic group that was repeatedly condemned by the Church.

THE SECTARIAN MIND-SET EVEN WITHIN ORTHODOXY IN OUR OWN TIME

The ongoing allure of the sectarian mind-set is evident in the fact that even within Orthodoxy in the 20th century, two major examples of this mind-set developed: in certain parts of the Russian Orthodox Church Outside Russia (ROCOR), and in the Greek Old Calendarist Movement. Both movements emerged in the aftermath of World War I, with strong political motivation involved. The first one was dominated by a fiercely anti-Soviet position that favored the restoration of the Russian monarchy, and the second one was fueled partly by monarchist sentiment against the democratizing efforts of the Venizelists. Each of the movements broke away from its Mother Church, with an independent schismatic ecclesiastical structure of its own. And in varying ways and to varying degrees, each of these groups have been characterized by some, if not all, of the typical traits of the sectarian mind-set which we've identified in this chapter.

The sectarian mind-set of a portion of ROCOR was revealed after the reconciliation in 2007 of most of the ROCOR parishes with the Patriarchate of Moscow, as at least nine parishes or groups of parishes have refused to accept that reconciliation, and still abide in schism. And in Greece, the several Old Calendarist groups continue to abide in schism from the Mother Church and from each other. One of them, the Matthewites, even claims that no other Orthodox body besides themselves has the saving grace of God.

So, may we all take to heart the vivid lessons that Tertullian and these modern movements give us concerning the dangers of the temptation to yield to the harsh, rigorist, judgmental, separatist, sectarian mind-set.

Chapter Seven

THE CANONIZATION OF THE NEW TESTAMENT: THE CHURCH DECIDES

EARLY CHURCH COUNCILS: INTRODUCTION

THIS IS THE FASCINATING STORY, though sketched out here only briefly, of the long, complex, and critically important process by which the established, hierarchical Church, guided by the Holy Spirit, determined which writings would become known as the *New Testament*. These writings were seen as fulfilling and superseding the sacred Scriptures of the Hebrews, which the Church retained as the *Old Testament*.

In the first centuries after Christ there were many writings in circulation in Christian circles that claimed apostolic authorship and authority. But not all of them were trustworthy as really conveying the truths of the Christian Faith. Especially in response to heretics who claimed their own writings to be authoritative, the Church had to decide *which* of all these books in circulation would be finally accepted as the definitive, divinely inspired written Word of God. The entire process lasted nearly 400 years.

Whether consciously or not, anyone who accepts the 27 books of the New Testament as we have them today implicitly trusts the judgment—the *spiritual discernment*—of the established Church of the first four centuries in having *correctly made* the many decisions which She had to make during this long canonization process. These decisions concerned not only every book which She ultimately accepted, but also every book which She rejected as being less than the inspired written Word of

God. And as we will see, it was not always easy to determine whether any certain book should be included in the New Testament canon or not.

At first, it wasn't readily apparent that the life and words of Jesus Christ would need to be recorded in written form at all. The first Christians relied on "word of mouth" to spread the Gospel. They remembered and passed on to others the various oral traditions about Christ and His teachings that circulated among the original disciples of the Lord. As long as the early Christians had the original Apostles still living in their midst, they could ask them to rehearse once again the glorious story of their days walking with the Savior. And also, the early Christians had a vivid expectation that the Lord would return very soon. Hence, there was little thought of preserving His life and words in written form for future generations.

It was probably not until the decade of the 60s AD, some thirty years after Christ walked on this Earth, that the four Gospels began to be written and circulated among the Churches. Meanwhile, St. Paul only wrote his first epistle—probably 1 Thessalonians—around the year 50 AD. It's very interesting to observe that the early Church thrived for at least 17 years without a single word of the New Testament having been written! And probably at least another ten years passed by before any of the four Gospels were written.

MANY BOOKS IN CIRCULATION AMONG CHRISTIANS

It was only during the second century that the Church gradually began to realize the need to establish a permanent, authoritative list of writings about Christ and the Christian life that could be depended upon to contain only the Truth—Truth about the Father, Son, and Holy Spirit; about the Church; and about everything relating to the way of salvation and the spiritual life. The problem by that time was, as we mentioned above, that a lot of writings claiming apostolic authorship and authority were in circulation in the Christian world, but many of them were laced with errors of one sort or another. So despite their claims to be connected with various Apostles, these writings could not be accepted as trustworthy sources of Christian Truth. These books were not, in reality, written by Apostles or close disciples of Apostles. Instead, they were composed by others—some with clearly heretical ideas—who falsely claimed such apostolic connections. Such works included the Gnostic-oriented *Gospel of Thomas*, another work used by Gnostics called the *Gospel of Philip*, the strange *Arabic Gospel of the Infancy of the Savior*, the *Acts of Peter*, and the so-called *Gospel of Truth* written by the major Gnostic heretic Valentinus, among many others.

THE IMPETUS GIVEN BY MARCION

Interestingly, the first list of New Testament books was compiled around the year 150 by a heretic, the Semi-Gnostic Marcion. His understanding of traditional Christian teaching was so distorted that he actually completely rejected the entire Old Testament, because he believed that the God written about there was really a fallen angel. Reflecting his rejection of the Old Testament and its God, Marcion's New Testament "canon" only included an expurgated version of the Gospel of St. Luke, and similarly altered versions of ten of St. Paul's epistles.

Marcion's movement became so widespread that the Church had to take him very seriously. Many bishops wrote polemical works against him and his heretical ideas. But his list of canonical books, defective and truncated as it was, helped to stir the Church to eventually compile Her own list of authoritative New Testament books. As the *Oxford Dictionary of the Christian Church* puts it, "his rejection of three of the Gospels was an important factor in compelling the Church to differentiate between true and spurious works and construct its own Canon" (third revised edition [2005], p. 1040).

THE IMPETUS GIVEN BY MONTANISM

Another similarly compelling factor in the latter part of the second century that helped to spur the Church to compile the New Testament Canon was the rise and spread of Montanism. As we recall from Chapter Five, this rigorist, apocalyptic heresy was overemphasizing the role of prophets and prophetesses, to the point of giving the utterances of their prophets more authority than even the epistles of St. Paul. And as we noted there, concerning the issue of fleeing in a time of persecution, they even went beyond the words of Christ Himself.

THE ROLE OF ST. IRENAEUS

The first step in the canonization process of the New Testament by the hierarchical Church was the united, emphatic proclamation that there are four, and *only four*, authentic Gospels—those written by Saints Matthew, Mark, Luke, and John. For only these Gospels measured up to the four criteria that the Church used to discern between authentic and spurious works: 1), they were indeed directly associated with the original Apostles; 2), they were the gospels that were being used liturgically by the various Churches across the Empire; 3), they were the gospels being quoted by the various leaders of the Church; 4), and they clearly presented the Truth as preached by Jesus and His Apostles.

We recall from Chapter Four how St. Irenaeus of Lyons, the bishop there from about 177 to about 202 , heartily asserts in his very influential work, *Against Heresies* (III.11.8), that only these four are the true gospels. Henry Chadwick, in his fine book entitled *The Early Church,* observes that St. Irenaeus "was the first writer whose New Testament virtually corresponds to the canon that became accepted as traditional" (revised edition [London: Penguin Books, 1993], p. 81). This is a great testimony to the discernment of this first major Church Father as to which Christian writings in circulation in his day were trustworthy as Scripture, and which ones were not.

THE MURATORIAN CANON

The earliest extant list of New Testament books compiled within the Church dates from around the year 180 . It reflects usage in the Church of Rome at that time. This list appears in an 8th century Latin manuscript which was discovered by L. A. Muratori in the early 1700s. Hence, this list is called the Muratorian Canon. Originally written in Greek, the list includes the four Gospels, the Acts of the Apostles, 13 Pauline epistles (not including Hebrews), Jude, 1 and 2 John, and the Revelation of John. So we see that this early list did not include Hebrews, James, 1 and 2 Peter, and 3 John.

On the other hand, the Muratorian Canon most likely included the *Apocalypse of Peter* (though some think the reference is to 1 Peter), which was not accepted by the Church as a whole as being part of the New Testament. And in this document the *Shepherd of Hermas* is specifically disallowed to be part of the New Testament canon, though it is still recommended to be read: "it ought also to be read; but it cannot be publicly read in the Church to the people" (Henry Bettenson, ed., *Documents of the Christian Church,* second edition [London: Oxford Univ. Press, 1963], pp. 28–29).

THE ACCOUNT OF THE MARTYRS OF LYONS AND VIENNE

The lengthy *Account of the Martyrs of Lyons and Vienne,* written in 177 , also gives impressive testimony to the discernment of the Church in this part of Gaul (modern-day France) as to which writings could be trusted as New Testament Scripture. In the words of G. A. Williamson,

> This document, whose authenticity need not be doubted, contains a remarkable number of open or disguised quotations from the Bible. The great majority come from the New Testament, showing that

within a century of its composition it had already ousted the Old Testament from the affections of the Gallic Christians at least. Two disputed books, 2 Peter and the Revelation of John, are quoted from as freely as the rest (G. A. Williamson, trans., *Eusebius: The History of the Church* [Harmondsworth, England: Penguin Books, 1965], footnote 1, p. 193).

ST. DIONYSIUS THE GREAT AND THE REVELATION OF ST. JOHN

In the middle of the third century, St. Dionysius the Great, the illustrious Bishop of Alexandria. Egypt, from 247 to 264, expressed considerable reservation about including the Revelation of St. John in the New Testament canon. This part of the story of the canonization of the New Testament vividly demonstrates how complex and difficult this process of discernment was, at least concerning certain of the books in question.

Bp. Dionysius wrote, concerning the Revelation of St. John, that "some of our predecessors rejected the book and pulled it entirely to pieces, criticizing it chapter by chapter, pronouncing it unintelligible and illogical and the title false. They say it is not John's, and that it is not a *revelation* at all, since it is heavily veiled by its thick curtain of incomprehensibility." He himself was convinced, from observations that modern Biblical critics might make, that its author was a different John from the one who wrote the Gospel and the Epistle of 1 John. As he writes,

> Anyone who examines their characteristics throughout will inevitably see that St. John's Gospel and his first Epistle have one and the same color. But there is no resemblance or similarity whatever between them and the Revelation. It has no connection, no relationship with them; it has hardly a syllable in common with them. Nor shall we find any mention or notion of the Revelation in the Epistle (let alone the Gospel), or of the Epistle in the Revelation....
>
> By the phraseology also we can measure the difference between the Gospel and the first Epistle, and the Revelation. The first two are written not only without any blunders in the use of Greek, but with remarkable skill as regards diction, logical thought, and orderly expression. It is impossible to find in them one barbarous word or solecism [that is, an error in grammar or idiom], or any kind of vulgarism. For, by the grace of the Lord, it seems their author possessed

> both things—the gift of knowledge and the gift of speech. That the other author saw revelations and received knowledge and prophecy I will not deny. But I observe that his language and style are not really Greek: he uses barbarous idioms, and is sometimes guilty of solecisms. There is no need to pick these out now; for I have not said these things in order to pour scorn on him—do not imagine it—but solely to prove the dissimilarity between these books.

Still, St. Dionysius says, with noteworthy humility,

> But I myself would never dare to reject the book, of which many good Christians have a very high opinion. But realizing that my mental powers are inadequate to judge it properly, I take the view that the interpretation of the various sections is largely a mystery, something too wonderful for our comprehension. I do not understand it, but I suspect that some deeper meaning is concealed in the words. I do not measure and judge these things by my own reason, but put more reliance on faith, and so I have concluded that they are too high to be grasped by me. I do not condemn as valueless what I have not taken in at a glance, but rather I am puzzled that I have not taken it in (quoted by Eusebius in *Ecclesiastical History* 7.25).

Also in this long excerpt given by Bp. Eusebius of Caesarea, the first great Church historian, St. Dionysius alludes to another reason why there was much hesitation about the book in the eastern parts of the Roman Empire. This was that the book fueled the heresy of *millennialism* (or *chiliasm*), which claimed that Christ would return to establish a sensual kingdom on earth to last literally for one thousand years. This heresy is based mainly on a faulty interpretation of Revelation 20:1–7.

For reasons such as these, the Book of Revelation will be the last of the books of the New Testament to be generally accepted in the East. The Church in Antioch does not finally accept it until some time during the early 5th century. This is a major reason why it is not read to this day as part of the Church's lectionary (the list of Scripture readings designated for every day of the year), since these readings were decided upon mostly during the 4th century.

Interestingly, the Book of Revelation had always been favored in the West. By contrast, the Book of Hebrews was always highly regarded in the East, with its authorship generally attributed to St. Paul, while its authenticity was questioned in the West. According to Henry Chadwick, "The West disputed Pauline authorship of Hebrews and only accepted it 200 years later on the authority of the Eastern Church" (*The Early Church*, p. 43). It seems that somehow an unofficial *de facto* kind of exchange was ultimately made, with the East accepting Revelation in return for the West accepting Hebrews.

THE TESTIMONY OF EUSEBIUS OF CAESAREA

In the celebrated *Ecclesiastical History* written by Bp. Eusebius of Caesarea, we find two especially important passages concerning the canonization process of the New Testament. In both of these, he indicates the status of the process in his time and place—early 4th century Palestine. And in both passages, we see how the overall process is still quite a bit in flux:

> Of Peter, one epistle, known as his first, is accepted, and this the early Fathers quoted from freely, as undoubtedly genuine, in their own writings. But the second Petrine epistle we have been taught to regard as uncanonical; many, however, have thought it valuable and have honored it with a place among the other Scriptures. On the other hand, in the case of the 'Acta' [i.e., the *Acts of Peter*] attributed to him, the 'Gospel' that bears his name, the 'Preaching' called his, and the so-called 'Revelation' [of Peter], we have no reason at all to include these among the traditional catholic Scriptures, for neither in the early days nor in our own has any Church writer made use of their testimony....
>
> These then are the works attributed to Peter, of which I have recognized only one epistle as authentic and accepted by the early fathers. Paul, on the other hand, was obviously and unmistakably the author of the fourteen epistles [meaning that the Epistle to the Hebrews is included]. But we must not shut our eyes to the fact that some authorities have rejected the Epistle to the Hebrews, pointing out that the Roman Church denies that it is the work of Paul. What our predecessors have said about it I will quote at the proper time. As for the 'Acta' attributed to him, no one has ever suggested to me that they are genuine.
>
> Since the same apostle, in the salutations that conclude the Epistle to the Romans, has referred among others to Hermas [Rom. 16:14], the reputed author of the 'Shepherd,' it is to be noted that this, too, has been rejected by some authorities and therefore cannot be placed among the accepted books. Others, however, have

> judged it indispensable, especially for those in need of elementary education. Hence we know that is has been used before now in public worship, and some of the earliest writers made use of it, as I have discovered (EH 3.3).

The second quotation, given below, contains Eusebius's famous four categories in which he placed the various writings circulating within the Christian world in his day:

> It will be well, at this point, to classify the New Testament writings already referred to. We must, of course, put first the holy quartet of the gospels, followed by the Acts of the Apostles. The next place in the list goes to Paul's epistles, and after them we must recognize the epistle called 1 John; likewise 1 Peter. To these may be added, if it is thought proper, the Revelation of John, the arguments about which I shall set out when the time comes. These are classed as *Recognized Books.* Those that are *Disputed, yet familiar to most,* include the epistles known as James, Jude, and 2 Peter, and those called 2 and 3 John, the work either of the evangelist or of someone else with the same name.
>
> Among *Spurious Books* must be placed the 'Acts' of Paul, the 'Shepherd,' and the 'Revelation of Peter'; and also the alleged 'Epistle of Barnabas' and the 'Teachings of the Apostles' [i.e., the *Didache*; these last two, along with the *Shepherd of Hermas,* are among the writings of the Apostolic Fathers; see Chapter Two above], together with the Revelation of John, if this seems the right place for it. For as I said before, some reject it, and others include it among the Recognized Books. Moreover, some have found a place in the list for the 'Gospel of Hebrews,' a book which has a special appeal for those Hebrews who have accepted Christ. These would all be classed with the *Disputed Books,* but I have been obliged to list the latter separately, distinguishing those writings which according to the Tradition of the Church are true, genuine, and recognized, from those in a different category, not canonical but disputed, yet familiar to most churchmen.
>
> For we must not confuse these with the writings published by heretics under the name of the Apostles, as containing either Gospels of Peter, Thomas, Matthias, and several others besides these, or

> Acts of Andrew, John, and other Apostles. To none of these has any churchman of any generation ever seen fit to refer in his writings. Again, nothing could be farther from apostolic usage than the type of phraseology employed, while the ideas and implications of their contents are so irreconcilable with true orthodoxy that they stand revealed as *the forgeries of heretics*. It follows that so far from being classed even among *Spurious Books,* they must be thrown out as *impious and beyond the pale* (EH 3.25; my emphasis).

HESITATION ABOUT CERTAIN BOOKS

We see from these quotations by Eusebius that Hebrews, James, 2 Peter, 2 and 3 John, Jude, and the Revelation of St. John all were still in dispute in the early 4th century. We've seen some of the reasons for the hesitation about the Revelation and the Epistle to the Hebrews. But what about these other books? The Epistle of St. James was always regarded in the East as the work of St. James, the first bishop of Jerusalem. But in the West, its authorship was doubted, and it may have been observed that apart from three verses (1:1, 2:1, and 5:14), there is little that is specifically Christian in the book. The authorship of 2 Peter was questioned, probably because its style and quality of Greek are different from the style and quality of Greek in 1 Peter. There was hesitation about 2 and 3 John because these were referred to or quoted from very seldom by the early Christian writers, but this is probably because they are so short. And the Epistle of Jude was questioned because it contains a direct quotation, with the source given, from the non-canonical book of 1 Enoch (Jude 14–15). But in the end, these books were accepted by the whole Church as genuine parts of the New Testament, with their apostolic authorship and truthful content recognized.

On the other hand, the books that were regarded as Scripture for a while by some parts of the Church—books such as 1 Clement, the *Shepherd of Hermas,* the *Didache,* and the *Revelation of Peter*—were rejected by the Church as a whole as being of late, non-apostolic origin. And the churches which had been using them liturgically stopped doing so.

THE ROLE OF ST. ATHANASIOS THE GREAT

The earliest extant list of New Testament books which gives exactly the 27 books which comprise the New Testament as we know it today was compiled by St. Athanasios the Great, the illustrious bishop of Alexandria, Egypt, in the middle of the 4th century. In those times it was the custom for the Bishop of Alexandria to write to all the Churches at the beginning of each year to announce the date of Pascha for the upcoming year, and to give any other pastoral recommendations he wished to convey. In the year 367, St. Athanasios chose to include in his annual letter the list of books recognized and used as the New Testament in his Church in Alexandria.

WORLDWIDE ACCEPTANCE OF ST. ATHANASIOS' LIST

Within fifty years or so, this list came to be accepted by the worldwide canonical Church. A council in Rome in 382 accepted this list, as did a council in Carthage in 397. Interestingly, the Nestorian Church, which broke away from the established, hierarchical Church after the Third Ecumenical Council (held in Ephesus in 431), still omits 2 Peter, 2 and 3 John, Jude, and Revelation from their New Testament.

Even though this whole process lasted into the 5th century, and even though it was marked by much hesitation and considerable dispute, we can clearly discern the presence of the Holy Spirit in guiding the entire Church towards unanimity on this critically important issue. It's a great marvel that unanimity was reached without any mandate or decree being pronounced from an authority from on high. This is a great example of the early Church's implicit trust in a non-dictatorial, conciliar, Spirit-led approach concerning all matters relating to the life of the Church. Indeed, the New Testament as we have it today was the result of the entire Church for many years patiently seeking the guidance of the Spirit, with quiet trust in the truthfulness of the words of Jesus spoken to His Disciples about the Holy Spirit: "when He, the Spirit of truth, has come, He will guide you into all truth" (John 16:13). Henry Chadwick observes, as he concludes his account of this story, "Sometimes modern writers wonder at the disagreements. The truly astonishing thing is that so great a measure of agreement was reached so quickly" (*The Early Church*, p. 44).

EPILOGUE—RELEVANCE OF THIS STORY ESPECIALLY FOR PROTESTANTS

In their complete, unquestioning acceptance of the New Testament Canon, Protestants—whether they realize it or not—are showing profound trust in the established, hierarchical Church of the first four centuries. For it is that very Church which decided which books would comprise the New Testament that we have today. If Protestants can be helped to realize that they indeed are trusting that Church to a profound degree on this matter of such immense importance, perhaps they might become open to trusting the wisdom and spiritual discernment of that same Church concerning *other matters* relating to the Christian life—such as the hierarchical structure of bishops, priests, and deacons; the central importance of Baptism/Chrismation/Eucharist; the development of the Church Year and the great richness of the Church's hymnography and liturgical life in general; the veneration of Saints and relics; prayer for the departed; iconography; monasticism; and so on. For all these things were a vibrant part of the life of the institutional Church of the first four centuries. And they still are all very important in the present-day Holy Orthodox Church, which is the direct, organic continuation of the Church of the first four centuries.

Chapter Eight

THE RISE OF PAPAL PRESUMPTION

EARLY CHURCH COUNCILS

FROM THE VERY BEGINNING of the Christian era, the structure of the Church was a Spirit-led blend of hierarchy and conciliarity. As we saw in Chapter Two, the three-fold ministry of bishop, priest, and deacon was firmly in place at least in Antioch by the opening years of the second century. And we saw in Chapter One the conciliarity of the apostles at the first Church council—in Jerusalem in 49 AD—where each apostle, including St. Peter, had an equal voice, and where St. James, the first bishop of Jerusalem, summarized and pronounced the final decision.

By the second half of the second century, various regional councils of bishops, with each one representing his local Church, were meeting fairly often in western North Africa. This began happening in the other parts of the Roman Empire during the third century.

THE FIRST ECUMENICAL COUNCIL

The first Empire-wide council met in Nicea, in western Asia Minor, in 325. By that time, the three most major cities of the Empire—Rome, Alexandria, and Antioch—had emerged as the most important Christian cities in the Empire as well. As such, it was recognized that the Churches in each of these cities would have jurisdictional authority over the Churches in their neighboring provinces. This is explicitly declared in the Sixth Canon from this Council:

> Let the ancient customs in Egypt, Libya, and Pentapolis prevail, that the Bishop of Alexandria have jurisdiction in all these, since the like

> is customary for the Bishop of Rome also. Likewise in Antioch and the other provinces, let the Churches retain their privileges (NPNF, second series, vol. XIV, p. 15).

This is the heart of the *patriarchal/episcopal principle* or *pattern* by which the Orthodox Churches are organized and governed to this day.

THE SECOND ECUMENICAL COUNCIL

By the time of the Second Ecumenical Council, held in Constantinople in 381, that city had become the capital of the Empire, so naturally the Church there would assume preeminence in the East, while "Old Rome" was still being honored as the "first among equals" in the whole Church. Hence the Third Canon of this Council states, "The Bishop of Constantinople shall have the prerogative of honor after the Bishop of Rome, because Constantinople is New Rome."

In the Second Canon from this Council, the patriarchal/episcopal pattern outlined in Canon Six at Nicea is reaffirmed in considerably more detail:

> The bishops are not to go beyond their dioceses to Churches lying outside of their bounds, *nor bring confusion on the Churches.* But let the Bishop of Alexandria, according to the canons, *alone* administer the affairs of Egypt; and let the bishops of the East manage the East *alone,* with the privileges of the Church of Antioch, which are mentioned in the canons of Nicea, being preserved; and let the bishops of the Asian Diocese [meaning the Roman province of Asia in western Asia Minor] administer the Asian affairs *only;* and the Pontic bishops [in the Roman province of Pontus, in northwestern Asia Minor] *only* Pontic matters; and the Thracian bishops [in the Roman province of Thrace, which today is European Turkey] *only* Thracian affairs. *And do not let bishops go beyond their dioceses for ordination or any other ecclesiastical ministrations, unless they are invited.* And the aforesaid canon concerning dioceses being observed, it is evident that the synod of every province will administer the affairs of that particular province as was decreed at Nicea (NPNF vol. II, ch. XIV, pp.176-177; my emphasis).

And Canon Six of the Second Ecumenical Council decrees that any dispute against a bishop may be taken *only as far* as a synod in the relevant province or diocese. No appeal to any bishop outside the disputant's province or diocese is allowed.

Hence, we see very clearly that no one bishop is given jurisdictional authority over all the rest of the Churches, according to the Fathers of both the first two Ecumenical Councils. And these Councils, as well as all the rest of the Seven Ecumenical Councils, all of which together hold the highest authority in the universal Church, all have been officially accepted by the Roman Church.

THE THIRD ECUMENICAL COUNCIL

At the Third Ecumenical Council, held in Ephesus in 431, again we find the patriarchal/ episcopal pattern reaffirmed. This time it is ardently defended against the Bishop of Antioch's attempt to hold ordinations in Cyprus, a province that was not under his authority. Here is the full text of the relevant canon, Canon Eight:

> Our brother bishop Rheginus, the beloved of God, and his fellow beloved of God bishops Zeno and Evagrius, of the Province of Cyprus, have reported to us *an innovation* which has been introduced *contrary* to the ecclesiastical constitutions and the Canons of the Holy Apostles, and *which touches the liberties of us all.* Wherefore, since injuries affecting all require the more attention, as they cause the greater damage, and particularly when they are transgressions of an ancient custom; and since those excellent men, who have petitioned this Synod, have told us in writing and by word of mouth that the Bishop of Antioch has in this way held ordinations in Cyprus; therefore the Rulers of the holy Churches in Cyprus shall enjoy, without dispute or injury, according to the Canons of the blessed Fathers and ancient custom, *the right of performing for themselves* the ordination of their excellent bishops.
>
> The same rule shall be observed in the other dioceses and provinces everywhere, *so that none of the God-beloved Bishops shall assume control of any province which has not heretofore, from the very beginning, been under his own hand or that of his predecessors.* But if anyone has violently taken and subjected a province, he shall give it up—lest the Canons of the Fathers be transgressed, or the vanities of worldly honor be brought in under the pretext of sacred office, *or we lose, without knowing it, little by little, the liberty* which Our Lord Jesus Christ, the Deliverer of all men, has given us by His own blood.
>
> Wherefore, this holy and ecumenical Synod has decreed that *in every province* the rights which heretofore, from the beginning, have belonged to it, *shall be preserved* unto it, according to the old prevailing

> custom, unchanged and uninjured—with every Metropolitan having permission to take, for his own security, a copy of these acts. And *if anyone shall bring forward a rule contrary to what is determined here, this holy and ecumenical Synod unanimously decrees that it shall be of no effect* (NPNF vol. 11, XIV, pp. 234–235; my emphasis).

So here we see even stronger emphasis on the jurisdictional rights of the leading bishops in every province, with none of them being subject to any other bishop.

THE FOURTH ECUMENICAL COUNCIL

Canon Nine at the Fourth Ecumenical Council, held in Chalcedon, near Constantinople, in 451, extends Canon Six of the Second Ecumenical Council with these words:

> And if a bishop or [other] clergyman should have a difference with the metropolitan [the leading bishop in a province] of the province, let him have recourse to the Exarch of the Diocese [comprised of several provinces], or to the [patriarchal] throne of the Imperial City of Constantinople, and there let it be tried (NPNF vol. 11, XIV, p. 274).

And Canon Seventeen repeats the intent of Canon Nine: "And if anyone be wronged by his metropolitan, let the matter be decided by the Exarch of the diocese or by the throne of Constantinople, as aforesaid" (*Ibid.*, p. 280).

We see in these texts that the highest court of appeal, according to the Ecumenical Councils which Rome herself accepted, is Constantinople, and not Rome. As Johnson notes in the NPNF volume, concerning Canon Nine,

> Let the reader observe that here is *a greater privilege given by a General [i.e., Ecumenical] Council to the see of Constantinople than ever was given by any council, even that of Sardica [in 343], to the bishop of Rome*, that is, that any bishop or clergyman might at the first instance bring his cause before the bishop of Constantinople if the defendant were a metropolitan (*Ibid.*, p. 274; my emphasis).

THE PRIMACY OF THE BISHOP OF ROME

It is with this conciliar patriarchal/episcopal pattern of the Early Church clearly in mind that we now turn to the controversial issue of the proper jurisdictional authority of the bishop of Rome. Occupying the "throne of St. Peter," the bishop of Rome came to be popularly known as the "pope" of Rome from early in the 6th century onwards.

Certainly St. Peter was the leader of the original Twelve Apostles, as seen multiple times in the Gospel accounts. But the most famous declaration of Christ concerning Peter—"Thou art Peter [*Petros*], and on this rock [*petra*] I will build My Church" (Matt. 16:18)—refers to *the faith* of Peter, in the Orthodox understanding. This is partly because the word "rock" in the Greek is in the feminine gender, so it cannot possibly refer to Peter; and also because just a few lines further in the same chapter in St. Matthew's Gospel, Jesus castigates Peter for his misunderstanding and obstruction, even calling him "Satan"! (Matt. 16:22–23). So we understand that Christ will build His Church on Peter—and on all the Apostles—*as long as they stay grounded in the faith and will of Christ.*

And when Christ tells Peter, "And I will give you the keys to the Kingdom, and whatever you bind on earth will be bound in heaven, and whatever you loose on earth will be loosed in heaven" (Matt. 16:19), this must be understood in association with John 20:22–23, where Jesus bestows the Holy Spirit *upon all the Apostles*: "Jesus breathed on them, and said to them, 'Receive the Holy Spirit. If you forgive the sins of any, they are forgiven them; if you retain the sins of any, they are retained.'" Here we see that Christ bestows the grace for absolving sins in the Sacrament of Confession to all the Apostles, and by extension, to *all* their ordained successors—not just to Peter and his successors on the throne of St. Peter in Rome. And as is well-known, Peter first stayed in Antioch after leaving Jerusalem, yet the Church of Antioch has never claimed to be "the throne of Peter" with universal jurisdiction over the entire Church.

Now there are many natural reasons why the Church of Rome should have a certain preeminence in the worldwide Church. Not only do we see Peter as the leader of the Apostles in the Gospel accounts, but also in the first half of the Book of Acts (through chapter 12) he is clearly the leader. For instance, he initiates the election of St. Matthias to be Judas's replacement (Acts 1), he gives the first several Christian sermons (Acts 2–5), and he leads the first Gentile converts into the Christian Faith (Acts 10–11). After his time in Antioch, he does travel to Rome, where it is assumed that he leads the Church. And he ends up being martyred there under Emperor Nero on June 29, probably in the year 67 AD—with his grave becoming a great place of pilgrimage in the following years.

In addition, Rome, of course, was the capital of the Roman Empire, and it was by far the largest, most illustrious city in all of western Europe. So the Church there would very naturally have a certain preeminence in the worldwide Church.

Also, unlike in the East, where hundreds of churches were established by St. Paul and other Apostles, in the West only the Church in Rome was associated with the presence of any of the original Apostles. So it alone in all the West had the right to call itself an "Apostolic See."

So it was completely understandable that the Church in Rome would have prominence in Western Europe. And by extension, even the Churches in the East quite willingly gave the Roman Church first place in honor and respect—hence the standard description of the Roman bishop as being "the first among equals." But in the East this never implied a willingness to allow the Roman bishop to have *jurisdictional authority* over the Churches there, as we've seen in looking at the canons of the first four Ecumenical Councils. This was unlike what happened in the West, where eventually, although never without a long and hard struggle, the bishop of Rome finally did establish his jurisdictional control over all the Churches in all the various regions of Western Europe, by about the middle of the 9th century.

It's also relevant that beginning with chapter 13, the focus in the Book of Acts shifts away from St. Peter to St. Paul, who stands at the center of the entire remainder of the book, with the exception of chapter 15. And Paul also journeyed to Rome, where he also was martyred under Nero—most likely on the same day of June 29 exactly one year later, in 68. Saints Peter and Paul were both always commemorated together on that day; and both of their graves became important places of pilgrimage. In the icons, they very often are portrayed together, jointly holding the same church. This graphically illustrates that they both are equally responsible for the establishment of the Church as a whole. And we recall how St. Paul had to publicly rebuke Peter when Peter refused to eat with Gentile Christians (Gal. 2:11–21). So again, Peter is not to be followed when he does not do the right thing!

THE APOSTOLIC FATHERS REGARDING THE BISHOP OF ROME

When we turn to the Apostolic Fathers, we find St. Clement, Peter's third successor as bishop of Rome, addressing a letter to the Corinthian Church, as we saw in Chapter Two. But he does not write in the name of the throne of Peter, or even with any reference to his office as bishop. In fact, he does not even write in his own name, but only in the name of "the Church sojourning in Rome, to the Church sojourning in Corinth." This equality of designation indicates the equality of dignity and the jurisdictional independence that each of these Churches had. And Clement does not command or demand anything of the Corinthians; he only exhorts, urges, and begs them, but never with a dictatorial or imperious tone or stance.

So it is quite inaccurate for Johannes Quasten, the greatest Roman Catholic patrologist of the 20th century, to claim that "the Epistle of St. Clement is also of supreme importance for another point of dogma, the primacy of the Roman Church, of which is furnishes unequivocal proof" (*Patrology*, vol. 1 [Westminster, Md.: Christian Classics, 1983], p. 46). He is quite obviously projecting back upon the early Church a much later claim of the Roman Church to have jurisdiction over all the Churches of Christendom.

The second great Apostolic Father, St. Ignatius of Antioch, wrote his famous seven letters only about 11 years after 1 Clement was written, and yet in none of them is there any indication that he expects the Roman Church to have jurisdiction over all the rest of the Churches. One of these seven letters is addressed to the Church of Rome directly, and yet still, in this letter there is no hint of deference to the bishop there as being somehow above all the other bishops. Indeed, he makes no mention of any bishop in the Church of Rome in this letter.

St. Polycarp, the third of the three great Apostolic Fathers, visited the Roman Church in the middle of the 2nd century, where he met with Bishop Anicetus. They discussed a number of issues which divided their two Churches—especially the issue of when to celebrate the Paschal (Easter) feast, since the long-held tradition of the Christians of western Asia Minor was to celebrate it on the 14th of the Jewish month of Nisan (the day when Christ actually was crucified), no matter what day of the week that day fell on. In contrast, the Roman Church, along with most of the rest of the worldwide Church, always celebrated Pascha on a Sunday. But there is no indication that Anicetus even thought about trying *to dictate* to the Church of Smyrna concerning what to do in regard to this issue. Rather, both men agreed to disagree, and they maintained intercommunion despite their differences in opinion and practice.

BISHOP VICTOR AND THE QUARTODECIMAN CONTROVERSY

It's not until we reach the last decade of the second century that we find a bishop of Rome who actually tries to exert dictatorial authority over a Church located beyond his immediate jurisdictional territory—which by then perhaps extended across parts of central Italy. This occurs when Bishop Victor of Rome (r. 189–198) threatens to excommunicate the Christians in western Asia Minor over their practice of celebrating Pascha on the 14th of Nisan (for which they were called Quartodecimans, using the Latin word for "fourteen"). Rather than agreeing to disagree, as his predecessor Anicetus had done with Polycarp, and rather than trying to persuade with tactfulness and an appeal to brotherly love, as Bishop Clement had done in his letter to the Corinthians, Bishop Victor actually tried to *excommunicate* the Christians of western Asia Minor—to compel them to accept the Roman usage by force.

The bristling, indignant response by the rest of the Christian world to this arrogant and unjustified attempt by Bishop Victor to dictate to a Church beyond his region makes it obvious that nowhere in the Christian world was it accepted that the Church of Rome had, or ever would have, jurisdictional authority over them. For instance, Bishop Polycrates of Ephesus vigorously protested, appealing to all the saintly figures of his region in western Asia Minor, who all celebrated Pascha on the 14th of Nisan:

> We for our part keep the day scrupulously, without addition or subtraction. For in Asia great luminaries sleep who shall rise again on the day of the Lord's advent, when He is coming with glory from heaven and shall search out all His saints—such as Philip, one of the twelve Apostles, who sleeps in Hieropolis with two of his daughters, who remained unmarried to the end of their days, while his other daughter lived in the Holy Spirit and rests in Ephesus. Again there is John, who leaned back on the Lord's breast, and who became a priest wearing the mitre, a martyr, and a teacher; he too sleeps in Ephesus. Then in Smyrna there is Polycarp, bishop and martyr; and Thraseas, the bishop and martyr from Eumenia, who also sleeps in Smyrna. Need I mention Sagaris, bishop and martyr, who sleeps in Laodicea; or blessed Papirius; or Melito the eunuch, who lived entirely in the Holy Spirit, and who lies in Sardis waiting for the visitation from heaven when he shall rise from the dead?
>
> All of these kept the fourteenth day of the month as the beginning of the Paschal festival, in accordance with the Gospel, not deviating in the least but following the rule of the Faith. Last of all I too, Polycrates, the least of you all, act according to the tradition of my family, some members of which I have actually followed; for seven of them were bishops and I am the eighth, and my family has always kept the day when the Jews put away the leaven. So I, my friends, after spending sixty-five years in the Lord's service and conversing with Christians from all parts of the world, and going carefully through all the holy Scripture, *am not scared of threats*. Better people than I have

> said: "We must obey God rather than men" [Acts 5:29] (quoted by Eusebius in EH 5.23; my emphasis).

Bishop Eusebius, the great Church historian, reports these events in this way:

> Thereupon Victor, head of the Roman Church, attempted at one stroke to cut off from the common unity all the Asian dioceses, together with the neighboring churches, on the grounds of heterodoxy, and pilloried them in letters in which he announced the total excommunication of all his fellow-Christians there. But this was not to the taste of all the bishops: they replied with a request that he would turn his mind to the things that make for peace and for unity and love towards his neighbors. We still possess the words of these men, *who very sternly rebuked Victor*. Among them was Irenaeus, who wrote on behalf of the Christians for whom he was responsible in Gaul. While supporting the view that only on the Lord's Day might the mystery of the Lord's resurrection be celebrated, he gave Victor a great deal of excellent advice, in particular that he should not cut off entire churches of God because they observed the unbroken tradition of their predecessors (EH 5.24; my emphasis).

In the end, nothing came of Bishop Victor's attempt to cut off the Quartodecimans. Victor apparently either rescinded his excommunication of the Quartodecimans, or else he did not try to enforce it (how could he, living so far away from Asia Minor?). And through the succeeding decades most of the Quartodecimans apparently did gradually come to accept the practice of the rest of the Churches. By the time of the Nicene Council, which stipulated that Pascha must always be celebrated on a Sunday, there were few Quartodecimans left. Those who stubbornly refused to accept the Council's decision were cut off—but this was by the authority of an Ecumenical Council, and not by the authority of just one of the bishops of the worldwide Church.

TERTULLIAN AND THE BISHOP OF ROME

At about the same time that Victor was the Bishop in Rome, we find Tertullian as the leading voice in the Church in western North Africa. And in all of his voluminous writings, nowhere does he talk about the Churches of his area, or of anywhere, being subject to the authority of the Bishop of Rome. Indeed, it is Bishop Zephyrinus of Rome (r. 198–217) whom he openly castigates for allowing repentance for the sins of adultery and fornication, as we saw in Chapter Five.

THE BAPTISMAL CONTROVERSY BETWEEN BISHOP STEPHEN OF ROME AND BISHOP CYPRIAN OF CARTHAGE

Half a century later we come to the heated dispute between St. Stephen, the Bishop of Rome (r. 254–257), and St. Cyprian, Bishop of Carthage (r. 248–257), over the question of whether those coming into the Church from schismatic and/or heretical groups should be baptized, or simply chrismated (anointed with oil), or even simply received through a statement of faith. Stephen defended the Roman practice of accepting the baptism of heretics and schismatics if done in the proper way, making re-baptism unnecessary. In contrast, Cyprian ardently defended the practice in his region (western North Africa) of re-baptizing people coming into the established Church from such groups. This was because for him and his Church, all baptisms done outside the established Church had no merit or validity whatsoever, even if done with the proper form.

But Bishop Stephen feels that as the Bishop of Rome he has *the right to demand* that the Church in North Africa accept the Roman practice. To justify his claim, he appeals to the text, "Thou art Peter, and upon this rock I will build My Church" (Matt. 16:18). (It is interesting that apparently Bishop Victor had not appealed to this text when he tried to excommunicate the Quartodecimans fifty years earlier.) So now for the second time, we find a Roman bishop attempting to impose a Roman practice upon Christians living outside his jurisdictional territory; and again, the attempt is rejected with extreme indignation.

St. Cyprian, as the bishop of the leading city in western North Africa, leads the resistance there against Bishop Stephen's imperialistic attitude. He, of course, feels that each bishop is equal with the others in matters of jurisdiction. In fact, he had written some years earlier, concerning Matt. 16:18, that these words are "describing the honor of a bishop"—meaning *each bishop*—for he then wrote, "the Church is founded *upon the bishops*, and every act of the Church is controlled by these same rulers.... The Church is established in the bishop and the clergy, and all who stand fast in the Faith" (Epistle XXVI; ANF V, p. 305; my emphasis). And in his famous treatise entitled *On the Unity of the Church*, he describes the preeminence in honor and importance of Peter *and at the same time* he asserts the absolutely equal authority of each of the bishops:

> Christ builds His Church on one man; and although after His resurrection He confers an equal power on all the Apostles and says, 'As My Father has sent Me ...' [John 20:21–23], yet, in order to display the unity, He has by His authority ordained the source of the same

> unity, which originates from one man. The other Apostles were, to be sure, what Peter was, *endowed with an equal share in honor and power,* but a beginning is made from one man, so that the Church may be shown to be one....
>
> If a man does not hold this *unity of the Church,* does he believe himself to hold the Faith? If a man withstands and resists the Church, is he confident that he is in the Church? ... This unity we ought firmly to hold and defend, especially we who preside in the Church as bishops, that *we may prove the episcopate also to be itself one and undivided* (qtd. Bettenson, p. 264; my emphasis).

In a letter to Pompeius, whom Cyprian calls his "brother," he writes, in regard to the baptismal controversy,

> I send you a copy of our brother Stephen's answer. When you read it *you will be all the more cognizant of his error,* for he tries to maintain the cause of heretics against Christians and the Church of God. For among *arrogant claims, irrelevancies, and inconsistencies*—he is an inexpert and careless writer—he goes so far as to add, "If anyone comes to you from any heresy whatever, let there be no novel additions to the traditional procedure, namely the imposition of hands for repentance" ... Thus he judged the baptisms of all heretics to be valid and regular. And although particular heresies have their own baptisms and different sins, he, holding communion with the baptism of all, *gathered up the sins of all, heaped together into his own bosom* (Epistle LXXIII; ANF V, p. 386; Bettenson, *The Early Christian Fathers,* p. 270; my emphasis).

According to Fr. Schmemann, in response to Stephen's attempt to dictate to the Church of western North Africa on this issue,

> The African bishops through Cyprian of Carthage answered:
>
> *"None of us claims to be a bishop of bishops or resorts to tyranny* to obtain the consent of his brethren. *Each bishop in the fullness of his freedom and his authority retains the right to think for himself; he is not subject to any other* and he does not judge others."
>
> Stephen was answered still more sharply by Bishop Firmilian of Caesarea in Cappadocia, one of the pillars of the Eastern Church:

> "There are many distinctions within the Church, but what is important is spiritual unity, unity of faith and tradition. What boldness to claim to be the judge of all! Stephen by this claim excludes himself from the universal unity of the episcopate" (*Historical Road of Eastern Orthodoxy,* p. 84; my emphasis).

So far was St. Cyprian from accepting Roman hegemony over his Church that he probably would have broken communion with Stephen if the controversy had not been cut short by the outbreak of the Valerian Persecution in 257, in which Cyprian (and possibly also Stephen) was martyred.

BISHOP JULIUS OF ROME AND THE MARCELLUS AFFAIR

Another nearly one hundred years go by before a bishop of Rome once again tries to exert authority over any Churches that are located beyond his natural territory. In this case, Bishop Julius I (r. 337–352) gave shelter to two bishops—St. Athanasius of Alexandria, and Marcellus of Ancyra—both of whom had been condemned and exiled by Church councils in the East. Julius's efforts to restore these two men to their sees were vehemently rejected by the Eastern bishops as being unprecedented interference in the internal affairs of Churches beyond his territory. The Eastern bishops were so adamant in their opposition to Bishop Julius that they refused to attend the Council of Sardica in 343, which Julius had participated in summoning. This council did go on to speak about the Roman Church as a final court of appeal in certain cases, but this legislation was never accepted in the East as meaning that the Roman bishop had jurisdictional authority over any Churches in the East.

Besides refusing to attend the Council of Sardica, the Eastern bishops then called their own council, held at Philippolis in Thrace. And for some time thereafter, relations between the Roman Church and the Churches of the East were severely strained.

BISHOP INNOCENT I OF ROME

Bishop Innocent I (r. 401–417), in a letter to the bishops of western North Africa, falsely claimed that

> the Fathers ... decreed, not with human but with divine judgment, that no decision—even though it concerned the most remote provinces—was to be considered final unless this See [i.e., the Roman

> See] were to hear of it, so that all the authority of this See might confirm whatever just decision was reached. From this See the other Churches receive the confirmation of what they ought to ordain, just as all waters proceed from their source and through diverse regions of the world remain pure liquids from an uncorrupted source (Neuner and Dupuis, eds., *The Christian Faith in the Doctrinal Documents of the Catholic Church* [N. Y.: Alba House, 1982), p. 216).

In reality, not only did the Fathers never declare such a thing, but they repeatedly asserted the opposite—that every major bishop has full jurisdictional authority in his own region—as we have seen in looking at the relevant canons of the first four Ecumenical Councils. And we recall that Canons Nine and Seventeen of the Fourth Ecumenical Council stipulated that the Church of Constantinople—not Rome—would be the final court of appeal for cases involving metropolitan bishops.

BISHOP CELESTINE OF ROME AND THE BISHOPS ASSEMBLED AT CARTHAGE

One further example in the first 400 years of the history of the Church of an attempt by the Bishop of Rome to interfere in the internal affairs of a church beyond his recognized territory came during the reign of Bishop Celestine I of Rome (r. 422–432). This occurred when Celestine received into communion a priest named Apiarius who personally appealed to him after having been excommunicated by the Church in western North Africa. When Apiarius then returned to Carthage seeking to be reinstated based on Bishop Celestine's acceptance of him, a council of bishops was held in Carthage which sent a letter to Celestine containing these words:

> Premising, therefore, our due regard to you, we earnestly implore you, that in the future you do not readily admit to a hearing persons coming to you, nor choose to receive into your communion those who have been excommunicated by us—because you, venerable Sir, will readily perceive that *this has been proscribed even by the Nicene Council.* For though this seems to be there forbidden in respect of the lesser clergy, or the laity, how much more did that Council will this to be observed in the case of bishops—lest those who had been suspended from communion in their own Province might seem to be restored to communion hastily or unfitly by your Holiness.

> Let your Holiness reject, as is worthy of you, the *unprincipled* way that presbyters [i.e., priests] likewise, and the lesser clergy, have been taking shelter with you—both because *by no ordinance of the Fathers has the Church of Africa been deprived of this authority,* and because the Nicene decrees have most plainly committed not only the clergy of inferior rank, but the bishops themselves, to their own Metropolitans. For *the Nicene Fathers ordained, with great wisdom and justice, that all matters should be terminated in the places where they arise.* For those Fathers *did not think* that the grace of the Holy Spirit would be so lacking in any Province that the bishops of Christ anywhere could not wisely discern, and firmly maintain, what is right. This is especially so since whoever thinks himself wronged by any judgment may appeal to the council of his Province, or even to a general council [i.e., of Africa]—unless it be imagined that God can inspire a single individual with justice, *and refuse it to an innumerable multitude of bishops assembled in council* (NPNF vol. II, XIV, p. 510; my emphasis).

So here again we see the indignant response to the rise of "Papal presumption," even in the West in the 5th century.

CONTINUING EXPANSION OF PAPAL AUTHORITY OVER THE WESTERN CHURCHES

During the subsequent centuries, the Roman bishops—or more accurately, only the stronger ones—gradually expanded their direct authority over the Churches of the various regions of Western Europe. As we noted earlier, this long and difficult process was not completed until roughly the middle of the 9th century. One key means of doing this was imposing Roman rites and practices on the Churches in these areas, a process first begun by Pope Innocent I (r. 401–417), who was the first to declare that "all Latin churches should follow Roman rites" (Henry Chadwick, *The Early Church,* p. 240). Ironically, the greatly beloved Pope Gregory the Great (r. 590–604) "expressly disapproved of the policy of imposing the Roman liturgy on all other churches" (*Ibid.*).

A major boost in this process came when Pope Leo I (r. 440–461) "secured from [the Western Emperor] Valentinian III a rescript which recognized his jurisdiction over all the Western provinces" (*Oxford Dictionary of the Christian Church,* third revised ed., p. 972). Chadwick calls this "a thunderous rescript … which decreed that all bishops in the Western provinces must submit to papal authority on the pain of secular penalties" (*The Early Church*, p. 242). It was Pope Leo I who, with the aid of this imperial decree, deprived the Church of Arles, in Gaul [today's France], of its status as a metropolitan center, thus doing much to bring an end to the jurisdictional independence of the Church in Gaul. It was also Leo I who first officially claimed the title "Pope" for himself and all his successors.

CONTINUING ESCALATION OF PAPAL CLAIMS OVER THE EASTERN CHURCHES

The stronger Roman bishops also through the centuries tried to claim jurisdictional authority over the Eastern Churches as well, in direct contradiction to the spirit and the letter of the canons of the first four Ecumenical Councils. Bishop Julius I (r. 337–352) was the first to make such a sweeping declaration, in a letter written to the Eastern bishops:

> Do you not know that the custom is that we should be written to first, and that judgment is rendered here? What I write to you and what I say we received from the blessed Apostle Peter (quoted by Fr. Schmemann, *Historical Road of Eastern Orthodoxy*, p. 86).

Bishop Damasus I (r. 366–384) is the next strong Roman bishop: "From Damasus onwards there is a marked crescendo in the expression of the [universal] claims made by the bishops of Rome" (Chadwick, *The Early Church*, p. 238). Under him, "papal letters began to take the form of decretals [i.e., decrees]" (*Ibid.*, p. 240).

Then there is Bishop Innocent I of Rome (r. 401–417), who wrote in a letter to the bishops of western North Africa, as we quoted above: "The Fathers ... decreed ... that no decision—even though it concerned the most remote provinces—was to be considered final unless this [Roman] See were to hear of it" (Neuner and Dupuis, eds., *The Christian Faith in the Doctrinal Documents of the Catholic Church* [N. Y.: Alba House; 7th Rev edition, 2001], p. 216).

The next strong bishop of Rome is Pope Leo I (r. 440–461):

> Leo believed himself to be the successor of St. Peter in more than any merely historical sense. When he preached or wrote a letter, he believed that St. Peter himself was speaking and writing—or at least, that his hearers and readers should receive his words as such. Because the pope is legal heir of all that St. Peter was, there is no diminution of the power of the keys [Matt. 16:19], but a *plenitudo potestatis* [a plentitude of power] ...

> When Leo sent to the Greek East the Tome [Letter] which was to be received at Chalcedon in 451 [at the Fourth Ecumenical Council], he forbade the bishops in council to subject it to the scrutiny of discussion. Now that the matter had been defined, there was nothing to discuss, and they were humbly to receive the Tome as an utterance of blessed Peter himself. Although in practice and for tactical reasons Leo might occasionally appeal to the decisions of Church councils, his theory of authority allowed them little weight. The Greek bishops could hardly have looked at the matter in the same way. At Chalcedon the Tome was approved as a truly worthy and Petrine utterance, but [only] on the clear ground that *examination had shown it to be in conformity with received standards of orthodoxy. The Council retained their independence of judgment* (Chadwick, *The Early Church*, p. 244; my emphasis).

Pope Gelasius (r. 492–496), the next strong bishop of Rome,

> claimed that "the see of blessed Peter has the right to loose what has been bound by the decisions of any bishops whatever." The support which the Eastern patriarchs were receiving from the Emperor Anastasius I led Gelasius to expound a bold doctrine of the relation between ecclesiastical authority and kingly power: just as in mundane matters, he wrote, the clergy are bound to obey the emperor, so in ecclesiastical affairs the emperor ought to submit his neck to the prelates, and above all to the pope as chief prelate, who must give account to God for the manner in which the emperor discharges his responsibilities (*Ibid.*, p. 245).

The next strong one was Pope Hormisdas (r. 514–523), who was able to exact the signatures of some 250 Eastern bishops to a statement of loyalty to the Roman See, "in which the whole, true, and perfect security of the Christian religion resides." But the Eastern bishops only signed this statement because of the extremely intense political pressure that the new Emperor Justin I (r. 518–527) subjected them to, since he was so desirous of ending the schism that had officially separated the Western Church from the Eastern Churches for the previous 34 years. And the fact that the Eastern bishops had been refusing to accept Rome's terms during all the years of that schism certainly proves the fact that the Eastern Churches did not accept any papal claims to have jurisdictional authority over all the Churches of the world.

POPE GREGORY THE GREAT AND THE TITLE OF ECUMENICAL PATRIARCH

Even though the highly influential Pope Gregory the Great (r. 590–604) did much to expand the power and prestige of the Papacy in the West, he was a very humble man, unlike many of his predecessors and successors. In fact, he reacted with shocked indignation upon hearing that Patriarch John of Constantinople was being called "Ecumenical Patriarch" in the East, not understanding that the Easterners were using this title merely in an honorific way, in acknowledgment of the position of the patriarch of Constantinople as "first among equals" in the East, but without having jurisdictional authority over his fellow bishops in the East. But Gregory interpreted the title *literally*—as meaning that Patriarch John was claiming to have jurisdictional authority over the entire worldwide Church. Very tellingly—and very properly—Gregory was scandalized about this, *not* because he thought that only the Roman bishop had the right to have this title, but because it was an affront to the dignity, honor, and authority of all the other bishops *for any bishop* to claim such a higher status over all the others.

In a letter to Patriarch John, Gregory excoriates John for his "*execrable, profane, and rash presumption*" in claiming to be "head of the universal Church." He also says in this letter, in referring to the bishops of Rome before him, "*But yet none of them has ever wished to be called by such a title, or has seized upon this ill-advised name, lest if, in virtue of the rank of the pontificate, he took to himself the glory of singularity, so that he might seem to have denied it to all his brother bishops.*" And also, "to assent to *that atrocious title is nothing else than to lose the faith*"; and, "But far from Christian hearts be *that name of blasphemy*, in which *the honor of all priests is taken away*, while it is *madly arrogated to himself.*" And also, to make it perfectly clear that he was not only castigating the title but also its implication that Patriarch John was indeed claiming to rule over the entire universal Church, Gregory writes in this same letter,

> Concerning the Apostle Paul, when he heard some say, "I am of Paul, I of Apollos, but I of Christ" [1 Cor. 1:13], he regarded *with the utmost horror* such tearing to pieces of the Lord's body, whereby they were joining themselves, as it were, to other heads ... If then he shunned the subjecting of the members of Christ partially to certain heads, as if besides Christ, even though this were to the Apostles themselves, what will you say to Christ, who is the Head of the universal Church, in the scrutiny of the Last Judgment, *having attempted to put all His members under yourself by the appellation of Universal*? ...

> Certainly Peter … and Paul and Andrew and John, what were they but heads of particular communities? And yet all were members under one Head [Christ]" (Bk. v, Epistle 18; NPNF vol. II, vol. XII, pp. 166–169; my emphasis).[3]

What a far cry the spirit and content of this letter are from the explicit claims of the Roman Church in later centuries! For example, the Council of Lyons in 1274 declared as dogma: "The Holy Roman Church possesses also the highest and full primacy and authority over the universal Catholic Church … To Her, all the Churches are subject" (Neuner and Dupuis, p. 19). And in 1302 Pope Boniface VIII promulgated a papal bull in which "Boniface goes on to assert that *Christ and the Pope* ***form one head; the Pope is therefore the head*** *of the mystical Body* [of Christ]." Boniface also states in this bull, "Furthermore we declare, state, and define that it is absolutely necessary for the salvation of all men that they submit to the Roman pontiff" (Neuner and Dupuis, p. 218; my emphasis).

SOME CONCLUDING THOUGHTS

Thankfully, the Roman Church has significantly moderated this rigidly exclusivistic view concerning the possibility of salvation outside of communion with the Papacy, beginning with the Vatican II Council of 1962–1965. Now the Roman Church regards the Eastern Orthodox Christians as "separated brethren," rather than "schismatics." And the Vatican II Council also tried to reassert, at least to some degree, the importance of the conciliarity of all the bishops. These are two very important steps in the direction of reconciliation with the Orthodox Church, for which we should be grateful.

However, from the more thoroughly conciliar point of view of the Eastern Churches, as we have seen in this chapter, the gradual development of the idea that the Roman bishop must have jurisdictional authority over all the worldwide Churches was a huge aberration, a flagrant violation of the spirit and letter of the canons of the Ecumenical Councils. So from the Orthodox viewpoint, the only way the Roman Church can ever be reconciled with the rest of the universal Church is for Her to first renounce these claims. Then, many other very significant points of

---

[3] Pope Gregory also wrote, in a letter to Patriarch Anastasius of Antioch, in reference to St. Peter having been in Antioch, "But remember that you rule an Apostolic See … [and] that Saint Ignatius [of Antioch] is not only yours, but also ours. For, as we have his master, the Prince of the Apostles [i.e., Peter], in common, so also no one of us ought to have himself alone to be the disciple of this same Prince" (Bk. v, Epistle 39; NPNF vol. II, XII, p. 175).

difference in doctrine and practice would have to be addressed, the foremost being the infamous erroneous addition of the *Filioque* clause[4] into the Nicene Creed.[5]

Great progress could be made towards reconciliation if the Roman Catholics and the Orthodox resolved to get back to the spirituality, doctrine, liturgical life, and organizational structure of the undivided Church—as it was before the Great Schism of 1054. This is so because nearly all of the distortions in doctrine and practice in the Western Church entered into that Church after the Schism of 1054.

If all this were indeed to happen, then I believe the Orthodox Churches would still be willing to honor the bishop of Rome once again, as in the first thousand years, as "the first among equals"—as long as this title would only refer to a certain preeminence in honor and dignity, and not to jurisdictional authority over all the other Churches.

---

[4] This clause, meaning "and the Son," was first added to the paragraph on the Holy Spirit in the Nicene Creed in Spain at the Council of Toledo in 589. Pope Leo III (r. 795–816) allowed Charlemagne and the Franks to use it, but he was so sure that the *Filioque* was really improper that he had the original Creed engraved on silver tablets and hung in St. Peter's Basilica in the Vatican. The Church of Rome continued to resist Frankish/Germanic pressure to use the *Filioque* publicly all the way until 1014, when it was first used publicly in the Mass in Rome. Then, only 40 years later, at the time of the Great Schism of 1054, the Latins began accusing the Easterners of heresy for *not* using the *Filioque*, and they even tried to claim that the Filioque was part of the original Nicene Creed!

[5] Some of the other major errors of the Roman Church, from the Orthodox point of view, which would have to be rectified are the issues of papal infallibility, the dogma of the Immaculate Conception of Mary, the insistence on mandatory clerical celibacy, Purgatory and the granting of indulgences, and the practice of annulments concerning broken marriages.

Chapter Nine

THE HOLY MARTYRS LIVE AND DIE FOR CHRIST

CHRISTIANS AND THE GOVERNMENTAL AUTHORITIES

Despite the suspicions of many Romans, the Christians in the Roman Empire were not political revolutionaries. Jesus told His followers to "Render unto Caesar the things that are Caesar's" (Matt. 22:21). St. Paul exhorts, "Let every soul be subject to the governing authorities. For there is no authority except from God, and the authorities that exist are appointed by God . . ." (Romans 13:1–7). And we should remember that when Paul writes this, the Roman emperor is Nero! St. Paul also instructs the Christians to pray for the civil authorities, so "that we may lead a quiet and peaceable life in all godliness and reverence" (1 Tim. 2:1–3).

The Christians, of course, knew that the Lord wanted them to always strive to live godly, virtuous lives, which would benefit them spiritually. They knew that Christ had said, for instance, "If anyone loves Me, he will keep My word; and My Father with love him, and We will come and make Our home with him" (John 14:23); and, "If you keep My commandments, you will abide in My love" (John 15:10). And even though the Christians' main concern was to please the Lord of Glory, rather than the governmental authorities of the Empire, it was pretty much automatic that keeping God's commandments would also make them excellent, law-abiding citizens of the Empire. As we saw in Chapter Three, the Apologists in the 2nd century were quick to affirm to the emperor that the Christians, far from being a threat to the State and the surrounding society, are actually the Empire's best citizens, because they seek to live by the highest possible standards of godliness and morality, as mandated by their Christian Faith.

However, the Christians could not in good conscience participate in the civil religion, with its demands (thankfully, only intermittently enforced) that all citizens offer sacrifice and incense to the gods and goddesses, and to the emperor. Whereas the Jewish leaders had once cried out, "We have no king but Caesar" (John 19:15), the Christians have another King, infinitely higher than the Roman Emperor. So when compelled to reverence Caesar as a god, and to worship the idols of the gods and goddesses, they must refuse. But to the government and the surrounding society, this is treasonous, and it's asking for trouble with the various deities who they believe are protecting the State.

At the same time, the Romans were used to accepting all the deities of the various conquered peoples—to try to ensure, in a sense, that they would have all the spiritual powers, no matter what or who they might be, "on their side." (Alexander the Great had done the same thing in the 4th century BC; he even went many miles out of his way in Egypt, in the midst of his great military campaign to the East, to offer sacrifice at the shrine of a major Egyptian deity.)

So the Roman civil authorities are prone to try to be tolerant of the Christians. Bishop Eusebius of Caesarea in Palestine, in his great *Ecclesiastical History*, even recounts that when Emperor Tiberius (r. 14–37 AD) first heard the story about Jesus of Nazareth called the Christ, as related to him by his governor of Judea, Pontius Pilate, he responded favorably, and submitted a report to the Senate for them to consider voting to make this Christ a god (the Romans only deified certain men by a vote of the Senate). They refused, however, saying that they had not investigated the matter enough (EH II.2; pp. 38–39 in the Williamson/Louth edition).

Similarly, the Romans usually tried to be tolerant of the Jews. The biggest exception was Emperor Gaius (r. 37–41), whose persecutions against the Jews are recorded by Eusebius (EH II.5–6; pp. 41–43), where he quotes the great Jewish historian Josephus. We also know that Emperor Claudius drove the Jews out of Rome in about 51 AD (Acts 18:2), possibly because of disputes among them about Christ. The pagan Roman historian Suetonius (c. 75–160) reports, in his *Life of Claudius*, "Since the Jews were continually making disturbances at the instigation of Chrestus, he [Claudius] expelled them from Rome" (Ch. xxv.4; Henry Bettenson, *Documents of the Christian Church*, second edition, p. 2).

PERSECUTION UNDER NERO

As in all autocracies, official policies are maintained ultimately by the will of the emperor. If he decides to change things, who's to stop him? Hence, regarding the persecution of Christians, while the preceding emperors did not persecute them, Nero (r. 54–68) did. According to Tacitus (c. 60–c. 120), another early pagan Roman historian,

> Besides being put to death, the Christians were made to serve as objects of amusement; they were clad in the hides of beasts and torn to death by dogs; others were crucified, others set on fire to serve to illuminate the night when daylight failed. Nero had thrown open his grounds for the display ... All this gave rise to a feeling of pity, even towards men whose guilt merited the most exemplary punishment. For it was felt that they were being destroyed not for the public good, but to gratify the cruelty of an individual (*Annals*, xv.44; Bettenson, *Documents of the Christian Church*, p. 2).

In their writings, Suetonius and Tacitus also reveal typical attitudes on the part of the Romans towards the Christians. Tacitus called their Faith "a pernicious superstition," "evil," "sordid and degrading." And he called them "a class hated for their abominations" (*Annals*, xv.44)—by which he had in mind infanticide (probably from a literal misunderstanding of baptism as dying in Christ); cannibalism (from a literal misunderstanding of the Eucharist); and incest (from a misunderstanding of the kiss of peace and the *agape* meal, and from Christian husbands and wives calling themselves brothers and sisters in Christ). Over a century later the Apologists will still be defending the Christians from such charges—as we saw in Chapter Three. And according to Suetonius, "punishment was inflicted upon the Christians, a set of men adhering to a novel and mischievous superstition" (*Life of Nero*, XVI; Bettenson, *Documents of the Christian Church*, p. 2).

In large part because the Christians did not participate in the public spectacles and religious ceremonies of the Romans—and they probably generally tended to keep company mostly among themselves—Tacitus says they were accused of "hatred of the human race" (*Annals*, xv.44). And also because of their relative aloofness from the surrounding society, it was easy for the Romans to imagine that the Christians must be some kind of conspiratorial secret society, with revolutionary designs against the governmental authorities. The Christians' use of the word *sacramentum* added to this suspicion, since this word could also refer to an oath taken by political conspirators.

PERSECUTION UNDER DOMITIAN

The next major persecution of Christians occurs under Emperor Domitian (r. 81–96), who tries to set up a cult to himself as "master and God." During his reign, the customary oath "by the genius of the emperor" became officially obligatory. During this persecution, the granddaughter of Emperor Vespasian, Flavia Domitilla, is exiled, and her husband, Titus Flavius Clemens, is killed (he is a first cousin of Domitian). It is very possible that they were punished because of being Christians. She dies in about 100, and her property near Rome becomes a very early Christian cemetery called Coemeterium Domitillae, which still exists.

It is in this persecution that St. John the Evangelist and Theologian is exiled to the Island of Patmos in the Aegean Sea near the modern country of Turkey. He is allowed to return to Ephesus in the beginning of the reign of the next emperor, Nerva (r. 96–98). Nerva is considered the first of the "Five Good Emperors"—followed by Trajan (r. 98–117), Hadrian (r. 117–138), Antoninus Pius (r. 138–161), and Marcus Aurelius (r. 161–180), who was the Stoic "philosopher-king." (Domitian was so hated by the Romans themselves—in his later years he had launched a reign of terror against his own fellow citizens—that upon his murder in 96 AD the Senate voted to strike his rule from the official record of the Empire!)

EMPEROR TRAJAN AND PLINY THE YOUNGER DEAL WITH THE CHRISTIANS

Emperor Trajan was not insistent on the cult of the deified emperor being made a compulsory loyalty-test for all citizens. In 112 AD his governor in Bithynia (northwest Asia Minor), Pliny the Younger, writes to Trajan asking for advice about what to do concerning the Christians. Pliny had verified that the Christians were not committing incest or cannibalism (as they were commonly accused of), and they had obediently suspended meeting for a common meal when he published an imperial decree against secret societies. So he reports in a letter to Emperor Trajan, "I find nothing but a depraved and extravagant superstition" (quoted by Bettenson, *Documents of the Christian Church*, p. 4). In his reply, Trajan allows Christianity to still be a capital offense, but he urges Pliny not to press things against the Christians.

MARTYRDOMS IN THE SECOND CENTURY

Still, while none of the Five Good Emperors openly persecuted the Christians, all it takes is one private accusation to lead to martyrdom. Hence, martyrdoms do occur sporadically during the 2nd century. The most famous of these 2nd-century martyrs are:

St. Ignatius, Bishop of Antioch (died c. 107 in Rome; Feastday, December 20);

St. Telesphorus, Bishop of Rome (died c. 137; attested by St. Irenaeus, AH III.3.3; he is the only second-century Roman bishop whose martyrdom is well-attested; Feastday in the East, Feb. 22);

St. Justin Martyr (the great Apologist; in Rome, died c. 165; a court record of his trial comes down to us, as we saw in Chapter Three; Feastday, June 1); and

St. Polycarp, Bishop of Smyrna (died c. 157 in Smyrna; Feastday, February 23).

THE ACCOUNT OF ST. POLYCARP'S MARTYRDOM

A stirring *Account of the Martyrdom of St. Polycarp* was written by "the Church of God sojourning (*paroikousa*; from this word we get our word *parish*) at Smyrna to the Church of God sojourning in Philomelium [nearby], and to all the communities of the holy and universal Church sojourning in every place" (Salutation; in Fr. Jack N. Sparks, ed., *The Apostolic Fathers* [Nashville, TN: Thomas Nelson, 1978; Minneapolis: Light and Life, 2000], p. 139). This, and all the persecutions, are accepted by the Christians graciously and with deep spiritual understanding as a most glorious victory in Christ, rather than as a tragic defeat. The writers of this account say that this persecution has arisen so "that the Lord might show us again *martyrdom in accord with the Gospel*" (1:1; p. 139; my emphasis). And they also declare, "Blessed then and noble are all *the martyrdoms that have taken place by the will of God*, for we must devoutly ascribe to God power over all things" (2:1; p. 139; my emphasis). They go on to write,

> For who would not admire their nobility and patience and love of their Master? They endured being shredded with whips until the fabric of their flesh could be seen down to the veins and arteries within, so that even the by-standers felt pity and wept. But they themselves displayed such nobility that none of them muttered or groaned, showing us all that the most noble martyrs of Christ in that hour under torture were absent from the flesh, or rather, that the Lord was at hand and was conversing with them (2:2–3; pp. 139–140).

Chapter 4 (p. 141) explains how the Christians are not to "come forward of their own accord" seeking martyrdom, "for that is not the teaching of the Gospel." This accords with the general Christian teaching that we should not intentionally seek out trials and tribulations, but to accept them graciously when they come. As Christ enjoins us all, "In this world you shall have tribulations; but be of good cheer, for I have overcome the world" (John 16:33).

Bishop Polycarp has a vision shortly before his death. He tells the brethren, "I must be burned alive" (5:2; p. 141). Chapters 6:1–8:1 (pp. 141–142) tell of his arrest, his hospitality to his captors, and his two-hour prayer for everyone he can think of. In the stadium, when he is asked by the proconsul to swear "by the genius of Caesar ... revile Christ" in order to save his life, he answers, "I have served him 86 years and in no way has he dealt unjustly with me; so how can I blaspheme my king who saved me?" (9:2–3; p. 143; this probably indicates that Polycarp was baptized as an infant).

When it is announced to the crowd that "'Polycarp has confessed that he is a Christian,'" "the whole crowd of Gentiles and Jews who lived in Smyrna cried out with uncontrolled anger and with a loud shout: 'This is the teacher of Asia, the father of the Christians, the destroyer of our gods, the one who teaches many not to sacrifice nor to worship'" (12:2; p. 144; this is reminiscent of the fury of the crowd in Ephesus against St. Paul about a hundred years earlier [Acts 19:23–41]). The crowd cries out for him to be burned alive, and they themselves gather the wood for his funeral pyre (12:3–13:1; p. 144).

Chapter 14 (pp. 145–146) records Polycarp's beautiful prayer of thanksgiving for his martyrdom. Then the pyre is ignited, but the fire does not burn him. Instead, "the fire took the form of an arch like the sail of a ship filled by the wind and encircled the body of the martyr like a wall. And he was in the center of it not like burning flesh but like baking bread or like gold and silver being refined in a furnace; for we also perceived a fragrant odor like the scent of incense or some other precious spice" (15:2; p. 147). So then he is stabbed, and "a dove and a large quantity of blood came out so that it quenched the fire, and the whole crowd was amazed" (16:1; p. 147).

We also see in this account a remarkably clear understanding of the importance of relics. Even when the saintly bishop was still alive, "each of the faithful always hurried that he might be the first to touch his skin, for he was adorned with every power because of his goodly way of life even before his martyrdom" (13:2; pp. 144–145). Now, after his martyrdom, "there were many who wanted to do this [to take his body] and *have fellowship with his holy flesh*" (17:1; p. 148; my emphasis).

The centurion then burned Polycarp's body. Then the account says,

> We later took up *his bones, more precious than costly stones and finer than gold,* and deposited them in a suitable place. And there, in so far as it is possible, the Lord will grant that we come together with joy and gladness and celebrate *the birthday of his martyrdom* both in memory of those who have contended in former times, and for the

> exercise and training of those who will do so in the future" (18:2–3; p. 148; my emphasis).

So we see here an early indication of the practice of commemorating the Saints on the day of their glorious passing from the earthly into the heavenly life. This is still the practice of the Orthodox Church to this day.

We also see in this account another indication of the gradual assumption by the bishops of the role of the traveling prophets during the 2nd century (see above, Chapter Five):

> Of the elect was he indeed one, this most wonderful Polycarp—a man who in our times showed himself an apostolic *and prophetic teacher* and bishop of the catholic church in . Smyrna. For every word that he uttered was fulfilled and will be fulfilled (16:2; p. 147; my emphasis).

THE MARTYRS OF LYONS AND VIENNE

In 177, another vicious persecution of Christians flared up in Lyons and Vienne in the Rhone Valley of eastern modern-day France. This local persecution was precipitated by mob violence and backed by the civil authorities; apparently Emperor Marcus Aurelius gave at least tacit approval of it. Eusebius quotes at great length the *Account of the Gallic Martyrs of Lyons and Vienne* (EH V.1–2; pp. 139–149); this is the longest running quotation in his *Ecclesiastical History*.

The saintly, 90-year-old St. Pothinus, Bishop of Lyons, dies in this persecution (Feastday, June 2), along with the heroic young slave girl, St. Blandina (July 25); and a fifteen-year old youth named Ponticus. A number of others are mentioned by name, including the deacon Sanctus (July 25): "Sanctus was another who with magnificent, superhuman courage nobly withstood the entire range of human cruelty" (p. 141).

St. Irenaeus of Lyons presumably would have died in this persecution, but at that time he was in Rome, on a visit to the Church there, as we saw in Chapter Four.

A very noteworthy highlight of the *Account of the Gallic Martyrs of Lyons and Vienne* is the way a number of the martyrs at first denied Christ. But then, instead of being released, they were put back in prison, to be interrogated once again by the authorities before being set free:

> Their time of respite was not idle or unfruitful: *through their endurance the infinite mercy of Christ was revealed. For through the living the dead were being brought back to life, and martyrs were bestowing grace*

> *on those who had failed to be martyrs.* And there was great joy in the heart of the Virgin Mother,[6] who was *receiving her stillborn children back alive.* For by their means most of those who had denied their Master traveled once more the same road, conceived and quickened a second time, and learned to confess Christ. Alive now and braced up, their ordeal sweetened by God, *who does not desire the death of the sinner* [cf. Ezek. 18:23 and 32] but *is gracious towards repentance,* they advanced to the tribunal to be again interrogated by the governor.... They were individually examined with the intention that they should be released, but they confessed Him and so joined the ranks of the martyrs (p. 146; my emphasis).

This testimony is another indication that the Church as a whole is gradually realizing that She must offer the possibility of repentance for even the worst sins—murder, adultery, and apostasy. The *Account* itself very much emphasizes the great love and compassion for those who had weakened in the face of torture and death on the part of those who were strong in their faith in the same situation:

> This was the greatest war they fought against him *through the reality of their love,* that the Beast might be choked into bringing up alive those whom he thought he had swallowed already. They did not crow over the fallen, but *the things they themselves had in abundance they bestowed with motherly affection on those who lacked them.* Shedding many tears on their behalf in supplication to the Father, they asked for life and He gave it to them [cf. Ps. 20:5, LXX]. This they shared with their neighbors when triumphantly victorious they departed to God. Peace they had ever loved; peace they commended to our care; and with peace they went to God, leaving no sorrow to their Mother, no strife or warfare to their brothers, but joy, peace, concord, and love (p. 149; my emphasis).

And then immediately Eusebius comments:

> So much may profitably be said about the affection of those blessed ones for their brothers who had fallen from grace, in view of *the inhuman and merciless attitude* of those who later behaved so badly towards the members of Christ's body (p. 149; my emphasis).

---

[6] This is probably a reference to our Mother the Church, but it could also be a reference to the Theotokos.

This last remark was in reference to the rigorist, hard-line, schismatic Novatianists and Donatists, who, like the Montanists, refused the possibility of repentance for the worst sins, including denying Christ (see above, Chapter Six).

HOLY MARTYRS PERPETUA AND FELICITAS

Widespread yet still scattered persecution of Christians broke out under Emperor Septimius Severus (r. 193–211). Apparently it was the most severe in Alexandria and Carthage. Probably the most noteworthy martyrdom in Alexandria was St. Leonidas (d. 202; Feastday, June 5), the father of the tremendously influential theologian, Origen (185–254). In Carthage, the most famous of the martyrs were Perpetua and Felicitas, due to an account of their last days in prison and their deaths, which includes Perpetua's first-hand description of two visions she had concerning her impending martyrdom.

Perpetua was a young woman in her early twenties, with a babe in arms, from a well-to-to family. Despite the desperate pleas of her family—especially her father—to renounce Christ and save her life, she remained firm in her faith in and devotion to her Savior, even unto torture and death. And Felicitas was her handmaiden, who actually gave birth to a baby girl while in prison, just a few days before her death in the arena. They are both commemorated on February 1 in the Eastern Church.

THE DECIAN PERSECUTION

In 249 a Roman general named Decius defeated Emperor Philip in battle and took the imperial throne. Almost immediately he commanded that every resident of the Empire offer sacrifice to the gods and goddesses of the traditional State religion. This, of course, the Christians could not do with a clear conscience, and many of them died in the ensuing persecution—the first persecution of all Christians across the entire Empire. Some of the leading Christians who were martyred under Decius were St. Fabian, Bishop of Rome (Feastday, August 5); St. Babylas, Bishop of Antioch (September 4); and St. Alexander, Bishop of Jerusalem (May 16). The persecution ended when Emperor Decius was killed in battle in June of 251.

THE VALERIAN PERSECUTION

In 257 another Empire-wide persecution of Christians broke out under Emperor Valerian (r. 257–258). The most illustrious Christian to be martyred under Valerian was St. Cyprian of Carthage (August 31). This persecution ended with Valerian's death in the next year.

THE DIOCLETIAN PERSECUTION

Diocletian rules as the Roman Emperor from 284 until 305. He institutes a radical political, military, economic, and religious reorganization of the empire after almost 100 years of political unrest and economic decline, along with the beginning of the breakdown of the borders of the Empire through barbarian invasions, and the rise of a renewed Persian Empire to the east. In the preceding 49 years there were 22 emperors, most of whom were military men, so they are known as the "Barracks Emperors." Only one of them died a natural death, as so often a particular military legion with a particularly successful general would have more loyalty towards their general than towards the emperor, and would proclaim their general as the new emperor. He would then feel obliged to march on Rome, defeat the emperor in battle, and seize the throne. Some of the generals even ruled parts of the Empire temporarily.

As with the emperors Domitian (r. 81–96) and Decius (r. 249–251) before him, Diocletian attempts to revive the traditional State religion in order to restore Rome's ancient glory with the aid of the old gods and goddesses. Still, it's not until the year 303 that the last, longest, and most severe period of persecution of Christians begins.

This Diocletian Persecution is precipitated when Diocletian's co-ruler in the East, Caesar Galerius, begins to question the loyalty of the Christians in the army. He is influenced by Hierocles, the governor of Bithynia, who was a Neo-Platonist very hostile to Christianity. Then, at a large official public gathering in Nicomedia, the capital of the eastern part of the Empire, the *augurs* (official diviners) were not able to find the usual signs, or *auguries,* on the livers of the sacrificed animals. Diocletian consults the oracle of Apollo at Miletus, and the answer given is that the troubles were caused by the Christians who had been present (who could well have been making the sign of the cross on themselves).

On February 23, 303, the Christian cathedral opposite the imperial palace in Nicomedia is dismantled, and the next day an edict is posted, declaring: all churches are to be destroyed; all Christian Scriptures are to be confiscated and burned; all meetings for worship are forbidden; Christians of high rank were to lose their social and legal privileges; and sacrificing to the gods was required as a condition for bringing lawsuits.

Then, after some Christians are accused of plotting against the life of the Emperor, all the Christian clergy are incarcerated. Then they are ordered to make sacrifice. Finally, in 304, all citizens are required to sacrifice to the idols on pain of death. This final edict precipitates a fearsome persecution in the East that is to last over eight more years. Thousands of Christians receive glorious crowns of martyrdom, including St. Demetrius the Myrrhgushing (Feastday, October 26) and his friend St. Nestor (October 27) in Thessalonica, St. Katherine the Greatmartyr (November 24 or 25) in Alexandria,[7] St. Lucian of Antioch (October 15), and St. George the Trophy-Bearer (April 23) in Nicomedia.[8]

This wave of persecution was always much harsher in the East. In the West, only the first of these edicts was ever put into practice, and Constantine Chlorus, the western emperor, apparently only ever pulled down some churches.

In 305, when Diocletian abdicated, forcing his co-Augustus Maximian in the West to do so also, his caesar Galerius succeeded him as augustus, with the similarly bloodthirsty Maximin Daia becoming his caesar.

Finally, by the Spring of 311, Galerius was dying of a painful illness. Perhaps in desperation, he issued an edict of toleration for the Christians, and asked them to pray for him and the Empire. At his death two months later, his caesar Maximin Daia succeeded him as augustus, and the persecution was renewed.

The persecution is finally completely brought to an end in February of 313 with the famous Edict of Milan, which granted religious freedom to the adherents of all religions. This edict was issued jointly by St. Constantine the Great, who had become the sole ruler in the West, and Licinius, who had prevailed over Maximin to become the sole ruler in the East.

The Edict of Milan marks the end of State persecution of Christians in the Roman Empire, except for some incidents under Licinius—including the illustrious Forty Martyrs of Sebaste (March 9) being cast into a freezing lake in about the year 320—and under Emperor Julian the Apostate (r. 361–363). Very sadly, though, there will be more periods of Christians suffering persecution in the succeeding centuries—and tragically, such persecution will often be at the hands of other Christians.

---

[7] St. Katherine's famous disputation with fifty of the wisest philosophers of Alexandria, in which she won them over to belief in Christ, was a powerful indication that Christianity was getting close to the point when it would begin winning over the Roman Empire at the highest levels of intellectual and spiritual achievement.

[8] Aliki Kafetzopoulou has written a wonderful historical novel, entitled *The Purple Mantle* (translated by Efrosyni Zisimou Robinson [Platina CA.: St. Herman of Alaska Brotherhood, 2001]), which is set in the time of the Diocletian Persecution. In this gripping book the author skillfully weaves in the stories of many of the more famous martyrs of this era.

THE ONGOING GLORY OF CHRISTIAN MARTYRDOM

Around the year 200, the major Western theologian Tertullian declared, "The blood of the martyrs is the seed of the Church," as we saw in Chapter Six. All in all, the persecutions no doubt helped the Church to spread. The many public martyrdoms brought great publicity, and people marveled at the valor of the martyrs, their fearlessness in the face of torture and death, and the miracles which so often accompanied their martyrdoms. How often do we hear in the stories of the martyrs that their executioners, or by-standers, suddenly declared their faith in Christ!

According to Fr. Schmemann,

> The Church seemed to recognize martyrdom as the norm of the Christian life, as well as *the strongest proof of the truth of Christianity*.... The Christian martyr was ... *a witness* [the Greek word *martyr* actually means "witness"]; by accepting suffering and death he affirmed that the rule of death had ended, that life had triumphed.... The Church exalted martyrdom because it was *proof* of the most important Christian affirmation, the resurrection of Christ from the dead" (*Historical Road of Eastern Orthodoxy* [SVS Press, 1977] p. 37; my emphasis).

Being social outcasts, subject at any moment to arrest, torture, imprisonment, and death: this inevitably and indelibly shaped the experience of all the early Christians. Their faith was constantly tried and refined by the fire of this ever-present possibility. And when the crucial time came, the grace of God was always there to help them suffer and die in steadfast faith in the resurrection of the dead, and in the hope of living eternally with Christ in the Kingdom of Heaven.

How difficult this really is for us in America and Canada to understand today! And yet this has been the reality for millions of Christians through the centuries in many parts of the world. We think especially of those living under Communist rule in the 20th century, and those living in the Muslim world today. And as our own society and government in our time become more and more anti-Christian in outlook and policy, we Christians in America and Canada may well face varying degrees of outright persecution in the near future.

May we all always be strengthened and inspired, in the midst of whatever persecution and suffering we may be called to endure, by the example and the prayers of the vast army of Christ's holy martyrs, who are ever with us in prayer and spirit. In the words of two of the Church's hymns during the first week of Great Lent,

> The soldiers of Christ cast aside the fear of kings and tyrants; boldly and with courage they confessed Him as the Lord of all, their King and God; and now they intercede for our souls (Matins, Tuesday of the First Week of Lent).

> Thy martyrs, O Lord, forgetting the things of the present life, and despising torture in their longing for the life to come, were granted this eternal life as their inheritance, and now they rejoice with the angels. At their supplications bestow upon Thy people Thy great mercy (Vespers, Tuesday of the First Week of Lent).

And in all our trials and tribulations, even unto death, may we, along with Christ's holy martyrs, be fortified by Christ's immortal words, "Because I live, you will live also" (John 14:19); and, "I am the resurrection and the life. He who believes in Me, though he may die, he shall live" (John 11:25).

Holy Martyrs of Christ, pray to God for us![9]

---

[9] In chapter 8 of his excellent book, *The Rise of Christianity* (San Francisco: Harper, 1997), Rodney Stark, a sociologist by profession, gives a very cogent response to modern charges that the Christian martyrs were somehow suicidal or masochistic. This chapter is entitled "The Martyrs: Sacrifice as Rational Choice."

Chapter Ten

THE RISE OF MONASTICISM, THE NEW MARTYRDOM; AND THE WISDOM OF THE DESERT FATHERS AND MOTHERS

ORIGINS OF MONASTICISM

GIVING ONE'S LIFE IN MARTYRDOM for the sake of Christ was always considered to be the highest possible expression of one's love for and devotion to our Lord and God and Savior Jesus Christ. As Jesus Himself told His followers, "Greater love has no one than this, than to lay down one's life for one's friends" (John 15:13). Indicative of this understanding is the fact that the Church has always honored the martyrs as Saints, commemorating them on the day of their martyrdom.

With the end of the era of the violent persecution of Christians, which basically comes with the Edict of Milan in 313, as we saw in the preceding chapter, a new form of martyrdom arises—monasticism. This form of the Christian life involves dying in another way—dying to oneself, to one's self-will, to one's irrational passions, and even to one's natural desires, to the utmost degree, as seen in the three classic monastic vows of poverty, chastity, and obedience to one's superior/elder/abbot/spiritual father. Certainly, Christians are called to enjoy the good things of this life in moderation and with thanksgiving, yet with one's highest priority always on spiritual things—as St. Paul exhorts, "Set your affections on things above, not on things of the earth" (Col. 3:3). But the monastics voluntarily choose to live entirely *without* many of these good things, to help them devote all their time and energy to serving, worshiping, and praying to God. As St. Paul also writes (in a generalizing way), "He who is unmarried cares for the things of the Lord—how he may please the Lord. But he who is married cares about the things of the world—how he may please his wife" (1 Cor. 7:32–33).

Hence, very soon after the Edict of Milan, many Christians began going into the wilderness—especially into the desert regions of Egypt, Palestine, and Syria—seeking a life of either complete solitude, with one's fellowship only with the Lord and His angels; or to live in a community with similarly minded brethren to pursue together a life entirely devoted to serving, worshiping, and praying to God. In doing so, they were not denying the innate goodness of marriage or of life in the world. Indeed, the Council of Gangra, in Asia Minor, held in about 341, expressly condemned anyone who entered the monastic life based on a disdain for marriage. An even more important affirmation of the full goodness of marriage and marital relations occurred at the Council of Nicea in 325, when the saintly monk Paphnutius eloquently defended the right of priests and deacons to be married. The question of clerical celibacy never again became an issue in the Eastern Church, whereas mandatory clerical celibacy did come to prevail in the Western Church by about the end of the 12th century.

So, without denying the essential goodness of marriage, the monastics were simply choosing to live more simply, without the cares of marriage and of life in the world, in order to give all their time and energy directly to Christ and to praying for the entire world. In this profoundly important way they expressed their love for all their fellow humans—praying without ceasing for the salvation of all mankind. This makes it plain that living in solitude does not by any means automatically indicate some kind of hostile rejection of the rest of the world and humanity. And besides, the spiritual wisdom of certain monastics, conveyed in letters and various treatises, and collected in various compilations through the centuries, has brought enlightenment and guidance in the spiritual life to millions of Christians through the years. And through the ministry of hospitality, the monastics have provided countless pilgrims and other visitors through the centuries up to the present day with spiritual guidance and inspiration, and sometimes even with physical healing through their prayers.

ST. ANTHONY THE GREAT

The founder of *eremitic*, or solitary, monasticism is considered to be St. Anthony the Great of Egypt (251–356), whose whole life was radically changed as a young man when he was pierced to the heart by these words he heard one day in church: "If thou wouldst be perfect, go and sell what thou hast, and give to the poor, and come follow Me, and thou shalt have treasure in Heaven" (Matt. 19:21). In obedience to these words of Christ, he arranged for the welfare of his sister, his only sibling—both their parents had already died—and he sold all his possessions, giving the proceeds to the poor. Then after a time of living ascetically near his village, he went out into the desert near the Red Sea to live in isolation from the rest of the world, communing only with the Lord.

For the next approximately twenty years he lived in this way, seeing virtually no one else during that whole time. Then, as word spread about this amazing recluse who lived so close to God, people began to come to him for counseling and healing, and he began receiving them, with the love of Christ. And presently disciples began to gather around him. In the words of St. Athanasios the Great (298–373), in his famous biography of St. Anthony,

> And so for nearly twenty years he continued training himself in solitude, never going forth, and seldom seen by any. After this, when many were eager and wishful to imitate his discipline, and his acquaintances came and began to cast down and wrench off the door by force, Anthony, as from a shrine, came forth initiated in the mysteries and filled with the Spirit of God. Then for the first time he was seen outside the fort by those who came to see him. And they, when they saw him, wondered at the sight, for he had the same habit of body as before, and was neither fat, like a man without exercise, nor lean from fasting and striving with the demons, but he was just the same as they had known him before he entered seclusion.
>
> And also his soul was free from blemish, for it was neither contracted as if by grief, nor relaxed by pleasure, nor possessed by laughter or dejection, for he was not troubled when he beheld the crowd, nor overjoyed at being welcomed by so many. But he was altogether even as being guided by reason, and *abiding in a natural state.*
>
> Through him the Lord healed the bodily ailments of many present, and cleansed others from evil spirits. And He gave grace to Anthony in speaking, so that he consoled many who were sorrowful, and brought harmony to those who were at variance, exhorting all to prefer the love of Christ before everything that is in the world. And while he exhorted and advised them to remember the good things to come, and the lovingkindness of God towards us, 'Who spared

> not His own Son, but delivered Him up for us all' [Romans 8:32], he persuaded many to adopt the solitary life. And thus it happened in the end that cells arose even in the mountains, and the desert was colonized by monks, who came forth from their own people, and enrolled themselves for the citizenship in the heavens (*Life of Anthony*, ch. 14; NPNF vol. II, IV, p. 200; my emphasis).

The disciples who gathered around Anthony each lived according to his own unique prayer rule and work routine, with only a loose kind of organization binding them all together. This was the beginning of the *lavra* system of *semi-eremitic, idiorhythmic* monasticism (coming from the Greek word *idios*, meaning "one's own"). In this kind of system, typically the monks would live in seclusion in their cells during the week, and then each weekend they would come into the nearest town to sell the rush mats and reed baskets that they had woven during the week (the word *lavra* originally referred to the town market). And they would worship together on Saturday evening and Sunday morning, and have a common meal, the *agape*, afterwards.

One day, as Anthony wandered out into a more remote part of the desert, he came upon a hermit who had been in the desert longer than he had been. This turned out to be St. Paul the Hermit of Thebes (229–342; Feastday, January 15). His story is similar to Anthony's, for he also went into the desert to pursue the spiritual life as a young man after the death of his parents, after his pagan brother-in-law demanded that he give his inheritance to his sister. After meeting with St. Paul, Anthony gave this report to his own disciples: "'Woe is me, my children, I who am a sinful and false monk, a monk in name only. I have seen Elijah, I have seen John the Baptist in the desert, and I have seen Paul—in Paradise!'" (St. Nikolai of Zicha, *The Prologue from Ochrid*, vol. 1 [Alhambra, CA.: Serbian Orthodox Diocese of Western America; 2nd edition, 2008], p. 61 [for January 15]).

St. Anthony the Great, the first of the great Desert Fathers, continued to live in the Egyptian desert along with his beloved disciples for the rest of his very long life. He passed on to the next life, full of days, at the age of 105. His Feastday is January 17. And St. Athanasius's *Life of Anthony* became a "best-seller" all across the Empire, doing much to describe and spread the monastic ideal, especially in Western Europe.

ST. PACHOMIOS THE GREAT

Pachomios (c. 295–346) was born into a well-to-do pagan family in the Thebaid (in Upper Egypt), who made sure he was provided with an excellent classical education. At the age of twenty, he was conscripted into the army. He became so impressed by the loving care that Christians gave to the new conscripts (who were temporarily housed in the local prison) that he resolved to become a Christian himself. After his military service, he received Holy Baptism, and entered into a life of prayer in the nearby desert. Recognizing the need for ongoing guidance in the spiritual life, he asked the Elder Palamon, a fellow desert-dweller, to become his spiritual father.

In about the year 320 Pachomios was traveling through the town of Tabennisi, when he heard a voice saying to start a monastery in that place. He told Elder Palamon about this, and he agreed that this must be a directive from God Himself. So the two of them set about establishing a monastic center there. Soon thereafter, Palamon passed into the next life.

Not long after that, an angel, dressed in monastic garb, appeared to Pachomios and gave him a brief rule of prayer for his use and for the use of those who would gather around him. This is when disciples began to dwell with him at Tabennisi in great numbers.

After some time his sister Maria came to visit him, seeking guidance for a deeper spiritual life. He advised her to establish a similar monastery for women just across the Nile River, which she did.

His fame spread, and that of his community, so that by the time of his death some 7,000 disciples had gathered at Tabennisi and in the surrounding region, whom he supervised and cared for in seven monasteries for men and two for women.

St. Pachomios the Great is considered to be the founder of *cenobitic* (from the Greek word *koinos*, meaning "common"), or communal, monasticism, with all the monks living together and following the same prayer rule and work schedule. He is commemorated on May 15.

ST. AMMOUN

St. Ammoun (or Ammonios; c. 290–353) founded a large, semi-eremitic monastic community in the Nitrian Desert in Lower Egypt. Orphaned at a young age, he was raised by an uncle. When he was twenty-two, he acceded to his uncle's wishes and got married, even though he felt called to a monastic way of life. So from their wedding night, he and his wife lived together as brother and sister. Every evening they read the Vespers service together, and every morning they read the Orthros, or Matins, service. They supported themselves through gardening and farming.

One day, after living in this simple way for eighteen years, his wife spoke to him in words something like these: "I know you really want to live in the desert in compete devotion to our Lord Christ. Go, and pray, and be a means of salvation for others as you have been for me. I will stay here and start a monastery for women. Only, let us visit each other twice a year, so that I may still behold the face of the man I love."

So this is what they did. Ammoun became the first hermit in the Nitrian Desert. Many disciples gathered around him, and by the end of the fourth century this region was nearly as famous and important a monastic center as Sketis and Tabennisi.

St. Ammoun was a close friend of St. Anthony. When Ammoun died in 353, Anthony saw from the window of his cell Ammoun's soul ascending into the heights. He told the brethren who were with him, "Today Abba Ammoun has moved on, and I see his holy soul being borne by the angels into Heaven" (St. Nikolai of Zicha, *The Prologue from Ochrid*, vol. 4, p. 18 [for October 4]).

St. Ammoun is commemorated on October 4.

ST. HILARION OF GAZA

As a young teenager, St. Hilarion (c. 291–371) lived as a hermit in the Egyptian desert under the guidance of St. Anthony the Great. At the age of fifteen, Anthony blessed him to go into the desert of southern Palestine and live as a hermit there. Apparently, then, Hilarion was the first to bring the budding monasticism of Egypt into Palestine.

As with so many of the godly hermits who eventually became wonderworking elders, in time crowds of people sought him out for healing and spiritual guidance. In about 353, he returned to Egypt in quest of greater solitude. Later he went to Libya, Sicily, and Cyprus, where he died. His Feastday is October 21.

ST. MACARIOS THE GREAT

St. Macarios the Great (c. 300–390) established a semi-eremitic monastic center in about the year 330, in an area known as Sketis in Upper Egypt. From this name we get the word *skete*, which came to mean an offshoot colony from a larger monastery.

While St. Anthony and St. Ammoun left no writings, and St. Pachomios only wrote a very short prayer rule, the powerful, magnificent, eloquent, and deeply insightful *Fifty Spiritual Homilies* are attributed to St. Macarios and/or to his disciples. This marvelous work vividly describes many aspects of the spiritual life, including various dimensions of spiritual warfare with Satan and his minions. Here is a sample excerpt from this work, in which the tangible reality of intimate communion with the Lord, which is possible for every Christian through heartfelt prayer, is beautifully depicted:

> A man goes in to bend his knee in prayer, and his heart is filled with the divine influence, and his soul rejoices with the Lord, like a bride with her bridegroom, according to that word of the Prophet Isaiah which says, "As the bridegroom rejoiceth over the bride, so shall the Lord rejoice over thee" (Is. 62:5). And it comes to pass that being all the rest of the day otherwise engaged, he gives himself to prayer for an hour, and the inward man is rapt in prayer into the unfathomable deep of that other world in great sweetness, so that his whole mind is up aloft, rapt away thither, and estranged from things below. For the time being, forgetfulness comes to him in regard to earthly interests, because his thoughts are filled with and taken captive by divine and heavenly things, to things infinite and past comprehension, to wonderful things which no human lips can express, so that for that hour he prays and says, "Would to God that my soul might pass into Heaven along with my prayer!" (Homily VIII.1; Mason edition, p. 65).

St. Macarios, one of the very greatest of the Desert Fathers of Egypt, Palestine, and Syria, figures prominently in the collection of biographical vignettes and sayings known as *The Sayings of the Desert Fathers: The Alphabetical Collection*. Not only is the amazing austerity of many of the Desert Fathers and Mothers vividly conveyed in this work, but also their very inspirational compassion and humility. While some of their teachings may be too stark and severe to be readily followed by contemporary Christians, whether laity or monastics, most of their wisdom is directly applicable to our spiritual life today. And it always rings true, forged as it is by their own priceless experience of the power of the Holy Spirit, the grace of Christ, and the love of the Father. This is why we quote extensively from this work in the rest of this chapter.

Here is an excerpt from this work that demonstrates Macarios's humility, and provides some particular details of his life:

> One day Macarios the Egyptian went from Scetis to the mountain of Nitria [to visit] ... Abba Pambo [*abba* means *father*]. The old men there said to him, "Father, say a word to the brethren." He said, "I have not yet become a monk myself, but I have seen monks. One day when I was sitting in my cell, my thoughts were troubling me,

> suggesting that I should go [further] into the desert and see what I could see there. I remained for five years, fighting against this thought, saying, perhaps it comes from the demons. But since the thought persisted, I left for the desert.
>
> "There I found a sheet of water and an island in the midst, and the animals of the desert came to drink there. In the midst of these animals I saw two naked men, and my body trembled, for I believed that they were spirits. Seeing my shaking, they said to me, 'Do not be afraid, for we are men.' Then I said to them, 'Where do you come from, and how did you come to this desert?' They said, 'We came from a monastery and having agreed together, we came here forty years ago. One of us is an Egyptian, and the other a Libyan.' They questioned me and asked, 'How is the world? Is the water [of the Nile] rising in due time? Is the world enjoying prosperity?' I replied it was. Then I asked them, 'How can I become a monk?' They said to me, 'If you do not give up all that is in the world, you cannot become a monk.'
>
> "I said to them, 'But I am weak, and I cannot do as you do.' So they said to me, 'If you cannot become like us, sit in your cell and weep for your sins.' I asked them, 'When the winter comes, are you not frozen? And when the heat comes, do not your bodies burn?' They said, 'It is God who has made this way of life for us. We do not freeze in winter, and the summer does us no harm.'
>
> "That is why I said that I have not yet become a monk, but I have seen monks" (trans. Benedicta Ward [London: Mowbray's, 1975], p. 106).

And concerning the great power of humility, in spiritual warfare in particular, there is this story about St. Macarios from this same renowned collection of vignettes and sayings of the great Fathers and Mothers of the Desert:

> When Abba Macarios was returning from the marsh to his cell one day carrying some palm-leaves, he met the devil on the road with a scythe. The latter struck him as much as he pleased, but in vain. Then the devil said to him, "Do you know what your power is, Macarios, that makes me powerless against you? All that you do, I do, too: you fast, and so do I; you keep vigil, and I do not sleep at all. But in one thing you beat me." Abba Macarios asked what that was. He said,

"Your humility. Because of that I can do nothing against you" (Ward, pp. 109–110).

St. Macarios the Great's Feastday is January 19.

ST. BASIL THE GREAT

St. Basil the Great (c. 330–379) is best known as one of the greatest theologians of the Church: one of the three great Cappadocian Fathers—along with St. Gregory the Theologian (his best friend) and St. Gregory of Nyssa (his younger brother); and one of the Three Holy Hierarchs—along with St. Gregory the Theologian and St. John Chrysostom—who are honored together on January 30. But during his bishopric in the major Christian center of Neocaesarea in central Asia Minor, he also was known as an extremely skillful administrator, who did much to make sure that the burgeoning monastic movement remained securely within the fold of the established, canonical Church. He did this by working hard to keep the monastics and their abbots subject to their local bishops. And his *Longer and Shorter Monastic Rules* came to be the standard for all the monasticism of the Eastern Church to this day. Thus the *Oxford Dictionary of the Christian Church* can say that he "impressed on Eastern monasticism the structure and ethos which it has retained ever since" (3rd revised edition, p. 167).

Basil was raised in a solidly Christian home—indeed, both his parents are Saints in our Church: St. Basil the Elder, and St. Emmelia (their Feastday is May 8). For further studies Basil went to Athens, one of the greatest centers for classical education in the Empire. After his excellent education there, he returned home to Neocaesarea, intent on starting an illustrious career in governmental service. But his older sister St. Macrina the Younger (July 19) convinced him instead to devote his extraordinary talents and education to serving Christ and His Church.

His love for Christ, which he had imbibed in his youth from his parents, now burned ever more strongly in his heart, and he yearned to live in a fully dedicated Christian community. So he made an extended visit to some of the leading monasteries in Syria and Egypt, to learn about the monastic life in those areas. Apparently he was most impressed by the Pachomian communities in Egypt, for the influence of the prayer rule and way of life of those communities can be seen in his own monastic *Rules*.

Returning home, Basil began living a semi-monastic life on his family estate, along with other family members and friends. His dear friend from his school days in Athens, Gregory, would come for long visits. Later Basil became the bishop of the Church in Neocaesarea, which involved him heavily in administrative concerns and imperial politics. But it was his personal monastic experience which helped to convince him of the great importance of monasticism for the life of the Church as a whole.

St. Basil the Great, the most important monastic figure in the 4th century in Asia Minor, died on January 1, 379. He is commemorated on January 1.

ST. MARTIN OF TOURS

St. Martin of Tours (c. 335–397), in Gaul (today's France), was a Christian catechumen serving in the Roman army when one wintry day he saw a freezing beggar at the gate of the city of Amiens. Moved with compassion, he took his sword and cut his cloak—the only outer garment he owned—in half, and gave one of the halves to the beggar. That very night Martin saw a vision of Christ in a dream, in which He told him that the act of kindness he had done for the beggar had actually been done unto Himself. This vision inspired Martin to hasten to receive Holy Baptism, to resign from the army about two years later, and to enter monastic life as a hermit.

After a few years, in 360, he and St. Hilary, the Bishop of Poitiers (c. 315–367; January 13), established the first cenobitic monastery in Gaul, at Liguge. Martin continued to live there even after being made the Bishop of Tours in 371. As bishop he did much to strengthen monastic life, and Church life in general, in northern Gaul, through his powerful preaching and the many miracles wrought through his prayers.

Martin's biography was written by a priest who served under him named Sulpitius Severus (c. 363–420). It became extremely popular in the West, much like St. Athanasios's *Life of Anthony*.

St. Martin's Feastday in the East is November 12. He is considered to be one of the patron Saints of France.

ST. JOHN CHRYSOSTOM

Like St. Basil the Great, St. John Chrysostom (347–407; November 13) played an important role in the early history of monasticism, even though he is better known for his brilliant preaching—especially his exegetical sermons, going verse by verse through many books of the Bible—in the great cities of Antioch and Constantinople. But as a young man he lived the monastic life in the caves in the cliffs near Antioch, and only came back into the city when his health got seriously weakened from the austerities of his self-imposed ascetic discipline.

After returning to the city he was ordained a deacon. Six years later he was made a priest. Then he was given the principal preaching duties in the great church there, and in preaching to and caring for his large flock, most of whom were married, he realized that marriage—especially marriage that is centered in Christ—has its own particular glory. So while the monastic way of life always remained higher and dearer in his mind and heart, he recognized that married people have the same capacity for spiritual growth as the monastics, and he urged them to live prayerfully and virtuously in imitation of the monks as much as possible.

Chrysostom's enduring love for monasticism, and his understanding of it as the most direct avenue for spiritual growth, free from many of the cares and distractions so often associated with marriage and life in the world, is seen in this excerpt from one of his sermons on St. Paul's First Epistle to Timothy:

> To go to the monastery of a holy man is to pass, as it were, from earth to heaven. You do not see there what is seen in a private house. They all comprise a pure chorus ... These are truly saints and angels among men.... There is no dread of magistrates, no lordly arrogance, no terror of slaves, no disturbance of women or children ... Nothing of all these, but all there is full of prayer, of hymns, of spiritual savor. Nothing carnal is there (Homily XIV on 1 Timothy; NPNF vol. I, XIII, pp. 456–457).

And in a very similar way, he also says of the monks,

> For in nothing are their lodging-places in a condition inferior to the heavens; for the angels lodge with them, and the Lord of the angels. For if they came to Abraham, a man having a wife, and bringing up children, because they saw that he was hospitable, when they find much more abundant virtue, and a man delivered as it were from the body, and in the flesh disregarding the flesh, much more do they tarry there, and celebrate the choral feast that becomes them. For there is moreover a table amongst them pure from all covetousness, and full of self-denial....
>
> There is no fear there, or trembling; no ruler accuses, no wife provokes, no child casts one into sadness, no disorderly mirth dissipates, no multitude of flatterers puffs up. Rather, the table is an angel's table, free from all such turmoil.... as though living in another world, as though they had migrated into heaven itself, as living there, even so all their conversation is about the things there, about Abraham's

> bosom, about the crowns of the saints, about the choiring with Christ, ... about the King Who is above, about the war in which they are engaged, about the devil's crafts, about the good deeds which the saints have achieved (Homily LXIX on St. Matthew; NPNF vol. I, X, pp. 424–425).

But at the same time, Chrysostom repeatedly reminded his married parishioners that they also could live in holiness, just as the monks: "Paul commands us to put ourselves altogether on a level with the monks" (Homily VII on St. Matthew; NPNF vol. I, X, p. 49); and, "For even one dwelling in a city may imitate the self-denial of the monks; yea, one who has a wife, and is busy in a household, may pray, and fast, and learn compunction" (Homily LV on St. Matthew; NPNF vol. I, X, p. 344). And again,

> Would you like me to give examples of men whose lives were patterns of virtue, even though they lived in the world? ... I am referring to the holy men of the Old Testament. How many of them had wives and children, yet were in no way inferior to the greatest ascetic! (Homily XXI on Ephesians; *St. John Chrysostom, On Marriage and Family Life,* translated by Catharine P. Roth and David Anderson [Crestwood, NY: SVS Press, 1986], pp. 69–70).

He said on one occasion that the married have the capacity "to surpass all others":

> Seek the things of God, and those of man will follow with great ease. Instruct (*rhythmize*) your wife, and your whole household will be well-disciplined.... If we regulate our households in this way, we will also be fit to oversee the Church, for indeed the household is a little Church. Therefore, it is possible for us to surpass all others by becoming good husbands and wives (Homily XX on Ephesians; NPNF vol. I, XIII, p. 148).

And in a similar vein, he also once said:

> I am advising nothing burdensome. I do not say, "Do not marry." I do not say, "Forsake the cities, and withdraw yourself from public affairs"; but being engaged in them, show virtue. Indeed, those who are busy in the midst of the cities, *I wish to be* ***more approved*** *than those who have occupied the mountains* [i.e., the ascetic hermits].... Do not tell me, "I have a wife, and children, and am a master of a

> household, and therefore cannot duly practice all this." For if you had none of these things, if you are careless, all is lost; while if you are encompassed with all these things, if you are earnest, you will attain to virtue. For there is but one thing which is sought for—the preparation of a noble disposition. With this, neither age, nor poverty, nor riches, nor reverse of fortune, nor anything else, will be able to impede you (Homily XLIII on St. Matthew; NPNF vol. I, X, p. 278; my emphasis).

Chrysostom also gives a strong reminder to the monastics that bodily virginity/celibacy is valuable not so much in itself, but only as it contributes to the development of godliness, and that the true virginity is of the soul, which even the married can attain to. As he says, in commenting on 2 Corinthians 11:2 ("For I have betrothed you to one husband, that I may present you as a chaste virgin to Christ"),

> He said these things not in reference only to virgins, but to the whole body of the entire Church. For the uncorrupt soul is a virgin, though she have a husband; she is a virgin as to that which is Virginity indeed, that which is marvelous. For the virginity of the body is but the accompaniment and shadow of the virginity of the soul, which is the True Virginity.... let us then be virgins as to the True Virginity. For the Lord seeks after the virginity of the soul (Homily XXVIII on Hebrews; NPNF vol. I, XIV, p. 498).

St. John Chrysostom is commemorated on November 13 and January 27.

ST. JOHN CASSIAN

One of the greatest contributions of the monastics to the life of the Church over the centuries has been their frequent participation in theological debate and struggles against heresies. Flowing out of their personal experience of the truths of the Faith through their great ascetical efforts and their unceasing prayer and meditation on heavenly realities, the monks often have been able to affirm the traditional Christian teachings with a rare intensity and accuracy.

An especially important example of this is the life and work of St. John Cassian (c. 360–435), who as a young man spent about ten years with the Desert Fathers in Egypt, learning and imbibing their wisdom about the spiritual life. Later he became a deacon under St. John Chrysostom in Constantinople. From there he moved to southern France, where he established two monasteries based on Egyptian models. For the next two hundred years, eremitic, semi-eremitic, and cenobitic monasticism, permeated with the ethos of the monastics of the Egyptian desert, flourished in the wild ravines, caves, and hills of southern France.

After 415 Cassian wrote his two most important works—the *Institutes*, and the *Conferences*. Both are based on conversations that he had with the monastic Fathers in Egypt. In these works he endeavors to explain the Eastern understanding of *synergism*—that God and man must *work together* for man's salvation. While God makes salvation possible for every human being—both through the eternally efficacious work of Christ through His crucifixion in which He bears the sins of the entire world; and through His conquest of sin, death, and the devil through His resurrection from the dead—still, each person, through his or her *free will*, must freely accept and appropriate what the Lord has accomplished, for God does not *force* salvation on anyone. At the same time, the Holy Spirit is ceaselessly urging and enabling each person to choose the good—to choose to cooperate with God in the process of salvation.

The Western Church, just at this time, was caught in the throes of the Pelagian controversy, brought on by the British monk Pelagius's claims that man can save himself apart from the help of divine grace, sheerly through his determination and willpower to always choose the good. In response to this heretical teaching, the greatly influential Western Church Father St. Augustine of Hippo (354–430), in western North Africa, went too far to the other extreme, asserting that man is so totally depraved through Adam's Fall that he can do nothing in the process of salvation—that God, then, must do everything in this process. By the sheer force of logic, since not everyone is saved, this leads to the inescapable conclusion that God must have decided, before He created anyone, whom He would save for eternal life in Heaven, and whom He would condemn to eternal punishment in hell. This becomes known as the theory of double predestination, which the Eastern Church has steadfastly rejected whenever it has appeared in the history of Christianity.

Here is a glimpse of how Cassian describes the relationship of Divine grace and man's free will in the synergism of God and man working together in the process of man's salvation:

> And therefore it is laid down by all the Catholic Fathers who have taught perfection of heart not by empty disputes of words, but in deed and act, that the first stage in the Divine gift is for each man to be inflamed with the desire for everything that is good, but in such a way that the choice of free will is open to either side. And the second stage in Divine grace is for the aforesaid practices of virtue to be able to be performed, but in such a way that the possibilities of

> the will are not destroyed. The third stage also belongs to the gifts of God, so that the grace may be retained by the persistence of the goodness already acquired, yet in such a way that one's liberty may not be surrendered and experience bondage. For the God of all must be believed to work in all, so as to incite, protect, and strengthen, but not to take away the freedom of the will which He Himself has once given (*Conferences* XIII, ch. 18; NPNF vol. II, XI, p. 434).

And further,

> It cannot then be doubted that there are by nature some seeds of goodness in every soul implanted by the kindness of the Creator. But unless these are quickened by the assistance of God, they will not be able to attain to an increase of perfection, for, as the blessed Apostle Paul says, "Neither is he that planteth anything nor he that watereth, but God Who giveth the increase" [1 Cor. 3:7]....
>
> And therefore the will always remains free in man, and can either neglect or delight in the grace of God. For the Apostle would not have commanded saying: "Work out your own salvation with fear and trembling" [Phil. 2:12], had he not known that it could be advanced or neglected by us. But that men might not imagine that they had no need of Divine aid for the work of salvation, he adds: "For it is God Who worketh in you both to will and to do, of His good pleasure" [Phil. 2:13]. And therefore he warns Timothy and says: "Neglect not the grace of God which is in thee" [1 Tim. 4:14]; and again, "For which cause I exhort thee to stir up the grace of God which is in thee" [2 Tim. 1:6]. Hence also in writing to the Corinthians he exhorts and warns them not to show themselves unworthy of the grace of God through their unfruitful works, saying: "And we helping, exhort you that ye receive not the grace of God in vain" [2 Cor. 6:1] (*Conferences* XIII, ch. 12; NPNF vol. II, XI, p. 429).

Very tellingly, John Cassian is not considered to be a Saint in the Roman Catholic Church—except locally, in his own area of Marseilles, France. He is, however, honored not only as a Saint in the Orthodox Church, but also as a very important Church Father. His Feastday is February 29/28.

ABBA ACHILLES, ONE OF THE DESERT FATHERS

Here is a beautiful example of the charitable spirit, and the sensitivity to the feelings of others, of the Desert Fathers:

> Three old men, of whom one had a bad reputation, came one day to Abba Achilles. The first asked him, "Father, make me a fishing-net." "I will not make you one," he replied. Then the second said, "Of your charity make one, so that we may have a souvenir of you in the monastery." But he said, "I do not have time." Then the third one, who had a bad reputation, said, "Make me a fishing-net, so that I may have something from your hands, Father." Abba Achilles answered him at once, "For you, I will make one."
>
> Then the two other old men asked him privately, "Why did you not want to do what we asked you, but you promised to do what he asked?" The old man gave this answer: "I told you I would not make one, and you were not disappointed, since you thought that I had no time. But if I had not made one for him, he would have said, 'The old man has heard about my sin, and that is why he does not want to make me anything,' and *our relationship would have broken down*. But now I have cheered his soul, so that he will not be overcome with grief" (Ward, pp. 24–25; my emphasis).

ABBA BESSARION, ANOTHER OF THE DESERT FATHERS

Here is another example of the non-judgmentalism of the Desert Fathers, and their quickness to personally identify with sinners:

> A brother who had sinned was turned out of the church by the priest. Abba Bessarion got up and went with him, saying, "I, too, am a sinner" (Ward, p. 35).

ABBA ISAIAH, ANOTHER OF THE DESERT FATHERS

In accordance with the teachings of all the Saints of the Church, the Desert Fathers were very consistent in urging their disciples to accept suffering graciously, knowing that if they bear trials and tribulations nobly, God works through these things to instill humility in one's heart and mind and soul. And even if the soul at first rebels at such chastisement by the Lord (see Heb. 12:5–11), He uses it to bring the person back to Himself. Here is an example of such wisdom:

> Abba Isaiah also said, "When God wishes to take pity on a soul and it rebels, not bearing anything and doing its own will, He then allows it to suffer that which it does not want, in order that it may seek Him again" (Ward, pp. 59–60).

AMMA THEODORA, ONE OF THE DESERT MOTHERS

Women also went into the Egyptian desert to commune with God. One of the themes Amma Theodora used to talk about was the traits that are characteristic of good teachers:

> The same amma [meaning *mother*] said that a teacher ought to be a stranger to the desire for domination, vain-glory, and pride; and one should not be able to fool him by flattery, nor blind him by gifts, nor conquer him by the stomach, nor dominate him by anger. Rather, he should be patient, gentle, and humble as far as possible; he must be tested and without partisanship, full of concern, and *a lover of souls* (Ward, p. 72; my emphasis).

ABBA MATOES, ANOTHER OF THE DESERT FATHERS

This holy elder voices a universally held understanding of all the Saints and Fathers of the Church when he says, "The nearer a man draws to God, the more he sees himself a sinner." He then turns to the experience of the Prophet Isaiah to back up his statement: "It was when Isaiah the prophet saw God that he declared himself 'a man of unclean lips' (Is. 6:5)" (Ward, p. 121).

Abba Matoes also reminded those who would get too extreme in their asceticism that moderation is usually a better path: "Abba Matoes said, 'I prefer a light and steady activity to one that is painful at the beginning but is soon broken off'" (Ward, p. 121).

And we see his remarkable humility and wisdom about human relationships in this vignette:

> A brother questioned Abba Matoes saying, "What am I to do? My tongue makes me suffer, and every time I go among men, I cannot control it, but I condemn them in all they are doing and reproach them with it. What am I to do?" The old man replied, "If you cannot contain yourself, flee into solitude. For this is a sickness. He who

> dwells with the brethren must not be square, but round, *so as to turn himself towards all.*" He went on, "It is not through virtue that I live in solitude, but through weakness; those who live in the midst of men are the strong ones" (Ward, p. 123; my emphasis).

ABBA NILUS, ANOTHER DESERT FATHER

Abba Nilus gives us several pithy pearls of wisdom about prayer:

> He also said, "Prayer is the seed of gentleness and the absence of anger."
>
> He also said, "Prayer is a remedy against grief and depression."
>
> He also said, "If you want to pray properly, do not let yourself be upset, or you will run in vain."
>
> He also said, "Do not be always wanting everything to turn out as you think it should, but rather as God pleases; then you will be undisturbed and thankful in your prayer" (Ward, p. 129).

ABBA NISTHEROS, ANOTHER DESERT FATHER

More wisdom highly relevant for modern man comes from another one of the "ancients":

> A brother questioned an old man, saying, "What good work should I do so that I may live?" The old man said, "God knows what is good. I have heard it said that one of the Fathers asked Abba Nistheros the Great, the friend of Abba Anthony, and said to him, 'What good work is there that I could do?' He said to him, 'Are not all [good] actions equal? Scripture says that Abraham was hospitable and God was with him. David was humble, and God was with him. Elijah loved interior peace, and God was with him. So, do whatever you see your soul desires according to God, and guard your heart.'"...
>
> Abba Nistheros said that a monk ought to ... *Pray to God in His Presence, for He really is present.* Do not impose rules on yourself; do not judge anyone (Ward, pp. 129–130; my emphasis).

ABBA PAUL THE GREAT, A DESERT FATHER FROM GALATIA

Abba Paul said, "Keep close to Jesus" (Ward, p. 172).

ABBA POEMEN, ONE OF THE MOST PROMINENT OF THE DESERT FATHERS

It was very typical of the leading Desert Fathers that after many years of asceticism, prayer, and renunciation of their own will, the Lord would use them to bring physical as well as spiritual healing to many—including exorcising demons from the demon-possessed. But being so wary of the danger of pride, these wonderworking elders would often try to avoid being the means of such healing. Here is a wonderful account of how the brothers prevailed upon Abba Poemen to heal a terribly disfigured child through the power of his prayer and his humility:

> Many old men came to see Abba Poemen, and one day it happened that a member of Abba Poemen's family came, who had a child whose face, through the power of the devil, was turned backwards. The father, seeing the number of Fathers present, took the child and sat down outside the monastery, weeping. Now it happened that one of the old men came out and seeing him, asked him, "Man, why are you weeping?" He replied, "I am related to Abba Poemen, and see the misfortune which has overtaken my child. Though I want to bring him to the old man, we are afraid he does not want to see us. Each time he hears I am here, he has me driven away. But since you are with him, I have dared to come again. If you will, Father, have pity on me, take the child inside, and pray for him."
>
> So the old man went inside and behaved with good sense. He did not immediately present the child to Abba Poemen, but began with the lesser brethren, and said, "Make the sign of the cross over this little child." Having had him signed by all in turn, he presented him at last to Abba Poemen. Abba Poemen did not want to make the sign of the cross over him, but the others urged him, saying, "Do as everyone else has done." So, groaning, he stood up and prayed, saying, "God, heal your creature, that he be not ruled by the enemy." When he had made the sign of the cross over him, the child was healed immediately, and given back whole to his father (Ward, pp. 139–140).

Here is another example of the charitableness and compassion of the Fathers:

> A brother questioned Abba Poemen saying, "I have committed a great sin and I want to do penance for three years." The old man said to him, "That is a lot." The brother said, "For one year?" The old man said again, "That is a lot." Those who were present said, "For

> forty days?" He said again, "That is a lot." He added, "I myself say that if a man repents with his whole heart and does not intend to commit the sin any more, God will accept him after only three days" (Ward, p. 142).

And in a similar vein:

> Some old men came to see Abba Poemen and said to him, "When we see brothers who are dozing during the *synaxis* [the gathering in church], shall we rouse them so that they will be watchful?" He said to them, "For my part, when I see a brother who is dozing, I put his head on my knees and let him rest" (Ward, p. 151).

Concerning true silence:

> He also said, "A man may seem to be silent, but if his heart is condemning others he is babbling ceaselessly. But there may be another who talks from morning till night, and yet he is truly silent—that is, he says nothing that is not profitable" (Ward, p. 143).

Concerning a burning desire for the Eucharist:

> He also said, "It is written, 'As the hart longs for flowing streams, so longs my soul for Thee, O God' (Ps. 41:2, LXX).... It is the same for the monks ... they long for Saturday and Sunday to come to be able to go to the springs of water, that is to say, the body and blood of the Lord, so as to be purified from the bitterness of the evil one" (Ward, p. 144).

Concerning the constant watchfulness against unwanted, ungodly thoughts and the need for all of us to keep resisting them:

> A brother came to see Abba Poemen and said to him, "Abba, I have many thoughts and they put me in danger." The old man led him outside and said to him, "Expand your chest, but do not breathe in." He said, "I cannot do that." The old man said to him, "If you cannot do that, no more can you prevent thoughts from arising, but you can resist them" (Ward, pp. 143–144).

Concerning total reliance on the Lord in order to make spiritual progress:

> He also said, "To throw yourself before God, not to measure your progress, to leave behind all self-will: these are the instruments for the work of the soul" (Ward, p. 145).

Concerning the healing power of confession:

> It was said of a brother that he had to fight against blasphemy, but he was ashamed to admit it. He went where he heard some of the great old men lived to see them, in order to open his heart to them, but when he got there, he was ashamed to admit his temptation.
>
> But he kept going to Abba Poemen. The old man saw that he was worried, and he was sorry that the brother did not tell him what was wrong. So one day the elder forestalled him and said, "For a long time you have been coming here to tell me what is troubling you, but when you are here you will not tell me about it. Each time you go away unhappy, keeping your thoughts to yourself. Now tell me, my child, what is it all about?"
>
> The brother said to him, "The demon wars against me to make me blaspheme God, and I am ashamed to say so." So he told the elder all about it, and immediately he was relieved. The old man said to him, "Do not be unhappy, my child, but every time this thought comes to you, say, 'It is no affair of mine. May your blasphemy remain upon you, Satan, for my soul does not want it.' For everything that the soul does not desire, does not remain for long." And the brother went away healed (Ward, p. 151).

Concerning leading by example:

> A brother asked Abba Poemen, "Some brothers live with me. Do you want me to be in charge of them?" The old man said to him, "No, just work first and foremost, and if they want to live like you, they will see to it themselves." The brother said to him, "But it is they themselves, Father, who want me to be in charge of them." The old man said to him, "No, be their example, not their legislator" (Ward, pp. 160–161).

And here is an example of the gift of tongues among the Desert Fathers:

> Abba John, who had been exiled by the Emperor Marcian (r. 451–457), said, "We went to Syria one day to see Abba Poemen, and

> we wanted to ask him about purity of heart. But the old man did not know Greek, and no interpreter could be found. So, seeing our embarrassment, the old man began to speak in Greek, saying, "The nature of water is soft, and that of stone is hard; but if a bottle is hung above the stone, allowing the water to fall on it drop by drop, it wears away the stone. So it is with the word of God; it is soft and our heart is hard, but the man who hears the word of God often, opens his heart to the fear of God" (Ward, p. 163).

ABBA PAMBO, ANOTHER OF THE GREAT EARLY DESERT FATHERS IN EGYPT

A characteristic typical of very advanced holiness that has been a feature of Eastern spirituality from the earliest centuries has been one's face shining with the uncreated Light of God—as Christ shone on the Mount of Transfiguration, and as Moses's face shone when he came down from Mt. Sinai with the Ten Commandments. We see this occurrence in the Desert Fathers as well:

> They say of Abba Pambo that he was like Moses, who received the image of the glory of Adam [before the Fall] when his face shone. Pambo's face shone like lightning, and he was like a king sitting on a throne. It was the same with Abba Sylvanus and Abba Sisoes (Ward, p. 166).

And concerning the power of showing compassion:

> Abba Theodore of Pherme asked Abba Pambo, "Give me a word." With much difficulty he said to him, "Theodore, go and have compassion on all, for through compassion one finds freedom of speech before God" (Ward, p. 166).

ABBA PETER THE PIONITE, ANOTHER OF THE DESERT FATHERS

Some more advice concerning how to grow in and preserve one's humility:

> Abba Peter said, "We must not be puffed up when the Lord does something through our mediation, but we must rather thank Him for having made us worthy to be called by Him." He used to say it is good to think about each virtue in this way (Ward, p. 169).

ABBA SYLVANUS, A DESERT FATHER OF EGYPT, SINAI, AND SYRIA

A Palestinian by birth, Abba Sylvanus headed a band of twelve disciples in Scetis, before they all moved to Mount Sinai in 380. Later they moved to Syria, where he died by 414. His disciple Zacharias then took over the leadership of the small community.

Something of their relationship, and of Sylvanus's spiritual life, can be seen in this passage from the *Sayings of the Desert Fathers*:

> Another time his disciple Zacharias entered and found Abba Sylvanus in ecstasy, with his hands stretched toward heaven. Closing the door, he went away. Coming back at the sixth and the ninth hours, he found him in the same state. At the tenth hour he knocked, entered, and found him at peace, and said to him, "What has happened today, Father?" The latter replied [out of humility], "I was ill today, my child." But the disciple seized his feet and said to him, "I will not let you go until you have told me what you have seen." The old man said, "I was taken up to heaven, and I saw the glory of God, and I stayed there till now, and now I have been sent away" (Ward, pp. 186–187).

And this story, with some humor, shows the importance of down-to-earth stability, responsibility, moderation, and humility in the spiritual life:

> A brother went to see Abba Sylvanus on the mountain of Sinai. When he saw the brothers working hard [probably tilling the garden], he said to the old men, "'Do not labor for the food which perishes'" (John 6:27); and, "'Mary has chosen the good portion'" (Luke 10:42). So the old man, Abba Sylvanus, said to his disciple, "Zachary, give the brother a book and put him in a cell without anything else."
>
> So when the ninth hour came, the visitor watched the door, expecting someone would be sent to call him to the meal. When no one called him, he got up, went to find the old man, and said to him, "Have the brothers not eaten today?" The old man replied that they had. Then the brother said, "Why did you not call me?" The old man said to him, "Because you are a spiritual man and do not need that kind of food. We, being carnal, want to eat, and that is why we work. But you have chosen the good portion and read the whole day long, and you do not need to eat carnal food." When he heard these words

> the brother made a prostration, saying, "Forgive me, Abba." The old man said to him, "Mary needs Martha. It is really thanks to Martha that Mary is praised" (Ward, p. 187).

AMMA SARAH, ANOTHER OF THE DESERT MOTHERS

> It was related of Amma Sarah that for thirteen years she waged warfare against the demon of fornication. She never prayed that the warfare should cease, but she said, "O God, give me strength."
>
> Once the same spirit of fornication attacked her more insistently, reminding her of the vanities of the world. But she gave herself up to the fear of God and to asceticism, and went up onto her little terrace to pray. Then the spirit of fornication appeared corporally to her and said, "Sarah, you have overcome me." But she said, "It is not I who have overcome you, but my master, Christ" (Ward, p. 192).

AMMA SYNCLETICA, ANOTHER OF THE DESERT MOTHERS

Raised in the great city of Alexandria, Egypt, Syncletica had a noble and wealthy background. She was reputed to be a very intelligent and beautiful maiden, who was drawn to a contemplative life from a very young age. After her parents died when she was a young woman, she distributed her inheritance to the poor, and she and her younger sister began to live together in solitude, in a crypt. She died in about the year 350, at about the age of 80.

> Amma Syncletica said, "In the beginning there are a great many battles and a good deal of suffering for those who are advancing towards God, and afterwards, ineffable joy. It is like those who wish to light a fire. At first they are choked by smoke and cry, and by this means they obtain what they seek; as it is said, 'Our God is a consuming fire' (Heb. 12:29). So we also must kindle the divine fire in ourselves through tears and hard work" (Ward, p. 193).

And concerning the true asceticism:

> She also said, "If illness weighs us down, let us not be sorrowful as though, because of the illness and the prostration of our bodies, we could not sing. For all these things are for our good, for the purification of our desires. Truly, fasting and sleeping on the ground are set

> before us because of our sensuality. If illness weakens this sensuality, the reason for these ascetic practices is superfluous. For this is the great asceticism: to control oneself in illness, and to sings hymns of thanksgiving to God."

And:

> She also said, "There is an asceticism which is determined by the enemy, and his disciples practice it. So how are we to distinguish between the divine and royal asceticism, and the demonic tyranny? Clearly, through *its quality of balance.* Always follow a single rule of fasting. Do not fast four or five days completely, and break it the following day with any amount of food. In truth, lack of proportion always corrupts. While you are young and healthy, fast, for old age, with its weakness, will come. As long as you can, lay up treasure, so that when you cannot, you will be at peace" (Ward, pp. 194–196; my emphasis).

In a related way Amma Syncletica speaks about allowing for differing circumstances in this passage concerning pastoral care:

> We must correct those souls who are ruled by pride by providing them with higher examples to strive towards, just as we give the weaker souls encouragement, so that they might not be ruled by despair. Let us take an example from the work of the best gardeners, who, when they see that a plant is of small stature and sickly, water it profusely and care for it greatly, so that it will grow and be strong. But when they see in a plant the premature development of sprouts, they immediately trim the useless sprouts, so that the plant does not quickly wither. Likewise, physicians give rich nourishment to some patients, prescribing that they walk, while to others they give a strict diet and require them to remain at rest (*The Evergenitos,* trans. and ed. by Bishop Chrysostomos, et al. [Etna, Calif.: Center for Traditionalist Orthodox Studies, 1988], vol. I of the first book, p. 21).

ABBA HYPERECHIOS, ANOTHER OF THE DESERT FATHERS

Concerning keeping our mind and heart on heavenly things:

> He also said, "A monk's treasure is voluntary poverty. Lay up treasure in heaven, for there are the ages of quiet and bliss without end."
>
> He also said, "Let your thoughts be ever in the kingdom of heaven, and soon you will possess it as a heritage" (Ward, p. 200).

ABBA OR, ONE OF THE EARLY DESERT FATHERS OF NITRIA

Once more concerning humility, and being totally reliant on the Lord:

> Abba Or said, "The crown of the monk is humility." …
>
> He used to say this: "Do not speak in your heart against your brother like this: 'I am a man of more sober and austere life than he is.' Rather, put yourself in subjection to the grace of Christ, in the spirit of poverty and genuine charity, or else you will be overcome by the spirit of vainglory and lose all you have gained. For it is written in the Scriptures: 'Let him who stands take heed lest he fall' (1 Cor. 10:12). Let your salvation be founded in the Lord" (Ward, p. 207).

SOME CONCLUDING THOUGHTS

Fr. Alexander Schmemann summarizes the tremendous historical importance of monasticism in the life of the Church—an importance which it still has in the ongoing life of the Church today:

> The Christian world born out of Constantine's conversion not only did not reject the monastic movement but, in an almost paradoxical way, placed the monastic ideal, the monastic 'scale of values,' at the very heart of its own life and consciousness. Very soon indeed the 'desert' ceased to be limited to the wilderness at the outskirts of the 'inhabited world' (*oikoumene*) and implanted itself, in the form of numberless monasteries and convents, in the 'downtowns' of big cities [for instance, there were 76 monasteries in Constantinople by the middle of the 6th century], becoming thus the focus of spiritual guidance, leadership, and inspiration. The Fathers of the desert became the 'heroes' of the entire society, and their *vitae* [i.e., biographies] became the 'bestsellers' of Byzantine popular literature. The monastic liturgy, the monastic piety invaded and reshaped the liturgy of the whole Church, which, it can be said without any exaggeration, 'surrendered' herself to monasticism, just as, in another

> sense, she surrendered herself to the Empire. Monasticism was thus 'canonized' by the imperial-ecclesiastical organism as an integral part and expression of that Truth which, as we have seen already, formed the very basis of the Byzantine '*symphonia*' [the harmony of Church and State working together].
>
> And nothing reveals better the depth of that acceptance than the symbolic monastic tonsure of the emperor at the hour of his death. This ritual symbolized indeed the 'hierarchy of values' acknowledged by the Empire—its total subordination to the transcendent Kingdom of God, which the Empire as such does not inherit, of which it [only] can be an instrument or servant in 'this world,' but whose ultimate inheritance requires a total renunciation of everything 'earthly' (*Church, World, Mission* [Crestwood, NY: SVS Press, 1979], pp. 45–46).

Fr. Alexander also writes,

> The world receives a Christian sanction and is blessed by the Church, but monasticism became the 'salt' which does not allow the world to absorb Christianity and subject it to itself. In the light of this eternal reminder, the world already regarded itself as an image that passes—as a way to another, final reality which completes and judges all. The monks withdrew, but from the desert they bless the Christian empire and the Christian city, and they never weary of praying for them; they interpret this very abnegation as a service to the world for its salvation (*Historical Road of Eastern Orthodoxy*, p. 109).

* * *

Let us conclude this chapter with these words by Metropolitan Anthony Bloom, written in the Foreword to *The Sayings of the Desert Fathers: The Alphabetical Collection*, which has been our main source for the vignettes and sayings of the monastics that we've quoted in this chapter:

> If we wish to understand the sayings of the Desert Fathers, let us approach them with veneration, silencing our judgments and our thoughts in order to meet them on their own ground and perhaps to partake ultimately—if we prove able to emulate their earnestness in the search, their ruthless determination, their infinite compassion—in their own silent communion with God (Ward, p. ix).

CONCLUSION

We've made quite a journey together! From the Book of Acts to the wisdom of the Desert Fathers and Mothers, we've seen many ways in which the Lord Jesus Himself has guided the growth and development of His Holy Church in Her spiritual life, Her liturgical/sacramental life, Her doctrines and practices, and Her organizational structure through roughly the first five centuries of Her existence. And as we said in the Introduction, virtually all the basic elements of the life of the Orthodox Church today were in place by the end of the 5th century.

According to Rodney Stark's well-reasoned and well-documented study, at the beginning of the 4th century about 10% of the roughly 60 million residents of the Roman Empire had converted to Christianity (*The Rise of Christianity,* p. 7). This had come about, apparently, at quite a steady rate of about a 40% increase every decade. That rate most likely continued to the middle of the 4th century, when the Empire was over 50% Christian. And by the end of the 4th century, the Empire was well on its way to becoming a virtually totally Christian society.

How did the Christian Faith, starting with the tiny first group of Christians—only about 120 of them when dawn broke on the Day of Pentecost—come to literally conquer the entire Empire in only about 400 years? Of course, from our Christian perspective, this is above all the result of the sheer beauty and power of the life-giving Gospel of Christ as preached and lived by thousands and then millions of faithful Christians, which touched the hearts and minds and souls of millions more, turning them towards their own Creator and Savior. And of course, all this was only possible through the ongoing guidance and power of the Holy Spirit and of Christ Himself, as He fulfilled His promises that "I will build My Church, and the gates of hell will not prevail against Her" (Matt. 16:18); and, "I will send the Holy Spirit to you ... and He will guide you into all Truth" (John 16:7 and 13).

At a more specific level, perhaps we can look back and gather quite a number of particular factors within this general framework that all contributed to help spread the Christian Faith across the entire Empire and beyond. Many of these factors we've explored at some length in our study together in this book, while others we've just alluded to briefly, or not at all. These main factors could be listed as including:

1. The rich liturgical/spiritual heritage of the Jewish people, as seen in their cycles of daily prayer in the Temple and in their liturgical year with various Feast-days, which were continued and enriched with Christ-centered meaning by the early Christians, as we saw in our study of the Book of Acts (in Chapter One). Furthermore, the centrality of the weekly celebration of the Eucharist in the liturgical and spiritual life of the Church, with its profound mystical depth of meaning, was built upon the sacrificial system of the Jews as given to Moses by the Lord on Mt. Sinai, as recorded in Exodus and Leviticus. But as described especially in the Book of Hebrews, the entire system of sacrifices in the Mosaic Law was completely fulfilled through Christ's once-and-for-all sacrifice of Himself on the Cross.

2. The high quality of pastoral care and guidance provided to the early Christians by their bishops, as we saw in our study of the Apostolic Fathers (Chapter Two). This pattern continued in succeeding centuries, as seen in the lives and writings of such great teachers as St. Cyprian of Carthage (c. 200–257), St. Dionysius the Great of Alexandria (d. 264), St. Cyril of Jerusalem (c. 315–387), and St. John Chrysostom (347–407). St. Cyril wrote a marvelous series of homilies for catechumens based on the Nicene Creed, and then several "mystagogical" lectures for the newly baptized, while St. John Chrysostom wrote two instructions to candidates for baptism.[10]

3. The eloquent defending and explaining of the Faith to the surrounding society done by the Apologists, as we saw in Chapter Three. This effort continued in the following centuries as seen, for example, in the work of Origen (185–254), especially his *Against Celsus*; Lactantius (c. 250–c. 325), especially his *Divine Institutes*; and St. Augustine (354–430), with his monumental *The City of God.*

4. The powerful defense of the True Faith over against the Gnostic heretics and their dualistic mind-set, accomplished especially by St. Irenaeus, as we saw in Chapter Four. Many Christian writers persuasively and convincingly refuted heretical teachings in the succeeding centuries—for example, Tertullian in his *Against Marcion*; St. Hippolytus of Rome (c. 170–235) with his *Refutation of All*

[10] St. Cyril's catechetical lectures can be found in NPNF vol. II, VII; and St. John Chrysostom's two instructions can be found in NPNF vol. I, IX.

Heresies; St. Athanasios the Great (c. 298–373) in his various anti-Arian writings; St. Basil the Great (c. 330–379) in his *On the Holy Spirit,* directed against the Macedonians/ Pneumatomachians; St. Gregory the Theologian (329–390) in his writings against Apollinarianism; and St. Cyril of Alexandria (d. 444) with his writings against Nestorius.

5. The ability of the Church to resist and overcome the temptations of the judgmental, rigorist sectarian mind-set, as we saw in Her rejection of Montanism, as we saw in Chapter Five, and to learn from the tragic example of Tertullian (Chapter Six). St. Constantine the Great (c. 271–337) continued the tradition of the Church offering mercy instead of judgment to those repenting for even the worst sins, as when he told Acesius, a Novatianist[11] bishop, at the Nicene Council, when Acesius asserted that he would never offer forgiveness to anyone committing a mortal sin, "Acesius, take a ladder and climb up to Heaven alone." St. Gregory the Theologian (329–390), in a similar vein, eloquently exhorted the Novatianists of his day, "O new Pharisee, ... will you not give any place to weeping [in repentance]? Will you shed no tear? May you not meet with a Judge like yourself! Are you not ashamed of the mercy of Jesus, ... Who came not to call the righteous but sinners to repentance [Matt. 9:13], Who will have mercy rather than sacrifice [Matt. 9:13; Hos. 6:6], Who forgives sins till seventy times seven [Matt. 18:22]? ... Come and stand here on our side, that is, on the side of humanity" (*Oration on the Holy Lights*; NPNF vol. II, VII, pp. 358–359). And in Chapter Ten we quoted numerous passages from the Desert Fathers highlighting their humble, self-effacing non-judgmentalism towards others.

6. The crucially important canonization of the New Testament, accomplished by the Church during the first four centuries, as we observed in Chapter Seven. And with this comes the obvious understanding that it's only within the life of the same Church that wrote and compiled the writings of the New Testament that one can find *the proper interpretation* of these writings.

7. The adherence in the Eastern Church to the conciliar principle of every major bishop having jurisdictional independence, and the rejection of the growing presumption of the Roman Church to claim domination over the entire Church, as we saw in Chapter Eight.

8. The magnificent, heroic witness of the martyrs, who courageously and even joyfully endured torture and death, providing the surrounding society with *the*

[11] Novatianism, which broke out in Rome immediately after the Decian Persecution ended in 251, was a rigorist sect similar in many ways to the Montanists. Like the Montanists, they believed the Church could never offer the possibility of forgiveness and restoration to communion to those who had committed the worst sins, even if great repentance was demonstrated by the sinner.

greatest possible proof of the Truth of the Resurrection of the dead and eternal life in heaven with our Lord Christ, as we observed in Chapter Nine.

9. The ongoing witness of the monastics, the new martyrs, who continued to demonstrate proof of the reality of Christ's power through their ascetic feats, exorcisms, and the physical healings that they were able to accomplish, and their profound spiritual insights that have helped untold millions of Christians in their spiritual life to this day—as we discussed and provided examples of in Chapter Ten.

10. The conversion of St. Constantine the Great (c. 271–337) to the Christian Faith in 312, which made him the first Christian emperor. This makes possible the Christianization of the entire society, with Christian principles, for example, penetrating to the core of the legal system. As an early example of this, in 316 Emperor Constantine had a law passed that prohibited the branding of criminals on the face "because man is made in God's image." We should mention again his crucially important role in bringing to an end the fierce, decade-long Diocletian Persecution, with the Edict of Milan in 313 providing religious freedom for all. We can also mention some of the major ways he aided the recovery and flourishing of the Church after the era of persecution, such as his sponsoring the building of churches and the production of many copies of the Scriptures, entrusting large amounts of public funds to the Churches to provide social services to the poor, working towards the elimination in the Empire of animal sacrifice (which had been central to the State religion), and designating every Sunday to be a public holiday, thus greatly honoring and promoting the traditional day of worship of the Christians.

11. St. Constantine's summoning of the Council of Nicea in 325, which would prove to be the first of the tremendously important Seven Ecumenical Councils. These Councils—in Constantinople in 380, Ephesus in 431, Chalcedon in 451, Constantinople in 553, Constantinople again in 680–681, and Nicea again in 787—all gave the bishops of the worldwide Church the opportunity to meet together to examine and reject various heresies that sprang up through the years, and to address various issues concerning pastoral practice.

12. The visit of St. Constantine's mother St. Helen (c. 250–c. 330) to the Holy Land in 326 in her old age, and her discovery there of the True Cross and her working with her son in building churches and shrines in Jerusalem and throughout the Holy Land. All this does much to make Jerusalem a Christian city, and the world's most important center for Christian pilgrimage.

13. The ongoing example of service in Christ's name by thousands and then millions of Christians, as they sought with God's help to love Him with all their

heart and mind and soul and strength, and to love their neighbors as themselves (Luke 10:27). This was especially seen in the Church's outreach to the poor and downtrodden of society. As Igino Giordani writes,

> If, while it preached the life of paradise, Christianity had not regularly and effectively aided men to procure the means of earthly life also, especially through that long, vast, unceasing labor of redistribution of wealth known as charity, it would never have accomplished the revolution it did (*The Social Message of the Early Church Fathers* [Paterson, NJ: St. Anthony Guild Press, 1944], p. 254).

Two episodes that vividly demonstrated this brotherly love and service among themselves, and also for those beyond the Christian community, were the periods of widespread epidemics of "the plague"—perhaps smallpox and/or measles—from 165 to 180 and from 251 to about 259. During these terrifying epidemics, most of the pagans were so afraid of catching the disease that they often did not even provide minimal health care to their afflicted relatives and friends, preferring to throw them along the roadside, or even to flee from the cities, leaving the sick behind. Meanwhile, the Christians, due to their faith in Christ and His promises of eternal life, were unafraid to die, and so they willingly offered at least minimal care to the sick and dying—both to fellow Christians and to non-Christians as well. As a result, the Christians and those they cared for had a much higher survival rate, which greatly impressed the superstitious non-Christians, as did the highly risky service of love that the Christians showed to all during these times.

Not only did the poor find both spiritual and material aid in the Church, the lower classes in general found a remarkable elevation of their human dignity there, with the poorest and the richest communing from the same Chalice, and given the same kiss of peace from one another. Again, as Guardino states,

> The Church deliberately uplifts the lower classes, the majority … The intense community life of the Christians, from their prayers to God to their fulfillment of the precepts of charity, was fashioning a new social conscience, as the natural effusion of their religious life….
>
> Christianity realizes within its fold the peaceful, concordant living together of all classes (their collaboration with respect to labor) seeking order and harmony in every field on the basis of the original equality of souls and the actual brotherhood of the baptized (pp. 295–296).

14. The radiant joy, the deep peace, the touching humility, and the sweet savor of holiness of many of the Christians, spread across the Empire, in cities, villages, and countryside, among all classes, and working in all kinds of occupations (we recall the passage we quoted from the *Epistle to Diognetus* in Chapter Two). Surely this played a large role in the spread of the Faith, as all of us can attest how powerful, moving, and impressive it is to behold such characteristics in others—traits that only Christ can bestow and nurture in the hearts and minds and souls of His faithful followers.

* * *

It is my hope and prayer that this study of major themes in the history of the Early Church will inspire us to get to know better the Saints of this formative, foundational period—the Apostles, the Apostolic Fathers, the Apologists, the Martyrs, the Church Fathers, and the Desert Fathers and Mothers. May we all flourish more and more in our Christian Faith in and through our fellowship with them.

May we also be inspired to continue our study of Church History through all the centuries down to our own time. As we do so, may we seek to get to know better the Saints of all the ages. And may we marvel to see Christ's Hand throughout the Story, as He has guided and protected His Church in the midst of a myriad of attacks by the Evil One. Surely we will become more and more convinced that Christ's promise has been and ever will be indeed true, that "I will build My Church, and the gates of hell will not prevail against Her" (Matt. 16:18).

Epilogue

AN UNFORGETTABLE STORY FROM THE LIFE OF ST. JOHN THE THEOLOGIAN

BEFORE LEAVING YOU I would like to share one of the most touching stories from the annals of the Early Church, as quoted by Bp. Eusebius of Caesarea, the first great Church historian. It vividly demonstrates that the Apostle and Evangelist John the Theologian at the end of the first century, and Clement of Alexandria at the end of the 2nd century, and Bp. Eusebius at the beginning of the 4th century, all believed that repentance for even the worst sins, and forgiveness and restoration to the life of the Church, was possible through the infinite love and mercy of our Lord, as mediated through His pastors.

Here is the story, with Bp. Eusebius's introduction to it:

> Clement ... adds a story that should be familiar to all who like to hear what is noble and helpful. It will be found in the short work entitled *The Rich Man Who Finds Salvation*. Turn up the passage, and read what he writes:
>
> "Listen to a tale that is not just a tale but a true account about the Apostle John, handed down and carefully remembered. When the tyrant was dead [Emperor Domitian], and the Apostle John had moved from the island of Patmos to Ephesus, he used to go when asked to the neighboring districts of the Gentile peoples, sometimes to appoint bishops, sometimes to organize whole Churches, sometimes to ordain those who were pointed out by the Spirit. So

it happened that he arrived at a city not far off, named by some [as Smyrna], and after settling various problems of the brethren, he finally looked at the bishop already appointed; and indicating a young man he had noticed, of excellent physique, attractive appearance, and ardent spirit, he said: 'I leave this young man in your keeping, with all earnestness, in the presence of the Church and Christ as my witness.' When the bishop accepted him and promised everything, John addressed the same appeal and adjuration to him a second time.

"John then returned to Ephesus, and the cleric took home the young man entrusted to his care, brought him up, kept him in his company, looked after him, and finally gave him the grace of baptism. After this he relaxed his constant care and watchfulness over the young man, with the idea that the seal of the Lord he had set on him was a complete protection for him. But the young man snatched at liberty too soon, and was led astray by others of his own age who were idle, dissolute, and evil-doers. First they enticed him by expensive entertainments; then they took him with them when they went out at night to commit robbery. Then they urged him to take part in even greater crimes. Little by little he fell into their ways; and like a hard-mouthed, powerful horse, he dashed off the straight road, and taking the bit between his teeth, rushed down the precipice the more violently because of his immense vitality.

"Completely renouncing God's salvation, he was no longer content with petty offenses, but, as his life was already in ruins, he decided to commit a major crime and suffer the same fate as the others. He took these same young renegades and formed them into a gang of bandits of which he was the master-mind, surpassing them all in violence, cruelty, and bloodthirstiness.

"Time went by, and some necessity having arisen, John was asked to pay another visit [to Smyrna]. When he had dealt with the business for which he had come, he said, 'Come now, Bishop, pay me back the deposit which Christ and I left in your keeping, in the presence of the Church over which you preside as my witness.' At first the bishop was taken aback, thinking that he was being asked for money he had never received. He could neither comply with a demand for what he did not possess, nor refuse to comply with John's request.

But when John said, 'It is the young man I am asking for, and the soul of our brother,' the old man sighed deeply. Shedding tears, he said,

"'He is dead.'

"'How did he die?'

"'He is dead to God. He turned out to be wicked and profligate. In short, he is a bandit. And now, instead of the Church, he has taken to the mountain with an armed gang of men like himself.'

"The apostle rent his garment, groaned aloud, and beat his head. 'A fine guardian,' he cried, 'I left in charge of our brother's soul! However, let me have a horse immediately, and someone to show me the way.' He galloped off from the church, then and there, just as he was.

"When he arrived at the place, and was seized by the bandits' sentry-group, he made no attempt to escape and asked for no mercy, but shouted: 'This is what I have come for! Take me to your leader.'

"For the time being the young man waited, armed as he was, but as John approached, he recognized him, and filled with shame, he turned and fled. But John ran after him as hard as he could, forgetting his years [he was about 90 years old] and calling out, 'Why do you run away from me, my child—from your own father, unarmed and very old? Be sorry for me, child, not afraid of me. You still have hopes of life. I will account to Christ for you. If need be, I will gladly suffer your death, as the Lord suffered death for us. To save you I will give my own life. Stop! Believe! Christ sent me.'

"When he heard this, the young man stopped and stood with his eyes on the ground. Then he threw down his weapons; then he trembled and began to weep bitterly. When the old man came up the penitent threw his arms around him, pleading for himself as best he could. Being baptized a second time with his tears, he still kept his right hand out of sight.[12] But John solemnly pledged his word that the erstwhile bandit had found pardon through him from the Savior. John prayed, knelt down, and kissed the man's right hand as being cleansed by repentance.

"Then John brought him back to the church, interceded for him with many prayers, shared with him the ordeal of continuous fasting, and subdued his mind by the convincing power of many words. He did not leave him, we are told, till he had restored him to the Church,

---

[12] Presumably this was the hand that the young man had used to commit his acts of violence.

> presenting him as a perfect example of true repentance and a perfect proof of regeneration, a trophy of a visible resurrection."

Then Eusebius concludes this account by saying, "This story from Clement I have included both for its historical interest and for the benefit of future readers" (EH 3.23; quoting from ch. 42 of *The Rich Man Who Finds Salvation*, by Clement of Alexandria).

May we all be as eager, by the grace of our Lord, to give spiritual help to those around us as St. John the Theologian was to offer his own life for the salvation of the errant young man.

SELECTED RESOURCES FOR FURTHER STUDY

St. Basil the Great. *On Social Justice,* translated by C. Paul Schroeder. Crestwood, NY: St. Vladimir's Seminary Press, 2009 (Popular Patristics Series, vol. 38).

Bettenson, Henry, ed. *Documents of the Christian Church.* London: Oxford Univ. Press, 1963 (second edition).

_________. *The Early Christian Fathers.* New York: Oxford University Press, 1956.

_________. *The Later Christian Fathers.* New York: Oxford University Press, 1970.

Chadwick, Henry. *The Early Church.* London: Penguin Books, 1993 (revised edition).

Chrysostom, St. John. *Letters to Saint Olympia,* translated by David C. Ford. Yonkers, NY: St. Vladimir's Seminary Press, 2016 (Popular Patristics Series, vol. 56).

_________. *On Marriage and Family Life,* translated by Catharine P. Roth and David Anderson. Crestwood, NY: St. Vladimir's Seminary Press, 1986 (Popular Patristics Series, vol. 7).

_________. *The Cult of the Saints,* translated by Wendy Mayer and Bronwen Neil. Crestwood, NY: St. Vladimir's Seminary Press, 2006 (Popular Patristics Series, vol. 31).

St. Cyril of Jerusalem. *Lectures on the Christian Sacraments,* translated by Maxwell E. Johnson. Crestwood, NY: SVS Press, 2018 (Popular Patristics Series, vol. 57).

Eusebius of Caesarea. *The History of the Church,* translated by G. A. Williamson; revised and edited by Fr. Andrew Louth. Harmondsworth, England: Penguin Books, 1989.

Ford, David C. *Women and Men in the Early Church: The Vision of St. John Chrysostom.* South Canaan, PA: St. Tikhon's Monastery Press, 2017 (second, revised and expanded edition).

Hall, Christopher A. *Living Wisely with the Church Fathers.* Downers Grove, IL: InterVarsity Press, 2017.

Holy Apostles Convent, ed. *The Lives of the Holy Apostles.* Buena Vista, CO: Holy Apostles Convent, 1988.

St. Irenaeus of Lyons. *On the Apostolic Preaching,* translated by Fr. John Behr. Crestwood, NY: SVS Press, 1997 (Popular Patristics Series, vol. 17).

St. Macarius the Great. *Fifty Spiritual Homilies,* translated by A. J. Mason. Andesite Press, 2017.

Martin, Francis, ed. *Acts,* volume 5 in the Ancient Christian Commentary on Scripture (New Testament) series. Downers Grove, IL: IVP Academic, 2006.

St. Melito of Sardis. *On Pascha,* translated by Alistair Stewart-Sykes. Crestwood, NY: SVS Press, 2001 (Popular Patristics Series, vol. 20).

Musurillo, Herbert A., ed. *The Acts of the Christian Martyrs.* New York: Oxford University Press, 2000.

Schmemann, Fr. Alexander. *Historical Road of Eastern Orthodoxy.* Crestwood, NY: SVS Press, 1977.

Sparks, Fr. Jack N., ed. *The Apostolic Fathers.* Nashville, TN: Thomas Nelson, 1978 (Minneapolis: Light and Life, 2000).

__________, gen. ed. *The Orthodox Study Bible.* Nashville, TN: Thomas Nelson, 2008.

Stark, Rodney. *The Rise of Christianity.* San Francisco: Harper, 1997.

Waddell, Helen, translator. *The Desert Fathers.* Ann Arbor, MI: The Univ. of Michigan Press, 1957.

Ward, Benedicta, translator. *The Desert Christian: The Sayings of the Desert Fathers, The Alphabetical Collection.* New York: MacMillan Publishing, 1975.

Ware, Bp. Kallistos. *The Orthodox Church.* New York: Penguin Books, 1993 (second, revised and expanded edition).

__________. *The Orthodox Way.* Crestwood, NY: SVS Press, 1995.

STUDY GUIDE QUESTIONS FOR REFLECTION AND DISCUSSION

AT THE BEGINNING OF OUR STUDY TOGETHER:

1. Why do you want to learn more about Church History at this period in your life?
2. What do you hope to gain through this study?
3. Have you ever studied Church History before now? If so, what did that study involve, and how did it benefit you?
4. Why do you think it's important for Christians to know more about the history of Christianity – in particular, the story of what happened during the first 500 years or so of the Christian era?

FOR CHAPTER ONE

On the Book of Acts

1. Have you ever read the Book of Acts straight through in one sitting, or in a short period of time?
2. Would you be willing to do so now?
3. Why do you think this book could also be called The Acts of the Holy Spirit?
4. What do you think are the five or six most important episodes in the Book of Acts regarding the geographic spread of the Christian message?
5. What does the Book of Acts show us about the connection of the first Christians with Jewish liturgical and ritualistic practices?
6. In what ways can we understand the first Church council, described in Chapter 15, as being a paradigm for all the subsequent councils in the history of the Church?
7. What would be five or six additional passages that strike you as being particularly important and/or memorable, and why?

FOR CHAPTER TWO

On The Apostolic Fathers

1. Have you ever read any of the writings in the collection known as The Apostolic Fathers? If so, what were they, and what do you remember from that reading?
2. Why do you think we can trust the truthfulness of what is taught by The Apostolic Fathers?
3. Which of these writings do you think are most important historically, and why?
4. Which five or six themes seem to be most prominent in The Apostolic Fathers as a whole?
5. What is your favorite writing in this collection, and why?

FOR CHAPTER THREE

On The Apologists:

1. Before now, had you ever heard of any of the writers known as The Apologists?
2. Which of the Apologists do you find to be the most appealing, and why?
3. What do you think were the four or five most effective ways in which the Apologists refuted the misunderstandings that the surrounding society typically had concerning Christianity?
4. What role do you think the Apologists as a whole had in the eventual intellectual and spiritual conquest of the Roman Empire by the Christian Faith?
5. In what ways do you think the lives and works of the Apologists are most relevant for our attempts to spread Orthodoxy in our surrounding society today?

FOR CHAPTER FOUR

On St. Irenaeus and Gnosticism:

1. Which of the ways that St. Irenaeus used to refute the Gnosticism of his time do you think were the most important and effective?
2. Which aspects of modern-day Gnosticism do you think are most prevalent in our surrounding society today? And which of these aspects do you think are the most dangerous, and why?

3. How do you think the life and work of St. Irenaeus can be helpful for us as we try to resist and combat the various Gnostic influences in our surrounding society today?

4. How effective do you think the work of Rev. Philip J. Lee could be in helping our Protestant friends and/or relatives come closer to Holy Orthodoxy?

FOR CHAPTER FIVE

On Montanism:

1. What characteristics of Montanism do you think made it most threatening to the stability and health of the hierarchical Church in Asia Minor in the second century, and why?

2. What do you think are the most significant reasons why the Church had to condemn Montanism?

3. What do you think our Pentecostal and Charismatic friends and/or relatives might be able to learn from the story of Montanism?

4. What are the four or five most important things you would want to emphasize in talking to Pentecostals and Charismatics about Holy Orthodoxy?

FOR CHAPTER SIX

On Tertullian and the Sectarian Mind-set:

1. What do you think are the most important things we can learn from the story of Tertullian?

2. What do you think are the four or five most harmful aspects of the sectarian mind-set, and why?

3. Are there any aspects of contemporary Orthodoxy in America that you think might indicate a certain presence of the sectarian mind-set?

FOR CHAPTER SEVEN

On the Canonization of the New Testament:

1. What do you think were the three or four most important factors prompting the Church to create the canon of the New Testament?

2. What do you think were the most significant ways in which the Church decided which books to include in the New Testament canon, and which ones to reject?

3. Which Church Fathers played the most important role in the story of the canonization of the New Testament, and how did they do so?

4. How do you think this story might be helpful to Protestants in leading them closer to Holy Orthodoxy?

FOR CHAPTER EIGHT

On Papal Presumption:

1. What is the proper place and role in the worldwide Church of the bishop of the Church in Rome, according to the Fathers of the first four Ecumenical Councils?

2. In your opinion, which Roman bishops, by doing what things, contributed most to the rise of Papal presumption during the first six centuries of the Christian era?

3. How do you think this story might be helpful to our Roman Catholic friends and/or relatives in drawing them closer to Holy Orthodoxy?

FOR CHAPTER NINE

On Persecution and Martyrdom:

1. How would you describe the relationship of the early Christians with the civil authorities of their time and place?

2. How would you describe the ways in which the governmental authorities and the general populace viewed the Christians during the first three centuries of the Christian era?

3. How would you describe the early Christians' understanding of persecution, martyrdom, and relics, as seen especially in the Account of the Martyrdom of St. Polycarp?

4. How would you relate in your own words the way in which "through the living, the dead were being brought back to life" during the persecution at Lyons and Vienne?

5. How did the many martyrs for Christ aid the expansion of the Church during the first three centuries of the Christian era?

6. How can the Christian Martyrs inspire and strengthen us as we face opposition and even persecution in various forms in our contemporary, postmodern society, as we endeavor to uphold and proclaim traditional Christian beliefs and moral standards?

FOR CHAPTER TEN

On Monasticism and the Desert Fathers and Mothers:

1. In what ways do you think the monastic life can be considered a form of martyrdom?

2. What do you think are the three or four most important reasons for the dramatic rise of monasticism in the fourth century?

3. Of all the vignettes and sayings given in this chapter from the Desert Fathers and Mothers, which five or six are your favorites, and why?

4. How do you think people who have never heard of the Desert Fathers and Mothers might respond to these vignettes and sayings? Do you think their lives and words could be used as an evangelistic tool in the spreading of Orthodoxy?

FOR THE CONCLUSION:

1. In your opinion, which five or six factors were the most important/effective in Christianity's virtually complete intellectual and spiritual conquest of the Roman Empire by the end of the fifth century, and why?

2. How would you assess the role of St. Constantine the Great in the spread of Christianity?

FOR THE EPILOGUE:

1. How would you relate in your own words the story of St. John the Theologian rescuing the errant young man?

2. What does this story convey to us about the possibility of repentance for even the worst sins?

IN CONCLUSION:

1. What would you say are the four or five most important/significant things you've learned through this study, and why are these things important/significant?

2. Which five or six Saints do you feel closer to through what you've learned in this study, and why?

3. At this point, as (hopefully) you think about continuing your study of Church History, which two or three Saints from the first five centuries would you like to learn more about and draw closer to, and why?

4. Are there any particular aspects of the history of the early Church that you would like to delve into further at this point? If so, why do these issues have continuing interest for you?